To: Mother

Rich + Loretta 1997 Xmas

Through the Eyes of a Boy

Growing Up on an Eastern Oregon Farm After the Great Depression

Harlan Scott

Hells Canyon Publishing, Halfway, Oregon

Hells Canyon Publishing, Inc.
P.O. Box 646
Halfway, Oregon, 97834

Published by Hells Canyon Publishing, Inc., Halfway, Ore.
First printing, 1997

Printed in the United States of America.

10 9 8 7 6 5 4 3 2 1

Library of Congress Cataloging in Publication Data

Scott, Harlan N., 1931-
Through the eyes of a boy: growing up on an eastern oregon farm after the great depression / by Harlan Scott.
p. cm.
ISBN 0-9633919-2-5 (paper)
1. Scott, Harlan N. —Childhood and youth. 2. Farm life—Oregon. 3. Depressions—1929—Oregon. 4. Oregon—Biography. I. Title.
CT275.S3479A3 1997
979.5'04'092—dc21
[b] 97-33304
CIP

Book design and prepress: Steve Backstrom, Hells Canyon Pub.
Cover photo by Virgil Scott

This book is dedicated to Noel and Ethel Scott.

PROLOGUE

This book is an autobiography of my childhood with emphasis placed on depicting the lives of rural families during the heart of the Depression in the 1930s. It revolves around my folks and the incidents that can happen when a young couple is thrown into an occupation that they are not familiar with, an occupation that was not their choice and an occupation that perhaps they never really learned to like.

Despite these obstacles, my family and others raised their children with love and discipline. People managed to make the most of what they had, they enjoyed the socializing and were willing to share their meager resources with each other.

This story shares many humorous incidents with my readers and tells of how families and children entertained themselves, how schools differed from today and other interesting facts related to that time period.

The book is designed to entertain a broad spectrum of the reading public. Although it is localized in its dealing with particular people and specific locations, it is representative of similar situations occurring at that time throughout the United States. It should be appealing to all age groups.

The book is unique in that it employs an occasional poetic verse throughout its chapters. Verse is used here to capture a greater descriptive intensity in order to connect with the emotions of the reader.

The purpose of this book is to encourage readers living in a rapidly advancing society, where there is a growing dependency on material devices, to reflect on their past. It is hoped that in doing so they will put modern material ambitions in a more balanced perspective, particularly when setting goals and facing what they believe to be insurmountable obstacles. Also I feel that all age groups should go back in time, periodically, to review earlier lifestyles for the sake of preserving our heritage and culture.

I have dedicated this book to my deceased parents, Noel and Ethel Scott. It was with their guidance that I have been able to live an enjoyable and productive life. I would like to thank my uncle, Ralph Scott, my sister, Marilyn Thompson, my aunt, Fannie Halsey, my cousins, Don Gray, Jeff Halsey, and Warren Scott, and my wife, Rebecca, for their help in editing, research and other assistance.

They were the survivors that buried their roots in the soil,
Without electricity, cars, good soils or tractors for toil.
They united their efforts to help all pull through,
When they had nothing to give but their labor and friendship true.
Their children learned duties at an early age;
They respected their parents, they did not rage.
They enjoyed simple things that life had to share.
They pulled together with loving care.
These were the survivors of a rugged time and place,
That should be remembered from memories we can trace.

Table of Contents

Chapter 1

The Beginning

It may have been the most devastating day of my young mother's life when she and my father started unloading their belongings from the horse-drawn sled into the small weather-beaten house on Cricket Flat during the winter of 1933. It was during the peak of the Depression when poverty dictated people's lives. Such bleak conditions influenced their decisions on where they lived, what material things they could afford and overall, affected their entire style of living. It shattered dreams, and forced families to face challenges indescribable to today's generation.

My father and mother, Noel and Ethel Scott, were classic victims of the Depression. They had watched their nest egg of savings derived from the sale of a sweetshop in Joseph, Oregon, go down the drain in defaults by banks and loan companies. Instead of pursuing their dream of buying into another related business, they found themselves being hurled into a farming operation and life not of their choice nor one they were familiar with.

It had been my dad's father, Dave Scott, that had suggested that my parents take over this 160-acre ranch on the north end of Cricket Flat. It was a place my grandfather had acquired from a loan default. My parents, who had been existing with the aid of both of their parents and what sporadic low paying jobs that they could find, chose the ranch as a means of survival.

This 160-acre ranch was a much better site for growing trees than for farming, and even the soil that was most suitable for crops was shallow and rocky. Boundary fences were old and in ill repair or nonexistent. The only water on the place was in two hand dug wells and a small spring. Probably the most appealing part of the ranch was a small family orchard on a hill overlooking the house.

The old one bedroom house with its single wall construction of warped upright one by ten inch lumber and a leaking shed roof, had a woodshed and cellar. An old barn with sagging beams and rotting floors had already lost part of its roof of hand made shakes. The inside of the house was characterized by walls adorned with many layers of wallpaper and bare unpainted wood floors. The living room contained an old burned out wood stove with six inch stove pipe rising vertically through the ceiling and roof.

Charred wood and burnt paper around the pipe opening indicated that the house was living on borrowed time. A large wood cooking stove with a water heating reservoir and a large oven was located against the south wall of the kitchen. Woodrat droppings and the musky smell of the rats themselves indicated that the rats called this place their home. Bedbugs and wasps seemed to appear from every crack and crevice when the room was warmed up by the old wood heating stove.

A hand-dug well some 50 feet south of the house was covered by a platform of rotting planks. A hinged lid in the center of the platform provided an opening for lowering bucket on a rope to the water some 25 feet below. Since there was no electricity on the Flat at that time, water for both domestic use and livestock had to be drawn and packed to its destination.

It was this setting that we faced, my parents and I. I was only two years old when they unloaded their belongings into the old house. It was here that the harsh, wild and rural environment began shaping and imprinting my young life with everlasting memories. In my case, because of my youth, adjustments were easy and normal to make. In my folk's case, however, the adjustment from living in a small urban environment, to living in a rural setting without electricity, running water, motorized transportation and access to stores was a challenge.

My dad had spent some time as a young boy living in a rural environment when his dad operated a small sawmill on Smith Mountain. However this setting did not offer him any training in ranching. Also,

Some of the fields on the ranch and the layout of the land.

he had never been interested in mechanics so he had no background in operating and repairing farm equipment. My mother, having been raised on a ranch, knew some about farm animals but very little about farm equipment.

To make matters worse, the folks had no transportation when they first arrived. The sled and horses that hauled in their belongings were owned by someone else. They had no car during the first two years on the ranch. Their first transportation was a small trailer and a team of horses that my grandfather had helped purchase for them. They had to depend on neighbors and their parents for transportation to town until they purchased an old Oakland car in 1935.

The first few years on the ranch required some of the basic survival skills that were used by many of the pioneers arriving into Oregon during the late 1800s. A large well-insulated cellar was probably one of the most important buildings on the ranch. It allowed the folks to store large volumes of canned fruit and raw apples from the large orchard. A large garden provided fresh vegetables during the summer and canned vegetables during the winter. We rarely ate beef, since cattle could be sold for badly needed cash. After the first winter, we always had milk cows that gave us our dairy products.

Operating mainly on borrowed cash during the first two years, my dad was able to assemble the bare bone necessities to operate the ranch. Outside of a new disk plow, all of the other equipment was mainly scrounged from other ranchers' junk piles. Four horses with varying bad habits, plus some horses borrowed from the neighbors, formed the horse power for pulling equipment for the first five years. Old wire from an abandoned county roadway on an adjacent ranch was salvaged to reinforce existing fences and to construct new ones. A wooden trough was installed at the spring so as to collect more water for livestock. Increasing numbers of cows, pigs, and chickens were gradually introduced to the ranch, and this required the construction of a pond.

By the end of twelve years, in 1945, Dad had purchased more ground and developed more farmland from timber and pasture land until there were approximately 240 acres of farmland and 860 acres of timberlands and pasture. Four more ponds were built and by this time farming operations had mainly been converted from horses to tractor. We now owned our own combine and all the equipment needed for farming, although a lot of the equipment was old and hay-wired together. Dad had purchased a better secondhand car and had acquired his dad's pickup. He also purchased another old truck. We now had about 50 head of cattle and about 100 hogs. A new barn and combination shop and chickenhouse were built.

My mother's life in the house had also improved despite the extra challenge of having three more additions to the family. A new bedroom was added, water was piped into the house, hot water coils were installed in the cookstove and a light plant provided electricity for electric lights and a refrigerator. A make-shift shower was installed in my five by eight foot bedroom. My three new sisters were welcomed into our two-bedroom house: Rosalie was born in 1935, Marilyn in 1943, and Anita in 1946.

Despite all the improvements and land additions, our living standards were still just above the poverty level. Poor soils and insufficient farming acres seemed to put caps on farm income levels on

The second house the folks built on the ranch, built in 1948.

Cricket Flat. The old saying, "Misery loves company," seemed to apply on Cricket Flat, especially on the northern end where crop soils were the poorest. Most of our surrounding neighbors were in the same boat as we were. Most had old secondhand cars and farm equipment and barely subsisted from year to year.

In 1948, timber prices, which had been secondary to other farm produce, suddenly began to rise, enabling poor ranchers with timber on their property to breathe welcome sighs of relief. Now, these timber lands, which before had been cleared and burned like so many weeds, began to represent a cash crop. This new source of income allowed Cricket Flat residents to upgrade their incomes and buy material things that before had been unavailable. My folks were able to build a new house, buy a new tractor, buy some more land, and enjoy a progressively more comfortable lifestyle until 1960.

A government Soil Bank program, in which the federal government paid farmers to retire their cultivated lands in 1960, attracted most of the landowners on the Flat, including my folks. Since farmers were not allowed to pasture or hay their croplands under this program, my parents sold their cows and pigs and rented their pasture lands out. At this time my father started working for the Agricultural Soils and Conservation Agency and worked there until 1965.

The conservation program ended in 1965 and rather than go back to farming, my dad entered into a highly successful career in the real estate field. He set up an office in Elgin with my mother acting as his secretary and bookkeeper. He remained in the real estate business until his death in 1986. My mother achieved her life long ambition of writing a book when *Heritage of the Wallowas* was published in 1980. She passed away in April of 1989 after struggling with throat cancer.

I left my folks' ranch in 1953 when I married a La Grande girl and rented my uncle's ranch, which was located just north of my folks' ranch. After one year of farming, I was drafted into the Army where I served two years. I then attended Oregon State University in Corvallis, Oregon, completing a degree in Fish and Game Management. Upon graduation in 1959, I worked for the Oregon Department of Fish and Wildlife until my retirement in 1989.

Since then I have managed my 600 acre ranch and tree farm on Cricket Flat. Although I have had a productive and full life, my life experiences from the time I moved to the ranch in 1933 until I entered Elgin High School in 1945 have been permanently imprinted in my mind. This time period involved a way of living profoundly different from anything I experienced later in life. This period, along with my folks' guidance, shaped my moral values, my philosophy of life and my common sense judgment more than any other period of time.

I have often wondered why this twelve-year period had such a significant impact on my later life. Perhaps the ability of families to live in harmony with their hardships and make the most out of their limited resources were the most impressive aspects. Some other attributes of families living during this period, were the willingness to share their limited resources with others, the gregarious socializing and the ability to be happy with the limited recreational resources that were available.

Children, because of their early role in the work force, seemed to accept responsibilities at an earlier age. They also seemed to be much better than today's youth at entertaining themselves without the modern devices of television, video games, battery toys, four wheelers and other modern recreational playthings. They seemed to have more respect for their parents and teachers and poor behavior was not tolerated by adults like it is today.

In the following chapters I will try to recapture some of the experiences that will perhaps give the reader a better understanding of what rural life was like during my earlier years. Most of my experiences depict the way of life of that time period before I entered high school.

Today's lifestyles often seem to promote a widening gap separating those who lived during an earlier period. Modern technologies, a greater use of convenience items and material things, and changing philosophies on child rearing all contribute to this widening gap. Perhaps a visit to the past will both entertain and provide forgotten moral values and guidelines for future generations.

The following poem, which I have named "The House in The Swale," was written to give a more deeper look at the living atmosphere that surrounded our first house on the Flat:

It was this year in May when I happened to stroll,
Past the homestead where my memories took control.
A pile of broken old boards were all that remained,
Of a humble old house that was weathered and stained.
An old house that was dear to my heart;
For this was the house where my memories did start.
I was only two when our family did decide,
For the next fifteen years that they would reside
In this house called home at the end of the trail,
The last house on the road, the house in the swale.

As I stood there that day with nature in full prime,
My memories grabbed my soul and stepped back in time.
Suddenly the house was there and its presence did blend,
With mother nature's features that she decided to spend.
To the west was an orchard with a variety of trees,
Surrounded by a forest like an island in the seas.
In the bottom of the swale just to the south,
Was an old hand pump that pumped water from its mouth.

Its pipe reached down some 40 feet below,
Where clear cold water formed a small flow.
Between the well and the house stood a giant fir tree,
With huge spreading limbs growing long and so free.
They spread out over the house like a huge dark tent,
Shading the house from the sun that was sent.
One large limb, much enjoyment it did bring,
For tied to its middle was a long rope swing.
To the east of the tree was a rough lumber shed.
It housed the wood from which the stove was fed.
To the west of the tree was a shed dark and old,
That stored all the food from the heat and the cold.
Its double walls with sawdust were filled,
So in hot weather food could be chilled.
Directly north of the home stood this little outhouse,
That was used by all from husband to spouse.
Its nearest neighbor to the northwest,
Were a shop and a chickenhouse joined at their crest.
Further northwest, the newest one on the farm,
Was a large red building that we called the barn.
All these buildings, along with the trees,
My mind was full of memories as a wind-filled sail,
Oh this beautiful place with the house in the swale.

"Oh Harlan, I need water from the well."
I could hear these words as I was in a spell.
The walk from the well to the house inside,
Further caressed my mind to its swelling tide.
The small pantry room which would later become,
My own bedroom and a shower all in one,
Was attached to the kitchen on its south side,
And was crammed full of canned goods like hair on a hide.
An old painted door pointed the way,
To a larger living room that had seen many a day.
Layers of wallpaper were the main strength of the walls,

Without two by fours they were subject to the wind's calls.
A large wood stove sent its chimney straight and true,
Straight up through the roof where the gentle breezes blew,
The fragrant blue smoke from the wood of fir and pine,
To where it caressed our lives like the grapes that make the wine.
To the north of the living room was an old board door
That led to the bedroom with an old wooden floor.
This bedroom served all with only two beds.
It was homey and small with a couple of dreads.
One dread was cold nights for walls did not turn,
The sub-zero weather that chills like a burn.
Pitchers of water that would be set by the bed,
Would be in the morning as solid as lead.
The other dread was noise from woodrats in the loft;
They were as noisy as thirty hogs in a trough.
Their playing and running could be heard all night.
And they would only stop at the morning's first light
Memories so vivid they seemed to make me pale,
Of the little old house, the house in the swale.

My soul did churn as I stepped back in time,
When my body was young and in its prime.
My mind and soul were imprinted with this place,
And with my parents with their patience and grace.
I am eternally grateful that no one can take away,
The beautiful memories that visited that day.
Even though the house would be frowned on by most,
It was always clean with a gracious host.
Mom and dad seemed to make this place home,
With their love and guidance to all that would roam.
The house was always open to stranger and kin,
With a love that over-shadowed the structure within.
We never showed shame for what it did lack;
Even though we knew it was a wallpapered shack.
It was my home and my memories will never fail,
To think of that house, the house in the swale.

Chapter 2

Ranch Contributors

The following names and a brief description of each person and their contributions to the ranch are listed to give the reader a better perspective in reading the following chapters.

My father, Noel Scott, who was described briefly in the first chapter, was 27 years old when he moved to the Flat in 1933. He was five feet ten inches in height, sandy-haired, wore thick prescription glasses and weighed about 180 pounds. He resisted wearing the typical rancher attire throughout his ranch life and would commonly wear out-dated or worn dress pants and an old dress type man's hat for ranch work. He was well known for having a pessimistic outlook and was quite skeptical about accepting new ways or scientific breakthroughs. My mother said he would not believe television was real until he saw one.

He had a habit shared by many of the Flat residents and it was probably developed from necessity while living with little cash or spare time. This was to repair a broken tool or piece of equipment to its barest minimum level for operation. He almost seemed to enjoy having a growing list of equipment breakdowns by patching them together rather than spending time and effort for more permanent repairs.

Dad was tight with his money and was a shrewd speculator in acquiring land . He seemed to recognize that by putting every spare penny into buying land it would eventually lead to good financial gains. He was a hard worker and was not afraid of putting in long hours in inclement weather.

Dad seemed to have two different levels when it came to losing his temper. Around material objects and livestock, he seemed to let his hair down and vent his anger with well-chosen cuss words and sadistic abuse of his old felt hats. His hats were thrown, trampled, ripped, hand crumpled and talked to like they were living things during these outbursts.

Around most of our family and the neighbors, Dad seemed to keep his temper under control. Dad hated confrontations with neighbors or friends and would tolerate their verbal abuse without verbal retaliation. Around me, however—perhaps because I was with him most of the time—Dad did not hesitate to display his temper. In his arguments with my mother, even though he would get frustrated, he was always under control. In his discipline with my sisters and me, he was always calm and firm when administering corporal punishment.

He believed in God, but had varying degrees of skepticism about the Bible, various strict religions and the church in general. Dad placed high value on the sanctity of marriage. He probably was one of the most honest men that I have ever known. Although he was a Democrat, he seemed to vote for the person rather than the party. He used to keep a running oral dialogue with political speakers he disagreed with on the radio.

Dad had two years of college in electrical engineering at Oregon State College and had a better than average level of education for men at that time. He read a lot and had an excellent reading retention level. Sometimes, he would go through spells of depression, especially after some crop failures or other sad news.

My mother, Ethel Scott, was 25 years old when she moved to the ranch. She was a slender, pretty brunette of five feet five inches in height and weighed about 115 pounds. Mother was in bad health when she arrived at the ranch. She had been on heavy medication but had to stop it after arriving at the ranch because they could not afford the cost.

Ethel always wore long pretty dresses and kept her hair neatly brushed or combed at all times. She always kept a neat clean house and was very conscientious, considering our primitive accommodations, in maintaining high standards in dress and hygiene for herself and the rest of the family.

Mother had an exceptional ability to plan and prepare delicious nutritional meals with limited resources and always had the ability to prepare good fast meals for company with very little prior notice. She seemed to feel obligated to invite visitors, friends or strangers, to stay for the upcoming meal, with only had one exception to this habit, which I will explain in a following chapter.

Ethel was an excellent long-range planner in preserving and storing foods for the upcoming year. She seemed to be a nutritionist way ahead of her time in preparing well-balanced meals. Mother would force daily doses of castor oil and cod liver oil down our throats like a mother bird feeding her young.

She was an excellent seamstress and made a large share of our clothes. She often reconditioned hand-me-down clothes for Dad and me. What few clothes she bought for me were always purchased one to two sizes too large in hopes that I would grow into them before they wore out.

Mother countered Dad's pessimism by being an optimist in many ways. She was always pushing for improvements around the house, such as piped water in the house and a generator plant, while dad was telling her that it would not work. She bitterly resented Dad taking all the extra cash and investing it in land. Mother loved to reminisce about the past. She could entertain the family for hours with stories of her past and had an amazing capacity for remembering names and details. From as long as I could remember, she always talked about writing a book, which she eventually did.

My mother had much stronger beliefs about the church and God than my father did. She did not drink or smoke, but did not nag my father for his moderate use of alcohol or his heavy use of tobacco. Until I was twelve years old she made my sisters and me say our prayers before going to bed. She was quite emotional and easily shed tears in reaction to joy or sorrow. Her dad used to tell her that her eyes were too close to her bladder.

My mother graduated from Behnke Walker Business College in Portland, Oregon, after her graduation from Joseph High School. Although she did not complain in front of my sister and me about our ranch life, it was no secret that she would have much rather have taken advantage of her college training in some way.

My sister, Rosalie, was four years younger than I. She had a petite doll-like face with long brown hair and twinkling blue-green eyes. At a very young age she learned to hold her own with me despite my age advantage. She developed an uncanny ability to get me in trouble with my folks. She developed blackmail to its highest degree and frequently used it against me. She appointed herself as my watch-dog at school and would give my folks a detailed report of my daily transgressions. As she grew older, the folks gradually increased her role in doing the household chores where she proved to be a big help to my mother.

Rosalie grew up to be a very attractive girl and was very popular with the boys during her high school years. She married after attending Eastern Oregon College at La Grande for two years and eventually ended up working for Boise Cascade in Purchasing Inventory. Rosalie died in 1991 after a struggle with cancer. Following this chapter is a poem called, "Memories we Shared," that I wrote for Rosalie shortly before she died.

My sister, Marilyn, was twelve years younger than I. She was a bright, out-going child with long, light, blondish hair. Although she did not share most of my younger life because of her age, she and our younger sister, Anita, were always eager to please me. I used them shamelessly for running my many errands. Marilyn was a born leader, with a take-charge sort of personality and was very intelligent. She is now married and is working for an insurance company in La Grande. She and her husband, Miles, have recently moved back to the folks' second ranch house on the Flat.

My youngest sister, Anita, is fifteen years younger than I, and like Marilyn, did not spend many years living in the old house or being a part of my early life. Anita had dark reddish brown hair and had a trusting sweet nature that appealed to everyone. Anita attended Eastern Oregon College in La Grande and is now married and working for The State District Court in La Grande. Anita was a late bloomer as far as looks were concerned. She seemed to grow more attractive as she aged and is still a very attractive woman.

Dave Scott, my dad's father, made many major contributions to the ranch. He spent many weekends working on the new house and the new barn and many other ranch projects. He was a thin tall bald-headed man with a pronounced stoop to his shoulders and was a tireless worker. He was a reserved, religious man who tried hard to get along with his fellow man. He was honest and law abiding to the last letter of the law and caused my father to carefully conceal his poaching and home brew making activities while he was around.

Stella Scott, my dad's mother, spent many days assisting my mother around the house during the period when the folks first moved to the Flat and during sickness and child-birth periods. She was a short, slightly-stout built woman who wore her graying hair in a bun. She always had a twinkle in her eye and had a good sense of humor.

Bill Halsey, my mother's father, also contributed to our lives on the ranch. He did not spend a lot of time working on the ranch as he had lost a ranch near Joseph due to an Irrigation District foreclosure. But his visits were entertaining and he paid a lot of attention to my sisters and me. For the next few years he was quite busy establishing another place with a small dairy herd. He was a tall gray headed man with a keen sense of humor.

Vergie Halsey, my mother's mother, spent a lot of time assisting my mother during childbirth and periods of illness. She was a short, stoutly-built woman with black curly hair. She was a hard worker who could milk cows and do a lot of other work normally performed by men.

Jack Halsey, my mother's brother, spent a lot of time exchanging work with my dad on the ranch. He and his wife, Fannie, moved to the Flat when I was ten years old. Jack was a tall muscular man with curly brown hair. Jack had a keen sense of humor and could keep everyone in stitches with his quick-witted retorts. He was an outstanding mechanic and had the ability to invent and build equipment to facilitate work on the ranch. He used to become quite impatient with my dad's Band-Aid approaches to repairing equipment and fences. Jack spent many hours fishing and hunting with my dad and me. He loved the outdoors and actively enjoyed these hobbies until his death.

Fannie Halsey, Jack's wife, was an attractive red-haired woman who spent lots of time exchanging work visits and meals with our family. Fannie now lives in Elgin, where she spends most of her time visiting with her children and grandchildren.

Jack Halsey's barn, built in the 1940s. The roof was made entirely of materials from Jack's ranch.

Ralph Scott, one of my dad's younger brothers, spent the most time on the ranch and provided the most assistance to my folks. Ralph, an outgoing, self-confident, natural leader, was twelve years old when he began living on the ranch in 1933. He had a genuine love for the land and would work ahead in his schoolwork so they would let him out early in the school year to work on the ranch.

At a young age Ralph handled most of the ranch duties with the ability of a grown man. He was quite interested in horses and would jump at the chance to break and train them. He worked every year on the ranch until he was 19 years old. He married his wife, Jean, when he was 20 years old and joined the Navy in 1941. He later became a very successful public accountant in Kennewick, Washington, where he still lives today.

Harold Scott was another younger brother to my dad. He spent a lot of time on the ranch and was instrumental in leading the way in developing a piped water system in the old house. Harold was a studious young man with a tremendous knowledge in math. He later graduated from Oregon State College and joined the Navy. Harold had a very successful career with Shell Oil Company in California and upon retirement , he and his wife Katie moved back to Central Point Oregon, where they still live today.

Kenneth Scott was Dad's youngest brother, and like his other brother, spent quite a bit of time on the ranch. Ken helped with the water system and other ranch work. He served in World War II in a highly dangerous tour as an Army Ranger in Germany. He later worked in construction and lost his life in a car accident at a fairly young age. He was the first one in my dad's family of five boys and three girls to die.

Virgil Scott was my dad's oldest brother. He and his wife, Winn, spent one summer helping the folks on the ranch. Virgil built and installed new kitchen cabinets in the old house, helped with the haying and worked on the new barn. He was a short heavy set man with a keen mind. He taught school for a few years and then ended up working for Portland General Electric in Portland, Oregon. At 91 years of age. Virgil is the now the oldest member of the Dave Scott Family.

Obe Scott was my dad's uncle. Obe and his wife Gladys were established residents of the Flat when we moved there in 1933. Obe and Dad exchanged work and equipment during the first five years on the ranch. Obe taught Dad most of the techniques of ranching and was always willing to lend advice or a helping hand. Obe, a large heavily-built, balding man, spoke with a slow drawl. Obe was well known for his ability to get the most work out of his employees by well-timed flattery.

George Kennedy and his wife Georgie were our nearest neighbors on the ranch. Georgie was a first cousin to my dad. George spent a lot of time on the ranch. George, a black haired man with rugged weathered features, could have passed for a Mongolian. He always wore a heavy black beard and a pair of bib overalls. He wore long underwear year around and seemed to have an aversion to bathing. He always had a great rapport with small children.

George's biggest vice was that he loved to talk. He could ramble on all day and not tell the same story twice. Most of his stories were told for the truth and he had a list of sayings that provided entertainment for all. George never seemed to be real interested in farming their leased property. I think the reason that George helped Dad so much was that he used Dad for a sounding board for his stories. I know that

Dad never had enough money to pay George for all of his labor.

During my younger years, I was always small for my age. I had straight brown hair that always wanted to fall forward into my eyes. My blue eyes stood out in a face laden with large freckles. Due to my mother overestimating my rate of growth, my clothes were usually one to two sizes too large. To compensate for this, I always had about two rolls on both my shirt sleeves and pant legs. Somehow I always ended up with extra long shoe laces that were generally untied. During the summer months I went bare-footed and would develop tough soles on the bottom of my feet, comparable to shoe leather.

I had a very inquisitive mind and would shower my parents with an endless barrage of questions. I was very interested in wildlife and would continually ask my father which could win in a fight when two different species of animals were pitted against each other. I was a fair student at school but had a tendency to convince other students to perform acts that would get them in trouble with the teacher. I was continuously playing tricks on my sisters, which usually got me in trouble with my parents.

I was a daydreamer and would often try and put my dreams into actual practice. I was shy in meeting other children outside the farm environment, especially girls. I enjoyed athletic contests with other boys and did not hesitate to get into wrestling matches and fist fights with boys older and stronger than myself.

I learned at an early age to entertain myself without the company of other children . Fishing, hunting, building tree houses, watching wildlife, reading and carrying out some of my special projects were some of my solitary endeavors. Some of my fondest memories off the ranch were enjoying a milkshake or Coke at the Elgin Drug Store, which had a soda fountain at that time. Watching a cowboy movie at the Elgin Theater was always a great treat. Watching an air show at the La Grande Airport left a lasting impression on my young mind.

Some of my early day heroes were cowboys in the movies and my Uncle Ralph. I used to spend countless hours trying to train my hair to comb back and wave the way my Uncle Ralph's did. I used to dream about Shirley Temple as the ultimate girl.

I was very sensitive to pain and would take off running when I got hurt. My folks and uncles would often have to run me down to treat my wounds when I got hurt. I actively worked on the ranch until I was married in 1953, and thank those early years for teaching me discipline and work responsibilities at a very early age.

This is a summary of the persons that helped the folks out on the ranch at a very difficult time. Many of them did not ask for any returns except room and board and their being welcomed back for visits to our home at any time. I think that their help exemplifies the spirit of helping each other that existed during this time period.

The following poem, "Memories We Shared," is a poem that I am dedicating to the memory of my sister, Rosalie, who had the misfortune to lose her life to cancer. I presented the poem to her shortly before she died.

We started our acquaintance many years, before,
When you were just born and I was only four.
The childhood memories that we shared since that day,
Are etched in our minds in a selective way.
Times when we were happy or when we were downcast;
Only you and I can bridge to the past.
We shared the old house with our mother and dad.
When times were hard and weather was bad.
The house with one bedroom that was shared by all,
With rough wooden floors and paper on the wall;
Two beds with many blankets for cold winter nights,
With no heat in the room, only kerosene lights.
A living room with an old wood stove,
Where we huddled around like ships in a cove.
Winter snow storms that would blow in from the door,
And piled up snow drifts high on the floor.
Leaks in the ceiling in every room in the place,
Occurring during storms made us all race,
To place pots and pans under the drip,
And keep the floor from being as wet as a ship.
The old wood cookstove where meals were prepared,
And placed on the table that we all shared,
For eating our meals and playing card games,
A table that seated many different names.

The old washing machine that sent gas fumes through the house,
And the little old pantry where we often saw a mouse.
The hand-dug well with its old hand pump,
With an old iron handle that came down with a clump.
The crystal clear water that poured from its spout,
Filling a metal bucket that was large and stout.
Memories of deeds and thoughts declared:
Memories of the past, memories we shared.

We saw the seasons only Cricket Flat can provide,
Snows so deep, fence posts they did hide.
Temperatures so cold that trees would pop and snap,
From temperatures so low that they froze the sap.
Icicles from the eves touching the ground,
So much snow that it deadened the sound.
The thrilling yell of our voices as we glided down hills,
Crusted with snow to provide many thrills,
As our fast running sleds formed a cold breeze,
So cold on our faces it made our nose freeze.
The hard frozen ice that allowed us to skate,
On our pond's slick surface that often tempted fate.
Remember the ride on a cold winter night,
In a horse-pulled sleigh to an uncle's invite,
To his house up the road where we were to dine,
Via a snow covered path through the fir and the pine.
Nestled on snow in the bottom of the sleigh,
And covered with a blanket to keep cold away,
We smelled the horses and we heard the feet,
As they sprayed snow with a rhythmic beat.
Occasional peaks from our nest in the straw,
Would show only darkness or a star we saw.
Then we made a quick turn to our right,
And out of the darkness we saw a beautiful sight,
Lamp-lit windows decorated with lace,
Were like giant chandeliers suspended in space.
Then we arrived at our Uncle Obe's house,
As he helped us in with the aid of his spouse.
With a great relief we would see winter leave,
And spring burst forth with new things to conceive.
Buttercups of yellow nestled on hills of green,
Purple wild onions in every ravine,

Through the Eyes of a Boy

Flowers of every color bursting in bloom,
And the seeking of the morel mushroom.
We would see summer arrive with haying in the heat,
And occasionally sneaking off for a well-earned treat.
We would take a quick dip in the pond with frogs and snakes,
Or a potluck dinner with chicken and cakes.
Fall was a favorite with its colors of gold,
When grain was harvested and cattle were sold.
Wood was gathered and stored to dry,
And fruit was picked for our winter supply.
Those were the seasons that our memories compared,
Memories of the past, memories we shared.

Other events will always be a part of our past,
They can't be erased, they will always last.
The one room school that we did attend,
One teacher for all ages and the time they did spend,
Teaching us the basics of how to read and write,
And giving us homework to do in to the night.
The family closeness that we all had,
The sharing of the good as well as the bad.
The evening hours were the ones that seemed to bind,
The family together where memories were kind.
Huddled around together we would hear Dad read,
From books of interest, of adventure and deed.
Reading from the dim glow of a kerosene light,
We would be spellbound well into the night.
Hanging on each word we would always dread,
Hearing Dad say, "Let's go to bed."
The radio was another that made time go fast,
Listening to music and programs of the past.
Visiting the neighbors was a regular event,
And many Sunday afternoons were regularly spent,
With potluck dinners and card games to play,
With good food to eat and plenty to say.
As we grew older we often did chance,
A chaperoned ride to the clubhouse dance.
As we would arrive we would hear the beat,
Of the rhythmic pounding of dancing feet,
The high pitched wail of the violin,
As it sped up the pulse and the soul within,

The piano's pouncing like a high pitched drum,
Blending the sound like a honey bee's hum.
The shuffling feet and the gleeful yell,
Seemed to put the dancers in a spell,
As they formed a ring and swung to the right,
And weaved their way to the caller's delight,
And they would dance at a whistles blow,
It could be a partner they did not know.
Much fun was had until the middle of the night,
When the feet were tiring and the time was right,
To play the last song and home we would go,
And dream about dances from the fast to the slow.
Those were the memories, some thoughts prepared,
Memories of the past, memories we shared.

Perhaps the most vivid memories that we all had,
Were the memories that revolve around Mom and Dad.
Memories of discipline with love combined,
Memories of respect and tasks designed,
To teach commitment to a job well done,
And how the rewards can benefit one.
Their commitment to thrift and their disdain for waste,
And their language and behavior, always in good taste,
Their reverence for God and his written command,
And their respect for truth and the laws of the land.
Always well-liked by their friends and their peers,
They commanded respect throughout their years.
Many other incidents keep flowing through my mind,
Memories and thoughts starting to unwind,
Like a babbling brook weaving its way,
Through the rocks and the logs, cleaning each day.
Cleansing and washing with waters so pure,
Like memories on my mind, a therapeutic cure,
From the trials of the day and the tribulations we bare,
Memories we cherish, memories so fair.
Too many thoughts and events to cover all,
Just some mentioned, my favorite to recall.
And last but not least I feel honored to have spent,
My childhood days with one who has meant
A common bond to the past and of things which we cared,
Memories of the past, memories we shared.

Chapter 3

Farming and Farm Equipment

After moving to the ranch, my dad was advised by other ranchers living on the Flat to diversify his operation to balance fluctuating markets on the different farm products. Following this advice, we raised hay, grain crops, seed peas, some grass seed, cows, hogs and chickens.

The farm ground consisted of two types. One type was shallow and rocky and never was suitable for growing trees. The other soil type was mainly of volcanic ash origin and was where most of the trees were present. It was deeper and had very few rocks. Both types were less productive for growing crops than the richer soils further to the southwest towards Elgin. It was discouraging to put in all the work of farming and receive only about one-third the yield of ranches near Elgin and La Grande.

George Kennedy, one of our nearest neighbors, once sent a soil sample to Oregon State College to have it analyzed for mineral needs. When he was asked about the results he said, "They told me I needed 16 inches of new top-soil."

Growing and storing hay was always a difficult job. During the early years, hay was cut with a horse-drawn mower. Horses were often startled by the sudden explosion of blue grouse, lifting up into the air, when they were flushed right beneath the horse's nose. This would often result in short uncontrolled runaways by the horses. As the mowed section of the field would become smaller, the concentration of grouse would become greater, since the grouse tended to move to the standing hay for hiding cover.

My dad would carry a gunny sack on his mower to collect grouse that would be maimed or killed by the mower. These collected grouse would be saved for eating and provided a tasty variety in our diet. In the early years, we would often see over 100 grouse in a day. Now, blue grouse are seldom observed on Cricket Flat.

After the hay was mowed, it was raked into windrows by a horse-drawn dump rake. The rake was designed to dump its load of hay by depressing a foot pedal located beneath an old iron seat. The dumping assembly was a good place to get your heel if you didn't move your foot forward rapidly after tripping the assembly. A bar supporting the rake tines would grab your heel like a steel trap if you were not careful. The old rake ruined several pairs of my shoes and severely bruised my heel on a number of occasions.

After the hay was windrowed and shocked, it was bucked into large bunches of hay by a horse-drawn buck rake. This rake consisted of a series of poles resembling a table fork that slid along the ground in front of the horses. The hay was brought into the stack with this fork and then lifted onto the stack with the aid of a swinging boom pole with an attached Jackson fork. Hay to be put in the barn was pitched onto hay wagons from the large piles in the fields and transported into the barn by a method described in another chapter.

Horse-drawn rake, which was involved in several run-aways.

The hardest part of the haying operation was hand pitching the hay. Hand pitching was required by the person spreading the hay on the stacks, shocking the windrows, pitching the hay on the wagons and distributing the hay after it was deposited in the barn. The hay always contained a lot of dust and a sticky weed called tarweed, which would stick to your legs and cause a burning sensation. After tramping around in the hay, your legs would be black clear above your knees with dirt and tarweed stickers. It was a common practice to jump into our pond or a watering trough after we had completed haying for the day and bathe there, before eating our evening meal.

In later years we went to tractor-pulled mowers, side delivery rakes and a new tractor equipped with a device called a Farmland. This Farmland greatly sped up the haying operation because it could lift the hay onto our truck for hauling to the barn and could pick up the large bunches in the field and haul them to the stack and lift them onto the stack in one operation. This method made haying quite easy for the person driving the tractor but put more work on the person on the stack because it was able to haul the bunches in from the field at a much faster pace. Dad would put me on the stack and would rapidly bring in bunches of hay with this Farmland, as I scrambled to spread out the hay.

However, I did get revenge one summer when a knee injury prevented me from walking. Since I could not walk, Dad put me on the Farmland and he took the job spreading the hay onto the stack. It did not take me long to master the art of picking up the hay and delivering it to the stack where my dad was struggling in the dust and tarweed. As I became more familiar with the equipment, I increased the speed of my deliveries to the stack. It was not long before my dad was scratching his legs, and breathing heavily, sweat and dust covering his entire body.

"Slow that tractor down," my dad gasped, as he hurriedly tried to catch up with the mounting piles of hay.

Mimicking a phrase that I had often heard my dad say when I asked for a rest, I replied, "I think we had better keep rolling, Dad. There are clouds building up in the west and we need to get this hay stacked before it rains."

Needless to say, I did slow down and my father never repeated his rain phrase again during the following years when I was back on the stack.

Preparing the soil for seeding was a major job, especially when horses were used. Some of the tillage equipment, such as plows, springtooths and harrows, required walking behind the equipment and guiding the horses with long reins. Some of the fields that Dad would work up seemed to contain submerged reservoirs of rocks that found their way to the surface each time the ground was worked with equipment. From as long as I can remember, it would be my job to pick up these rocks from the field and stack them in piles at the field's edge.

Piling up rocks was one of my most discouraging and hated jobs on the ranch. As Dad drove the truck—or, during the earlier times, a horse-drawn trailer—I would pick up the rocks, pile them on the truck or trailer, and unload them. Seeing thousands of rocks scattered over the field during the first springtoothing operation in the spring and realizing that I was going to have to put my hands on every rock, was very demoralizing.

It was always a mystery to me where the rocks came from. It would appear that we had unearthed every rock each year that we plowed. Then, the following year another crop of rocks, appearing to be the same or larger in number would appear after the first plowing. Later in life, I told my kids and grandchildren, that my unusually short legs in relation to the rest of my body, was caused by packing too many rocks.

During the first three years on the ranch, grain crops were cut and bound into small clumps, and then hauled to a stationary thresher. Harvest operations were a cooperative effort of several ranchers pooling their labor, wagons and binders to work one ranch at a time. Gene Carver, an elderly gentleman who owned the only threshing machine on the north end of the Flat, ran and maintained the threshing machine.

The use of the thresher would leave huge piles of chaff and straw that would be used for feeding livestock. Apparently the threshers were not too efficient in removing all the seed from the grain heads. These piles were relished by livestock and various wildlife species. Dad told how rabbits, mice, songbirds, deer and a species of grouse no longer present on the Flat, would live on these stacks during the Winter months. He said the grouse species, which I suspect was the sharptailed grouse, disappeared shortly after the threshing machines were replaced by combines.

For a period of years after the use of the threshing machine was discontinued, Dad's uncle, Obe, harvested our grain fields with a horse-drawn combine. Since it took a number of horses to pull this combine, Obe used unbroken horses loaned to him in exchange for breaking them to work. Obe would use them in combination with work-broke horses to have better control. However, these unbroken horses provided many thrills with their frequent attempted runaways.

Dad purchased his first combine about 1944. It was a used Allis Chalmers combine with a five foot cutting swath, and we pulled it with an old Fordson tractor that he had purchased from his Uncle Obe. It was my job to sew the grain-filled sacks and slide them onto a chute. At a selected spot in the field, I would trip a retainer at the end of the chute and let the sacks slide to the ground.

After combining all day we would load up the old flatbed truck with the filled sacks of grain, which generally weighed about 120 pounds apiece. The next morning, while Dad was servicing and making needed repairs to the old combine, I would nurse the old truck loaded with grain to the Elgin Warehouse. I was about 13 years old when Dad taught me how to double clutch and downshift the old truck on the hills.

I did not have a driver's license when I first started driving the truck to town. I never did get stopped by the police, but I remember my Granddad Dave giving my dad a lecture on letting me drive the truck out on the highway.

We did not haul too much of our barley and oats to town as we mainly stored these grains on the ranch and chopped them up for livestock feed.

We started growing garden peas for seed the next year, 1945, and had to modify the combine to thresh peas. Unlike grain, the pea vines would lay flat on the ground. This meant that the combine header had to be placed close to the ground. We would often pick up rocks in the header that would funnel right into the heart of the combine where they could cause considerable damage. This usually caused costly delays and made us wonder why we ever grew peas.

The combine was finally retired one year when a large rock tore its insides apart and made repair impossible. The peas were a real gamble because a rain or hail storm during the ripe period would cause the pods to shatter and release the peas onto the ground. Dad was able to recover some of the value of the peas by letting our hogs fatten up on them when the harvest season was over.

Dad replaced the Allis Chalmers combine with an old, used International with a twelve-foot cutting swath and replaced the old Fordson tractor with a new Minneapolis Moline tractor. Replacing the old Fordson was another very happy moment for my dad. He spent many a frustrating hour trying to get it started and getting it unstuck from the mudholes in the fields.

The old Fordson tractor had already seen its best days when Dad purchased it from his Uncle Obe. Its main drawback was getting it started. Dad sometimes had to crank it for half a day before getting it to run. After about 15 minutes of cranking, Dad would begin to lose his composure and the air would be ringing with his emotional, verbal abuse of the tractor. His old felt hat would be subjected to foot stomping, hand-wringing, sailing through the air, and beating on the stubborn Fordson.

Dad's anger at the Fordson affected our black stock dog, Sug. Sug would go into a barking frenzy whenever Dad started cranking on the tractor and would race around the area biting trees, actually seeming to try to imitate Dad's anger. This did not seem to pacify my dad; he would often just transfer his verbal abuse from the tractor to the dog.

On cold, winter mornings, Dad would build a fire beneath the Fordson's oil pan to make it crank easier and to assist in its starting. The tractor had a component called a magneto bolted to its side. This unit seemed to cause most of the starting problems and, as they had quit making this particular part, it could not be replaced. Dad got to be an expert in taking this magneto apart and putting it back together again. Sometimes the tractor would start immediately after this procedure and sometimes it wouldn't. When it did not start he would repeat the procedure.

We had quite a few acres of land that we called pasture or timberlands. These pieces either had too many trees or too many rocks to cultivate or were too steep. This was the land where we pastured our range cattle. Most of it was located in Duncan Canyon, with access by horse or foot only.

Our farm crop portion of the operation often seemed to require a lot of hard work for us, with very little return. It was like playing Russian Roulette with mother nature. Late spring rains caused us to get our crops in too late. Little rain during the summer would reduce crop yields, hail or heavy rain during the late summer would shell out our peas, and rain on our down hay would reduce its food value. Farming on Cricket Flat was always a poor-odds gamble.

Chapter 4

Horses on the Ranch

Let a man with absolutely no experience with work horses work with four spoiled steeds with varying faults and you will have a prescription for mayhem. This was the situation that faced my father during his first few years on the ranch. Horse traders must have rubbed their hands in glee when they saw my father and granddad searching for prospective workhorses.

With Dad and his father knowing very little about horses, it was like leading two unsuspecting lambs into a lion's den. It was about a month after arriving at the ranch when they bought four workhorses for pulling the farm equipment and a two-wheel horse-drawn trailer. I cannot remember where or from whom the horses were purchased, but based upon the horses' idiosyncrasies, there must have been some happy and relieved sellers when they unloaded these steeds on my dad.

The four new horses that were added to our growing collection of animals were named Sparky, Dan, Charlie and Bird. Now Sparky turned out to be an uncontrollable kicker. One had to be extremely careful in harnessing and hitching him to equipment. Dad received several painful kicks and several pieces of equipment were torn up as a result of Sparkie's temper tantrums.

Dan and Charlie were the most gentle of the four. However, when either one was hitched to a team with another horse, they would hang back and let the other horse do all the pulling. When hooked together it was an on-going contest to see who could pull the least. This habit required the driver to constantly scold and whip the horses to get them to pull.

Probably the worst outlaw of the four was Bird. Now Bird, even though he was a gelding, imagined that he was a stallion. He was a fence jumper and was extremely hard to catch. He would use every available opportunity to escape from the ranch and join a group of semi-wild horses that were free-running in a timbered, rugged canyon located on some neighboring property. His escapes would require an all out effort by Dad and his younger brother, Ralph, to capture this renegade. Even when Bird stayed on the ranch, it was an all-family effort to capture him and the other horses.

Dad was unable to keep the horses tied up in the barn when they were not working because he did not have the extra hay and grain to feed them. He had to turn them out to feed in the pasture at night and then catch them the next morning.

It was these repeated and strenuous efforts to catch Bird and Bird's negative influence on the other horses that made Dad develop a real dislike for this horse. Dad, who was quite strong-willed, decided that he was going to break this equally strong-willed horse of his bad habits. After Dad would get Bird secured in a makeshift barbed wire corral, he would work for hours trying to train Bird not to run from him. Dad, while uttering a long list of profanities, would rush up to Bird and vigorously throw his hat at the feet of the trembling, wild-eyed horse. Bird, knowing that he could not escape, would stand like a scared soldier at attention for these sessions. Upon being freed from the confines of the corral, however, he would revert to his old ways.

Dad had old Bird in mind when he purchased a hobble strap attached to a thirty foot section of chain at an auction sale. He gleefully attached this strap and chain to Bird's front foot when he released him following the end of the workday. It was with great satisfaction that Dad would then watch the snapping action of the chain painfully pop Bird's legs when he would try to run away.

Although the chain greatly handicapped Bird's running abilities, he still attempted to flee for awhile. It was during these short flights that Dad would tirelessly pursue Bird while riding one of the other horses. Dad's main motives for these chase sessions were twofold: revenge and the hope that he could train Bird not to run from him.

It was during one of these "training sessions," with Dad immensely enjoying the whip-ping chain snapping against Bird's legs, when the chain broke loose from the leg strap. It was then Bird's turn for revenge as he raced straight as an arrow for the wild bunch of horses on the adjoining ranch. Following the trail of broken fences and an occasional glimpse of Bird's waving tail as he disappeared over hills, Dad grudgingly conceded defeat for the day. It took about two days of hard riding to eventually recapture the renegade horse and mend the broken fences.

One of the faults that all of the horses shared was their tendency to run away while pulling equipment. My first involvement in a runaway occurred when I was about five. My dad and I were traveling in a two-wheeled trailer en route to Uncle Obe's place when the runaway occurred. Dad had stopped along this primitive road to take down a rail gate and had given me the responsibility of holding the horses' reins. It was then that the horses decided it was time for some excitement. They jerked the reins out of my hands and plunged full speed ahead down the winding road. Moving faster than I had ever seen him move, Dad jumped onto the moving trailer, threw me out in one motion and desperately tried to regain control of the runaway team.

As I regained my footing, I watched my dad and the team disappear around the bend of the road like a Roman chariot in the Olympic Games. Not knowing exactly what to do, I slowly followed the primitive tree-lined road in the direction taken by the team. It was on down the road about 300 yards where I spotted the two-wheeled trailer at the base of a large fir tree. It almost appeared as if the trailer had attempted to climb the tree, as its eight-foot tongue and bed were pointed in a skyward direction, lodged against the tree trunk.

I fearfully searched for signs of their departure, but Dad and the horses were nowhere to be seen. I began following the pieces of harness and wood from the front part of the trailer tongue scattered along the road.

It was not too long before I heard my father admonishing the team in an unforgiving manner. As I came around the next bend in the road, I saw the two wild-eyed horses gasping for breath and cornered up against Obe's fence. Dad had each in tow with some old rope that he had borrowed from Obe. It took Dad considerable time and effort to patch up the harness and repair the trailer.

Another famous runaway occurred when my Uncle Ralph was raking hay with a horse-drawn rake. He was using one of Dad's horses and an older horse known to be weak in stamina and strength that Dad had borrowed from a neighbor. Ralph had been raking with this team for a considerable length of time and was getting concerned about the physical state of the team, especially the borrowed horse.

This animal was displaying all the signs of a horse about ready to die. It was stumbling, gasping for breath and was almost impossible to get started again after a rest stop. Ralph was so concerned about the horses that he stopped raking and left the physically exhausted team for an unattended rest while he voiced his concerns to my dad.

While Ralph was discussing the horse's plight with my dad, who was working in the adjacent field, the borrowed horse proved to Ralph that he had a lot to learn about horse endurance. It was also during the two men's discussion that old Shep, the family stock dog, decided that he would further establish his reputation as a fighter by testing his skills on a badger. Shep figured that he would give this impetuous, snarling rascal, which was only about one half his size, a sound thrashing.

Now the badger, which happens to be one of the most ferocious fighters for its size, had other ideas. It was not long before Shep and the badger were a rolling mass of fur, teeth and blood, claiming Ralph's and Dad's undivided attention. The winner of this fight was never known, as the fight was up-staged by another event.

It seemed that Ralph's unattended team was not quite ready to die of exhaustion after all. It was the sound of pounding hoofs that caused Ralph and Dad to switch their attention from the fight to the rear view of two seemingly refreshed horses as they gained speed with the rake in tow. Years of stored-up energy seemed to be released by the noise of the fight, as the runaway team raced at full speed around the inside of the field fence. The gathering of huge mounds of hay between the horses and the rake would gradually slow the horses down until the rake would suddenly catapult over the pile and land with a resounding clanging and banging sound.

The loud noise of the rake hitting the ground would inject new life into the racing team as they sped around the field with seemingly endless endurance. Perhaps they would still be running if the wheel of the rake had not caught in the fence that enclosed the field. The sounds of screeching wire, snapping fence posts and the clanging metal sound of the posts hitting the rake filled the air as the team tore out about 200 feet of fence. Finally, this team, believed to be dead tired several minutes ago, came to a grinding halt as wire from the fence finally halted their run.

Another notable runaway occurred one clear winter day during our return home from church. My folks, two neighboring boys, and my sister and I were passengers in our sled pulled by two of Dad's unpredictable horses. Dad's cousin and his wife were following close behind in another horse-drawn sled, as my folks had invited them to our house for dinner.

It was a beautiful, bright winter scene and the sun seemed almost to blind us by its reflection on the glistening snow. Clumps of snow-covered pine trees lined the snow packed county road leading towards our house. The rhythmic beat of the horse's hoofs was occasionally interrupted by flying snow, dislodged from the horses' hooves, pelting our wind-chilled faces.

The two neighboring boys and I were the primary cause of this particular runaway . We had barely left the church, when one of the boys joined up with a sled following ours and initiated a snowball fight. It was an ill-advised throw by my dad's cousin that scored a direct hit on the rump of one of our horses. This was all it took to give our horses an excuse to release some of their stored-up energy. Like sprinters leaving the starting blocks, our team was soon at full speed.

Amidst the sounds of pounding hoofs and popping harness leather, I could hear my mother's pleading cries to my dad to stop the team. As she tightly held my four year-old sister, she dropped to her knees on the straw-covered bed of the sled and told the other boy and myself to do the same.

Snow flying from the horses' hooves was now pelting the sled's passengers like giant hailstones. Dad, standing in a braced position in the front of the sled, was pulling as hard as he could on the reins. Fortunately our wild ride ended with no harm to passengers or equipment when Dad managed to steer the headstrong team into the four foot snow levels at the turnoff to our house.

It was about four years after Dad had bought the first four renegade horses that he purchased two more. One was a high-spirited black gelding named Prince and the other a white mare named Mollie. Mollie was the only good horse that he acquired while I was living on the ranch. She could be easily caught, she could be used for riding or working and was trustworthy and gentle. She was the main horse that my sister and I rode to school during the winter months. She only got out of control one time while she was on the ranch.

Because Mollie was trustworthy and gentle, she was used for putting hay in the barn. Our hay was transferred from the field to the barn by a wagon called a hayrack. From the face of the barn it was lifted vertically by hay nets that were hooked from each end to a carriage assembly attached to a cable.

This cable lifted the hay to an over-hang opening in the barn, where it locked into a horizontal track running the full length of the barn. Once the net load of hay reached the horizontal track, it followed the track to a selected point. Here it could be released by a long trip rope attached to the carriage assembly. The pull cable exited the back of the barn through two pulleys to where we could hook it to a harnessed horse. The horse then provided the pulling power to lift the hay by pulling in a forward motion.

This method for putting hay in the barn required well-coordinated equipment, including the carriage assembly, the track, and the tripping mechanism, that all had to be working perfectly for success. Just one little malfunction of one of these parts would create problems. One important aspect of this operation was maintaining a slow steady pull by the horse pulling up the load.

It was my job to hook the cable to Mollie's harness and maintain control over her pulling speed and the length of the pull. When I would hear my dad yell to stop, I would know that he had tripped the load from the net and I would then unhook the cable so that he could pull the nets back down to the load and re-hook them for the next load.

Dad and Uncle Jack had just gotten through spending a whole day overhauling the whole hay-lifting assembly to make it work properly for the season's first load of hay to the barn. I had just hooked Mollie to the cable and started pulling the load up when Mollie stepped on a yellow jacket's nest.

As one might guess, this was when the fireworks started. The angry wasps immediately stung both me and the horse. The normally gentle horse was instantly lunging and trying to gain speed against the load drag of the cable. It was not long before Mollie was at full gallop, with me behind, desperately trying to hold onto the reins.

I could hear both Dad and Jack screaming for me to stop. But halting Mollie at this time was about like trying to stop a speeding train. I was doing well just to keep my grip on the reins. It was only after we had jerked both pulleys off the back of the barn and pulled the carriage and nets through a small hole at the back of the barn that I was able to stop my runaway horse.

The scene at the back of the barn was matched in drama by the events occurring in the front. Apparently the sudden burst of speed by Mollie had caused Dad's hand to get tangled in the trip rope. Almost simultaneously Dad was jerked up on the remaining pile of hay. Just then the tension of the trip rope tripped the nets and dumped the net load of hay on my dad's prone body. Fortunately the trip rope had disengaged from my dad's hand when he was jerked up on the load. Otherwise Mollie would probably have pulled him through the back end of the barn with the nets and the carriage.

As I came reluctantly around to the front of the barn, my hay-covered dad, who was now stomping on his old felt hat and uttering profanities, shouted, "What in the name of hell happened back there?"

When I showed him the welts from the wasp stings, Dad reluctantly accepted my explanation. Later, Uncle Jack, who was at first feeling pretty glum about repairing the damage, laughed until he cried, recalling Dad being jerked up on the hay load and having the hay dumped upon him. He said that Dad looked like a mad troll who had just been tarred and feathered as he crawled out from beneath the hay.

Prince, the high spirited black horse, proved to be one of Uncle Ralph's favorite horses. Ralph had broken Prince to ride after some spirited riding sessions and did quite a bit of cow wrangling with him. Mollie later had two colts that proved to be fairly good riding horses, as well.

After Dad acquired an old second-hand tractor, he gradually phased the tractor into most of the farm work and sold off most of his horses. He then acquired a saddle horse named Snip from my mother's parents.

Snip was a spoiled horse that was difficult to catch and could be spooked at any strange-looking object. His rider would never know when Snip might suddenly bolt unexpectedly in any direction. All members of the family had occasion to part company with Snip's saddle during these sudden movements. Snip would also pretend to be frightened by some non-existent object in his path and would refuse to move forward until persuaded by a whip or spurs.

Catching Snip was a real problem. Attempts to bribe him with grain—the usual method of catching most of our horses—was unsuccessful with Snip. He would stretch neck and head out to their maximum reach to steal grain from its container. Upon attempting to put an arm or rope around his neck, he would bolt and wave his tail as if flaunting his pursuers. We found the best capture method for this horse was to drive him into a fenced-in field and chase him with a pickup until he got so tired he would give up and let us put a rope around his neck.

Snip was extremely intelligent. He had learned to open the metal latch assembly to the barn door leading to the grain bin and would help himself to a feast of grain. He seemed to be immune to foundering—the death of a horse from eating too much grain—and would often let the other horses in the grain. This finally led to the death of Mollie, when she foundered on chopped barley.

One of my favorite remedies for stopping Snip from opening the barn door was to attach the electric fence unit to the door latch assembly. It was very amusing and gratifying to watch Snip jump backwards about 20 feet upon grabbing the door latch. Snip did get some revenge however, as both Dad and I received some sinus-clearing jolts from this latch when we forgot it was electrically charged.

In reminiscing about horses and equipment that Dad owned, I find it truly amazing that he was able to operate the ranch with any success. The number of hours that he spent catching the horses and then working them until dark must have been extremely tiring. Later, he told how he would walk behind a four-horse team pulling a plow all day and then go to bed almost too tired to eat. It was a happy day in his life when he sold his four renegade horses and converted most of his farming operations to the tractor.

The "horse" I use on the ranch today.

Chapter 5

Cows on the Ranch

Raising cattle on the ranch served several purposes. The male calves were all castrated at a young age and sold as steers when they were two years old. For the first seven years the female calves and the mature cows were kept as breeding stock to build up the herd size. During the first ten to twelve years, from four to ten cows were maintained for dairy purposes. The milk products were used for family consumption. The cream was sold and the separated milk was fed to the dairy cows' calves and to the pigs.

When I was eight years of age, I was introduced to the cow milking program and by the time I was twelve, it was pretty much my entire responsibility. The job involved gathering the cows from the pasture, putting them in the barn, hand milking them and then transporting the milk to the separator.

The whole sequence of milking was performed mornings and evenings and took about two and one-half hours per session. When dad was not haying or combining or some other task that kept him away from the ranch, he generally helped with the milking and by cranking the cream separator. Early on we averaged about six cows for milking purposes. However, as beef cow numbers increased, we gradually cut down on our dairy herd size.

After the milk was separated, the separator had to be disassembled and washed. This job was quite an operation in itself because of the large number of parts that had to be washed once a day. Rosalie took over this job when she reached eight years of age. She did help some with the milking after the dairy herd size was down to three to five cows.

The separated milk that was not used for the family, was fed to the milk cows' calves, since these calves were taken from their mothers when they were about a week old. These calves had to be trained to drink milk from a bucket, as it was an unnatural thing for them to do. Bucket training calves sometimes was very time-consuming and difficult. These calves had to be kept in a separate pasture to keep them from robbing the milk from their mothers.

Milk not used for the family or the calves was fed to the hogs. It was dumped into a large wooden trough where there was always a squealing horde of hogs impatiently waiting for their precious share of milk. There was never enough milk to go around, so the strongest and most aggressive hogs ended up with most of the milk.

The cream that was separated from the whole milk was the driving economic force of the whole milking operation. The sale of this cream provided my folks with a much needed weekly income. Although the revenue was not great, it allowed them to survive gaps in income from crop and livestock sales. The cream that was separated from the milk was stored in our cellar in large cans until it was collected by a cream company representative.

The first cream company that collected our cream sent their truck from as far away as Pendleton, some 70 miles distant, on a weekly basis. This company made butter and cheese from the cream and did not care if it was sour or sweet. Even though our cellar was quite efficient in keeping produce cool, it would not keep cream from souring during a seven-day period during hot weather.

The Pendleton company discontinued collecting cream in the early forties and a La Grande based company that collected both milk and cream contracted to buy our product. Although some residents on the Flat sold the whole milk, my folks continued with the cream sales because they needed the milk for the calves and hogs. They also relied heavily on a certain percentage of the cream and its by-products for family use.

In connection with the milking, it was also my job to remove animal wastes from the barn. In the milking section of the barn was a six-by-twelve inch gutter that ran the full length of the barn. This gutter was positioned so that it ran directly behind the cows as they stood secured with their heads in stanchions.

The stanchions, which could be locked tightly around each cow's neck, were spaced so that a person milking the cows barely had enough room to slide a milking stool in between the cows for milking. This left the milker in a precarious position as he sat on the stool, sandwiched in between the cows and a sometimes uncleaned gutter just to his left.

Because milk cows are unpredictable in their reactions to certain events, our positions while milking left us at the mercy of the cows. We all, at one time or other, experienced kicks to the back, cows kicking our buckets over and swats to our faces by the cows' messy tails.

It was my dad that had the worst experience with milking. Once, he was snugly positioned between two of the gentler cows, listening to the pulsating milk squirts hit the bottom of the milk bucket, when one of our cats initiated a chain of events that was not good for Dad. Apparently the cat, one of several that lived in the barn, spotted a mouse trying to swipe some grain out of a grain box located near the cow's head.

With feline speed, the cat suddenly dived in around the cow's head in pursuit of the mouse. The sudden movement of the cat panicked the cows on each side of Dad and they sent out a barrage of kicks that would have put a kick boxer to shame.

It was only a matter of seconds that Dad had lost his glasses and was lying face-down in the gutter, which happened to be full of cow manure and urine. Amidst flying cow hoofs and cow manure, I helped roll Dad out of his unexpected bath in the gutter. Since he was nearly blind without his glasses, I had to retrieve them—unbroken but dirty—from beneath one of the cows. The first sign of a smile on my face following the incident prompted a stern lecture from Dad about neglecting my duties in cleaning the gutter.

Milking the cows was what I hated the most. Perhaps the lost opportunities in recreational pursuits due to my twice-a-day milking chores influenced my feelings on farming. By the time I had left the farm and gone into the Army, I promised myself that I would not pursue a career that included livestock.

As I grew older and the size of the beef herd grew, our milk cow numbers were reduced so that we kept only enough milk cows to provide for the family table. We further reduced our daily milking obligations by using the practice of turning the milk cows' calves back with them when we wanted to leave the ranch for some period of time.

While the milk cows saddled us with daily obligations, our beef cow operation confronted us with challenges that we were ill-equipped to handle. My father, not having a ranching background., did not construct or buy adequate facilities and tools for handling range animals. He was also a poor horseman and he could not rope from a horse. In addition, he did not have any good cow horses for rounding up cows. Our poor fences, or even lack of fences, allowed our cows to intermingle with the neighbor's stock.

Turning our range cattle out in the spring was no problem because the cows were anxious to migrate from the diet of old stale hay to one of green palatable grasses and forbs. Bringing them in for winter feeding was easy, too, because they were anxious to return to hay after a diet of diminishing dry grasses and shrubs.

It was the rounding up the two-year-old steers for sale during the late summer and early fall periods that presented the biggest problems. Separating them from the other cattle on the range without the use of a corral, driving them from the range to the ranch, and getting them loaded into a truck without adequate corralling and loading facilities, all presented problems.

On one occasion, I remember the steers presenting a lot of problems. We had chased them for two days before finally funneling them into the milking section of the barn. While trying to force them into the truck, which was backed up against the back section of the barn door opening, two steers managed to jump a two-foot square window in the barn and escape through a trail of broken fences, back to the range.

After about two days of chasing these increasingly wild steers through our fences and the neighbor's fences, we managed to get them into our neighbor's corral. After putting a rope around each one's neck, we were finally able to load and snub them up to the front end of truck racks.

It was at that time that my dad mistakenly thought we had won the battle with the steers. Even though the train car that hauled livestock from Imbler to Portland was not scheduled for four days, Dad decided to haul the steers to Imbler where he could board them in the Imbler stockyards until the train arrived.

We were just pulling into the Elgin city limits, when I glanced back and noticed that one of the steers had broken the rope securing him to the stock-rack. Knowing that there was a good chance that the freed steer would jump over the top of the rack and escape, we began to pull over to the side of the road.

The truck was just about to stop, when I told Dad that the 900-pound steer was attempting to jump out. I had just barely gotten the words out of my mouth, when the sudden acceleration of the truck rudely slammed my face against the rear window of the cab and sent the steer from its standing position to a prone position on the truck bed.

As the truck continued on through Elgin, Dad said matter-of-factly, "Tell me when he starts to jump again."

The steer, now a ton of pumped-up adrenaline, immediately got up and tried to jump again. I almost regretted relaying my message to Dad, as this time he hit the brake and sent me crashing into the front of the truck cab; and the steer hit the deck again.

This sequence of stopping and accelerating and stopping repeated itself most of the way through Elgin, with the old green truck closely resembling someone doing the bunny hop dance. The steer seemed to gain more resolve and energy with each body slam and would repeatedly rear up on its hind legs and attempt to climb over the battered, aging stock rack.

As wide-eyed pedestrians stared and other vehicle drivers scrambled to remain clear, we bunny hopped the old green truck all the way through town.

Now the other steer, who had also been taking a beating through our pulsating drive, decided he wanted in on some of the action. In a desperate back lunge, perhaps reinforced by Dad's accelerated start, the second steer snapped the rope securing him to the rack and joined the other steer in its jumping attempts.

My oral relays of jumping attempts by the steers were now being accelerated. Our whole sequence of actions was like someone speeding up the film speed of a movie projector.

I now had to really brace myself to keep from being hurled through the truck windshield. The glovebox door on the truck had opened and its contents were being scattered all over the truck cab. Tools that had been lost for years suddenly appeared from beneath the truck seat and just as suddenly disappeared again on the quick truck starts.

I had just asked Dad if we were going to drive this way over the next eight miles to Imbler, when one of the steers managed to break the top three truck rack boards. With the rack now lowered, despite Dad's best efforts on the bunny hop, the steers managed to jump over the rack to their freedom.

As we watched the two white-faced steers defiantly trot towards the town of Elgin, Dad looked for a moment like he was going to give up and go home. He had just watched three days of hard labor go down the drain. He was wondering how he was ever going to get these wild steers captured again. He did not have any horses immediately available, and he did not know where the steers would go or how to load them if they were caught.

Dad's four days of bad luck soon came to an end. As we were turning the truck around and temporarily blocking the highway, a couple of brothers that had just moved to the edge of Elgin from Cricket Flat stopped and inquired what had happened. Now these brothers, Ed and Burt Stowe, just happened to be the best cowboys in the Elgin area and they seemed to be homesick for some of their old Cricket Flat cow wrangling.

It did not take long, after learning what had happened, before they eagerly agreed to round up the steers and load them up by the use of a cattle chute located close by, near the Grande Ronde River. They told us to keep an eye on the steers while they went back to their place and got their horses.

In the meantime, our two wild-eyed steers with mucus flying from their nostrils had decided that a good offense was the best defense. Like two Mexican fighting bulls, they belligerently trotted down the main street of Elgin challenging anyone that moved. It did not take them too long to clear the street as they tried to figure which direction to go. They finally holed up under some cottonwood trees near the old Elgin Park.

It was after an exciting chase in and along the Grande Ronde that Ed and Burt were able to rope the two steers and drag them to the loading chute. With the aid of electric cattle prods and ropes, we again got the now somewhat subdued steers loaded and snubbed to the truck bed. This time we were able to successfully deliver them to the stockyards without any more problems. My father was a relieved man as we headed the old truck back to the ranch.

A similar incident happened with two other steers. We had just returned to our barn from the range with a bunch of steers earmarked for the market. We had managed to get the steers into one of Dad's make-shift corrals attached to the barn, when the fireworks started.

Two of the largest steers in the bunch managed to break out the side of the corral and let the whole bunch escape. After about two hours, we managed to repair the corral and capture all the steers except the two that had initiated the escape.

We gave up on the steers for the day; figuring that we would capture them for marketing when the cows were brought in for winter. It was a few days after the cows came in for winter feeding that we again attempted to capture these two steers. It did not take too much chasing before these wild ones jumped three fences and fled from the ranch. Although we made several searches for the steers, we did not see them again until we turned the rest of our cows out the following spring.

Apparently the steers had wintered out on the breaks of the Grande Ronde River and they joined the rest of our cows the next summer. The next time we went to gather our stock for wintering, the steers separated from the herd and stayed out another winter. We made several efforts to bring them in, but they became progressively wilder each time and acted more like elk than cows. They got so that they would take flight and run for miles at the first sight of a person or a rider on a horse.

It was during the following fall that Dad decided that he would never be able to catch these steers. By now they were too big to be

Farm ground reverting back to trees on Cricket Flat.

roped, even if a roper could get close enough to rope them. Dad and a neighbor solved the problem by stalking the steers and shooting them near the north end of our property. It turned our to be quite a job salvaging and packing out the meat because of the size of the animals. Dad estimated that they weighed close to 1,800 pounds apiece.

We had many adventures rounding up cattle—too numerous to tell them all. Every herd gathering, every branding operation and every incident requiring capturing and handling these range cattle with our limited knowledge and resources was an all-out adventure. I am sure that Dad was a relieved man when he sold his last cow in 1960.

Chapter 6

Pigs on Cricket Flat

Since pigs have the potential for rapid reproduction and are good foragers on crop residues, they were the popular farm animal for many of the Flat residents. Most of the Flat's farmers kept their hogs fenced in during crop growing and harvesting periods and then turned them out to freely roam throughout the community after the last grain crops were harvested.

Because the hogs had the free run of the community, it was an advantage to have a large number of pigs so that the owner could take advantage of grain and peas that escaped the harvest of the combines.

Residents often tried to discourage their neighbor's swine from trespassing on their fields by keeping a number of pig-chasing dogs. This method usually worked well in the daytime, but was not effective at night. Arguments often erupted over trespassing hogs and an occasional killing of the pigs by the dogs.

Far-ranging feeding patterns and the tendency of residents to buy breeding boars from their neighbors seemed to result in Cricket Flat hogs that were just one step removed from the European wild boar. These pigs were long, lean, fast runners. Sows liked to give birth to their young out in the thick timber.

Both sows and boars could be mean and dangerous, and many of these hogs had a tendency to attack one of their own that was in distress, especially if it started squealing. A squealing pig caught in a fence would often be torn apart by the other hogs. An old sow with young could also be extremely dangerous.

Since everyone had pigs, there were probably more good stories about hogs that were told around the Flat than about any other subject. My Granddad Dave told about walking down the side of a fence during a very dark night. As he was groping his way through the darkness, he heard the loud grunting sound made by a sow with little pigs. Thinking that the sow was right in front of him, he vaulted over the rail fence to escape being attacked. However, he picked the wrong side of the fence and jumped right on top of the angry sow. Motivated by the snapping and popping of the sow's jaws, Dave made a mockery of gravity as he jumped back over the fence.

My dad's Uncle John Scott, also a resident of the Flat, once broke his toe as a result of pigs. Hogs had been raiding his garden at night, and this one night had again come in for a snack. John, hearing them feeding, rushed out of his house to chase the pillaging swine away from his garden.

All the nightly raiders rushed away except a seemingly large, black one that appeared to be reluctant to flee. John, with a vengeful swing of the foot that would have made an 80-yard field goal, kicked this unmoving object with all of his might. However, the powerful kick with his bare foot, intended for a pig, met an unmoving large black stump that had no sympathy for a man's bare toe.

Probably the most famous hog on the Flat was a large white boar belonging to Uncle John. The boar, which everyone called Old Whitey, was a large, rangy boar that stood nearly as tall as a cow and had long protruding tusks. George Kennedy aptly described this boar when he said it was a cross between a greyhound and a race horse. Old Whitey freely roamed the Flat at all times of the year and had no respect for fences. He would jump a four-foot fence as easily as a person would walk through a door.

Now Old Whitey was one of my dad's worst enemies. The boar would come over during the winter and would eat hay and grain put out for our livestock. Whitey was mean and dangerous to both us and our livestock. He would inflict deep gashes with his tusks and caused some serious wounds to some of our cows. He was not afraid, even when dad fought him off with a pitchfork.

Dad had Palmer Kennedy, a brother to George Kennedy, come up and chase this boar off a couple of times. Palmer, a quick and nimble-footed man, would induce Whitey to charge and then at the last second he would step to one side and deliver a powerful rap to Whitey's nose with an ax handle. These blows would cause Whitey to leave for a few days, but he would always come back.

The usual method for chasing away trespass hogs was the use of one or more dogs. Whitey, however, would protect his back side by backing up against the side of the barn and fight the dog off rather than running. Dad was about ready to shoot Old Whitey until a sheep herder came by one day and asked Dad if he could use another dog. He said this large red dog, called Thor, was too rough on sheep, but thought he would make a good cow dog. He said Thor would grab a charging cow by the nose and would not back down from any animal.

As the sheep herder waxed eloquent with glowing accounts of Thor, I could see a gleam begin to brighten Dad's eyes. The herder could not even finish his laudatory comments before Dad interrupted him and said, "I will take him." Thor had scarcely been with us a week, when Old Whitey loped into the barnyard during our morning feeding chores.

It did not take Dad long to call Thor and our other dog, Sug, and sic them on the boar. Whitey wasted no time in backing up against the side of the barn. As Thor faced off against the boar, Whitey decided that he would give this new dog a good lesson by making a vicious forward charge. His forward charge ended up with his tender snout secured firmly between the flashing white canine teeth of 90 pounds of muscled dog.

Now a pig's most tender spot is right near the end of its nose, and this is exactly where Thor was hanging on as hard as he could. It did not take Whitey long to decide that flight was better than fight, as he painfully jerked loose from Thor's grip and raced out of the barnyard with the two dogs in hot pursuit. Running uphill, the fleeing boar launched his streamlined body over a four-foot fence and came down running on the other side.

As the boar and dogs raced out of our view, Dad and I quickly climbed over the boundary fence between George Kennedy's place and ours, putting ourselves in position to view Whitey's flight across a wide open field.

As the boar started to slow down, one of the dogs would give him a painful nip on the most tender spot of his posterior. These bites caused the boar to surge ahead with renewed speed and energy, putting distance between him and his pursuers. This nipping and squealing continued until the boar disappeared from our sight. Old Whitey never honored us with his presence again. We eventually had to give Thor away as he was too rough on our cows and hogs.

My dad generally had one of the largest number of hogs of anyone on the Flat. He, as well as most of the Flat residents, tried to raise more hogs than they had summer pasture or feed grain for feeding. Our hogs were always on the lean and hungry side, and it always took much longer than normal to raise a hog to selling weight, which was around 200 to 220 pounds.

There was a group of farmers around the Imbler area that called themselves the "Market at Six Club," which meant that they could bring their pigs to market weight at six months of age. George Kennedy used to jokingly remark that Dad qualified for that club because he marketed his hogs at six too—six years that is.

My Uncle Jack used to remark that my dad ran the only Hog College in the United States. He said that Dad's hogs could earn a degree in "Breaking Through Fences" in four months. He went on to say how Dad would always start out in the spring with a terrible hog fence. He added that by the time the hogs had learned to get through that fence, Dad would build the fence just a little bit better. Then the pigs would learn a bit more about breaking and entering. Jack added that, by the time Dad and his hogs had gone through several levels of improved fences, they could break into Fort Knox.

Jack always jokingly told the story about how he watched a group of Dad's graduate hogs approach a cattleguard. He said the first few hogs laid their bodies across the cattleguard like a group of soldiers using their bodies for crossing platforms. He said that the remaining hogs, using their fore runners as a bridge, crossed the cattleguard on their buddys' backs.

Dad finally got his revenge on Jack for all his pig stories. Jack was helping us load about 25 hogs that we were taking to the sale yard. We had finally managed to drive the unwilling restless pigs into a make-shift shed that had an attached loading ramp leading into our stock truck. Jack was holding the hogs in the shed with the aid of a four-by-six foot panel, which he was holding against a four-foot opening on the outside of the shed. Dad and I were inside the shed, trying to force the stubborn squealing pigs up the ramp and into the truck.

Apparently the pigs had gone out for football at Dad's pig college, as they all charged in unison and hit the panel held by my uncle. Like a team of professional football linemen, the pigs hit the panel with the combined force of a speeding locomotive. Jack did not have a chance, as he was knocked on his back into about twelve inches of pig manure and mud. Only the rickety panel protected him from 25 rampaging hogs using his body as a path to freedom.

It was the bubbles emerging from the quagmire that helped us find Jack. After pulling the splintered and broken panel from Jack's buried body, we were able to lift his mud-covered form from the slurping, sucking sounds of the pig manure and mud. Jack, who resembled movie shots of a monster arising from the depths of a mud swamp, was not in a very good mood.

Hurling his manure-laden hat into the side of the pig shed, he angrily shouted, "Noel, you and your toothpick fences." Fortunately, after a clothes-on bath in our pond, Jack regained his composure and we again rounded up the pigs and got them loaded.

Dad and I had several harrowing experiences with our swine, this time with the sows. We would entice the sows with their young pigs into our barn, and would concentrate them and their litters in small temporary partitions in the back. Here we kept the young and their mothers until they were large enough to withstand the rigors of cold weather and predatory coyotes.

The sows were always very protective, especially if we tried to handle the young in any way. Castration was one of the tasks that was performed on the young before being turned out of their pens. We would catch them with the aid of a noose attached to the end of a long pole so that we would not have to reach into the pens with the protective sows. After snaring the young male pigs, it was my job to hold the young pig securely on the barn floor while Dad castrated and ear-marked the squirming, squealing animal.

The squealing of the young pigs would drive the sows into a uncontrollable rage. It was a scary job, trying to confine the young pig while its mother was popping her teeth, emitting snorts of anger and charging the flimsy wooden panels.

On several occasions the sows lunged repeatedly against the wood panels, causing the panels to break. We would then have to drop the young pigs and scramble for our lives. We could often be observed running out the barn door with a mad sow snapping at our backsides. Fortunately, the sows would not chase us too far and we would generally escape without injury.

Dad, however, was not so lucky on one occasion. He was working the pigs by himself, and had just pulled a squealing pig from its mother. Before he could even turn around, the 400-pound sow broke through the panel and knocked my dad down. His first instinct was to protect his face with his arms and hands as the mad sow repeatedly tried to bite his face. Fortunately for my dad, a dog we called Spot heard the commotion and drove the sow away. Dad wore the marks of that attack for several years.

A sow once caused me to lose a large patch of skin from the side of my face. I had been riding my sled down a narrow trail in the snow. This hard-packed trail, which was made by cows traveling to their feed grounds, was confined on each side by a three foot wall of snow. This narrow trail led up a very steep hill and provided a thrilling fast sled ride for my sister and me.

I had launched my sled from the top of the hill and was speeding down the path like an Olympic bobsled contestant, when a large sow met me face-to-face around a curve in the trail. I don't think the sow moved one bit when my speeding sled crashed into her chest. On the other end, I was launched like a rocket over the startled, squealing sow, and landed on the side of my face in the hard crusted snow. I ended up with the side of my face looking like a giant, red strawberry.

We always had to play nursemaid to the newborn pigs. Some of the weaker, young pigs that were born in the winter had to be taken into the house and bottle-fed until they were strong enough to withstand the cold and compete with the rest of the litter. It was a common sight to see five or six little pigs housed in a cardboard box nestled behind our kitchen stove.

In the summer months, the sows would often give birth in the remote depths of the timber lands. We had to find these sows and their young in a very short period of time and move the litters to our barn to prevent the coyotes from eating the young pigs. Getting the sows and their young to the barn often proved difficult because of the protective nature of the sows. We would often wait until the sow left the nest for feeding, and then would capture the young pigs and haul them to the barn in a gunny sack.

A few of the Flat's residents would call on George Kennedy to assist in these pig moving operations. George would sneak up on the sow's litter, and grab a pig. When the pig squealed, the sow would start chasing George, who would artfully keep just ahead of the sow, heading back to the barn. While George was distracting the sow, the owner of the pigs would gather up the rest of the sow's litter in a gunnysack and follow. George had several narrow escapes in these captures, but was always willing to perform this service when it was requested.

During the last few years on the ranch we discovered that we could keep the coyotes from these forest-born litters by hanging a piece of our freshly worn clothing within twenty feet of the litter nest. This would work for about three days before we had to replace the apparel with another worn item. We found that dirty socks worked the best.

My dad and Uncle Jack became accomplished hog surgeons by watching the La Grande Veterinarian. By using an old sack needle, some sheep dip for sterilization, their pocket knives for scalpels and sack twine for sewing up their incisions, they would perform some rather complicated operations on the pigs. They would hoist their patients on the side of the woodshed and would cut and sew like a couple of surgeons in the emergency room. Despite their crude and unschooled methods, a surprisingly high percentage of their patients survived.

Probably the most depressing time of my dad's life was a result of our pig farming operation. It was in March one year that disaster struck our pigs. Dad had been feeling depressed all winter because the previous fall he had lost his pea crop to a hail storm. He felt somewhat relieved that he had a large number of hogs that had fattened up on the peas that were shattered out on the ground. He had wintered these pigs and would have sold them in about another month.

It was while we were feeding our cows one morning that we noticed three or four pigs were ill. The next day there were more hogs acting the same way. After calling the local veterinarian, we found that they were infected with hog cholera. The vet prescribed shots and sulfa pills for the rest of the pigs. This medication seemed only to prolong the agonizing drama of 80 hogs dying a slow death. We only managed to save five or six sows that were apparently immune to the disease.

Watching and trying to save the ailing pigs was just half of our problem. A state law required that we burn all the dead animals in order to eradicate the disease. We would spend days gathering dry fuel from our woods to burn the carcasses.

Hogs with cholera have a sickening pungent odor that made us nauseous just to be around. The odor from the burning carcasses seemed even worse. Several of the pigs crawled beneath our barn, and I had to crawl in where the odor was stifling to tie a rope to the hog's feet and pull them out.

The cholera epidemic dealt a major blow to my folks. For the second time in less than a year, Mother Nature took a cash commodity from our tightly budgeted income. We had to tighten our belts in almost every aspect of our lives. Mortgage payments on land purchased had to be deferred or reduced, planned equipment purchases were canceled, and a loan had to be taken out from the bank.

We had no type of insurance to cover our losses. Dad was very despondent for the next few months. He used to sit around in the evening after work, and stare into space. I believe that this was the worst year that we all experienced while living on the ranch.

He who milks the earth for its treasures to give,
Gambles with forces that selects who will live.
Forces thrown out like dice from the hand,
With God only knowing how they will land.

Chapter 7

Chickens on Cricket Flat

Chickens played an important role to most families living on the Flat. In addition to providing a cheap meat source to our diet, laying hens also provided eggs, which were used in many types of table dishes. Having eggs available on the ranch was also a big advantage over making a trip to town.

To a lesser degree, some of the Flat residents raised chickens for fighting purposes. Cock fights were another form of recreation enjoyed by the rural community.

Of all the livestock raised on the ranch, chickens and their culture were probably the least understood by my folks. They seemed to be way down on the priority list compared to the rest of the farm animals. Dad's time was mainly devoted to the more important revenue producers on the ranch, such as cows, hogs and the various crops.

Dad left my mother in charge of the chickens, garden and orchard. Leaving my mother in charge of chickens was like leaving a lamb in charge of a den of lions. She had been pecked and flogged by a protective mother hen when she was a child and had developed an powerful fear of chickens. I am sure she would not have assumed this chore if we had not needed the meat and eggs.

My mother's fear of chickens resulted in my being involved with the enterprise at a very young age. It was my job to feed them, gather the eggs, handle the hens with their broods and break up the setting hens. As I grew older, I assumed additional duties, including catching chickens for butchering, picking their feathers and preparing them for cooking.

My job of breaking up setting hens was one that had to be done quite often in the summer months. Once these hens started incubating eggs, they would steal the nests from the laying hens and would quit laying themselves. We did let some of the setting hens follow through with their incubation and raise chicks. When we had a sufficient number of hens incubating, we would have to break up the rest so that they could get back into egg production.

During the spring and summer periods it was common to have three to four incubating hens that needed to be broken up from incubating. We found that the best way to return these hens to the laying mode was to put them into a real wet gunnysack and hang the sack on the clothesline for about three days.

It did not take me too long to supplement my various forms of recreation by playing a betting game with these gunnysacked hens. I would wait until some of my friends came over and we would take the hens on a raft to the middle of our pond. We would then simultaneously release these hens into the water, making bets on which one would swim to the shore first.

There was one hen that could swim almost as fast as a duck, and would always reach the shore first. When company was expected, I would go out and catch this hen, regardless of whether she was incubating, so I could win bets with her.

Since we did not have a chicken house at first, we put up wooden boxes in our barn and woodshed for the hens to lay in. Although some of these hens used these wooden boxes, most of them preferred hiding their nests out in the timber or under buildings. I found a lot of these hidden nests by watching and following the hens.

There were a lot of nests that we did not find until the eggs had rotted or the hen showed up with a brood of chicks. Whenever I found rotten eggs, I would carefully stockpile them for use in war games with other kids. When I had company, we would choose up sides and evenly divide the eggs. Our war games were set up in locations where we could conceal ourselves for surprise attacks. The games were not designed for anyone having a weak stomach or sensitive nose, as all parties were generally hit several times by these vile-smelling bombs.

The failure of our chickens to lay eggs during the winter months prompted Mother to set up a management plan to reverse this trend. She had read in an agricultural bulletin about a method to stimulate hens to lay eggs during the winter months. Following the bulletin's instructions, we gathered up all our free-running hens and provided them with the straw litter and feed prescribed by the bulletin.

Most of these hens were older predator-wise survivors; some were so old that they had spurs and closely resembled roosters. Some had lost their combs and were battle scarred from fighting with other chickens, hawks and owls.

It was this group of ancient warriors that we expectantly fed and watered with such care that these hens must have felt like they had died and gone to heaven. After about three months of changing litter, feeding, cleaning roosts and doing all the things mentioned in the bulletin, we decided that something must be wrong.

"We have not gathered one egg since we have shut these hens up," my mother complained one day.

I had observed a few egg shells with traces of broken yolk on them, and it became apparent that the few eggs being laid were all being eaten by the hens. Mom then read the bulletin again and found that she had missed a section of some importance.

The part that she had missed mentioned that only young hens, birds of the year, should be used for laying hens, and that older hens did not lay well and would often eat the other hens' eggs. A quick inventory of our flock showed that we only had two young hens out of 25. This ended our egg production attempts for that winter, although we did have some limited success with winter egg production in succeeding winters.

One of the worst problems that we had in raising chickens was predators. Pigs, badgers, weasels, hawks, dogs, cats and owls all seemed to like chicken as well as we did. Probably the worst two predators were the goshawk and the great-horned owl. Most of the other hawks would light in a tree before they went after a chicken. This habit allowed us to shoot them before they could attack.

With the goshawk, however, intercepting them before they could attack our chickens was almost impossible. They would come flying into our barnyard at a high rate of speed, grab a chicken while in flight and pack the chicken off without ever slowing down. The only way that we could control them was when one would grab a chicken that was too heavy for the hawk to fly off with. When this happened, the hawk was reluctant to leave his kill, and this gave us an opportunity to shoot.

The other predator that really gave us problems was the great-horned owl. These owls would come in at night and pluck the chickens off their roosts. Since most of our chickens roosted in trees, they were vulnerable prey to the owls.

We found the best controls were penning the chickens up at night and setting traps on top of a twenty foot pole set up next to the tree roost. Once in a while these owls would even get into our chicken house with our chickens. My two younger sisters were surprised one morning when they opened the chicken house door and surprised an owl setting on the roost with the chickens.

The practice of raising game chickens for fighting purposes was practiced by a few of the Flat residents. Our participation in this sport was limited, although we did raise a few of the birds because of their increased ability to evade hawks and owls. These game birds were more like pheasants than chickens. They could fly for long distances, they were very wary in their feeding habits and they were quite successful in raising their young in the surrounding woods.

On the negative side, they were hard to catch, the roosters were mean and they were on the small side for eating purposes. We actually had one of our game roosters kill a goshawk when the hawk got his talons locked into a half grown chicken and was unable to fly. The roosters would sometimes fight each other until one of them was killed.

Cockfighting on the Flat was primarily held on one ranch. Participants would travel from up to 100 miles away to enter their birds in these fights. The fighting rings were located in a wooded canyon far from the view of a public road. Some of those present were there strictly as observers, some came to bet and some came to enter their roosters and wager. Although it was a cruel and illegal sport, attendance at these events was high. An estimated crowd of up to 200 in size was not unusual at these cockfights.

One of the funniest stories that I can remember relating to chickens is about an event that occurred one afternoon, when my mother had asked me to catch a rooster for her and prepare it for cooking. After a long hard chase, I had caught this large rooster that was very strong and difficult to hold. I struggled to contain this large bird in a still position so that I could make a clean head-detaching chop with my ax. Rube Witty, my dad's first cousin, saw my difficult struggle with the rooster and said, "Why don't you bite that chicken's head off? That's what I used to do when I was young."

Perhaps Rube would not have made this statement under normal circumstances. However, this particular afternoon, Rube, my Uncle Jack and dad had celebrated their completion of haying operations by tapping into a batch of Dad's home brew.

I don't remember how many bottles they had consumed, but it was enough to put them in a festive and talkative mood. Upon hearing Rube's remark about the rooster, Jack said in a challenging manner, "Rube, I would think you are better equipped to bite off a chicken's head now then when you were a boy. Why don't you show young Harlan how it is done."

Dad then joined in the good-natured bantering. Between him and Jack, they really started putting the pressure on Rube to back up his statement. I am sure that if Rube had been sober his pride would have been overcome by common sense. However, now he was backed into a corner, and with the help of the home brew and two unrelenting men, he reluctantly agreed to dispatch the rooster.

As Rube held the rooster up to a face-to-face standoff, there seemed to be about a minute pause in the confrontation. Perhaps Rube was wondering how he was going to get out of this without losing face, and perhaps the rooster was wondering why he was being stared at in such a fashion.

Then, striking suddenly like a rattlesnake, Rube had the chicken head in his mouth. What happened next was not too clear because my vision was blocked by the flapping wings of the rooster and an explosion of feathers. This was followed a by a bare-necked rooster hitting the ground at a dead run and squawking with every step as he raced out of sight.

Rube's mouth looked like the working end of a feather duster and his face looked like a road map of red lines from the rooster's claws. As Rube spit and coughed out feathers like the back of a combine spews out grain chaff, Dad and Jack rolled on the ground in laughter. The rooster, unhurt except for the loss of his feathers, was not observed again for about three weeks.

CHAPTER 8

TRANSPORTATION

Travel on the north part of the Flat during the early 1930s was time-consuming and difficult, especially during the winter months. For the most part, county roads were not graveled and maintenance by the county was minimal. Snow removal efforts were generally confined to the mail routes. Figure 1, a rough map of the county roads on Cricket Flat during 1935, shows quite a few more miles of county roads than we have today. However, they were primitive roads and many were rarely used except by just a few families. The map does not show the private roads in the area, or those roads, like the south end of Yarrington Road, that were changed to county roads after 1935.

Less than fifty percent of the families owned cars at that time and during the winter and wet spring seasons cars could not be used because of road conditions. Rubber-tired trailers pulled by horses, horse-drawn sleds, riding horses and walking were all common forms of travel. George Kennedy had a one-horse hack that was used by his family. My folks used a small two-wheeled trailer during the summer months and a sled in the winter. During heavy snowfall periods, travel was often restricted to saddle horses, snowshoes or skis.

Some of my most lasting memories were of the night trips made in the horse-drawn sleds. As my father braved the cold elements of the night from his standing position in the front of the sled, my mother and I would be nestled on a layer of straw covering the bed of the sled. Heavy blankets reinforced our cold weather clothing so that only

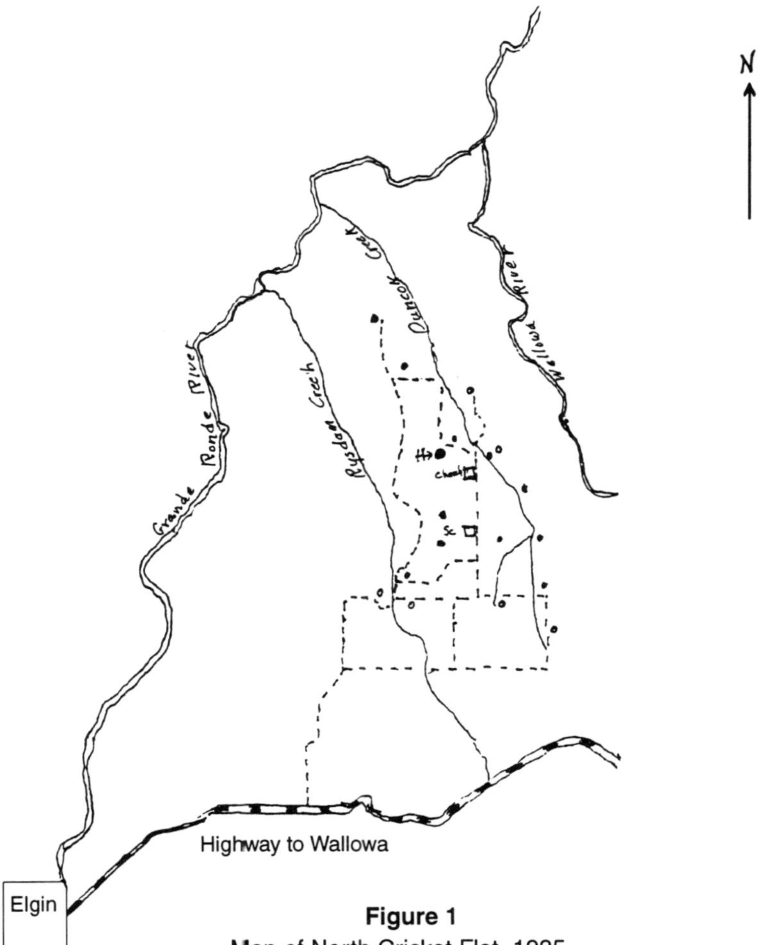

Figure 1
Map of North Cricket Flat, 1935

Legend
County Roads, 1935 _ _ _ _ _
Residential Houses •
School □ Sc
Church □
Our House H→ •
One Mile ├────┤

a small opening for our eyes exposed us to the cold night air and the spray of snow thrown by the horse's hooves.

The cold quiet of the night would be interrupted by the whirring sounds of the sled runners slicing through the snow. The creaking and jingling sounds of harness leather and tug chains almost drowned out the sounds of the snorting horses as their hooves drummed the packed snow. The solitary wail of a coyote and the hooting boom of the great-horned owl would sometimes join the sounds of the sled and horses.

As our sled would glide through the moonlit night, we would enter tunnels of darkness where heavy stands of fir and pine would shut out the moon rays of light like switching off a giant lamp. When we emerged from these forested tunnels, we could see the coal black silhouettes of trees creating jagged borders against a dark blue sky sprinkled with twinkling yellow stars. As our road left the forested areas, occasional farm houses would stand out like lighthouse beacons at sea, with their lamp-lit windows sending out warm messages of light.

When we arrived at a neighboring house after one of these evening rides, the man of the house would come out and help tie up the horses, while his wife would help my mother and me out of the sled and into the house. Blankets used during the ride would be brought in by the stove so that they would be warm and dry for the return trip.

Since car travel was limited during the winter months, trips to town for groceries and lamp fuel were almost impossible to make. Families usually tried to stock up on needed supplies in good weather so winter trips were not necessary.

Regardless of how much planning we did, some supplies were always needed during these winter periods. Fortunately, the mailman, a robust man by the name of Ed Mason, was willing to deliver needed supplies upon request by a note left in the mailbox. Apparently this was a free service that was commonly done by mail carriers at that time.

Mason would make his thirty-mile round trip from Elgin, often braving deep snowdrifts with a four-horse team and sled. He would often use a barn located at the far end of his route to house fresh horses for this tiring trip. Mason ran this mail route three days a week in the winter months. Since our mail box was over two miles from our house, it was still a chore retrieving the mail during inclement weather.

My folks bought their first car in 1935. This car, a secondhand Oakland, was purchased for $25.00. It lacked the necessary power to pull some of the hills around the Flat area and required accelerated speeds at the base of the hills. Ralph Scott told how the Oakland's lack of power trapped him between two hills. It was only with repeated backing and forward driving that he was able to finally gain enough momentum to conquer the hill.

Tires were a weak point on cars during the 1930s. It did not take much of a rock or stick to puncture their thin casings. Also, wear was rapid, with tires lasting only about one-fourth as long as they do today. Tire patching kits and tire changing irons were common accessories, even on short trips.

Batteries were also inferior to the ones we have now. If a car did not start right away, the battery would run down and the car would have to be hand cranked. Hand cranks were also called knuckle busters as the rotation of the crank would often result in one skinning his knuckles against the bumper supports.

During the late 1930s and the early 1940s, major improvements were make in the Flat's transportation system. The Union County Road Department, with assistance from a generous supply of WPA workers, upgraded the main county roads by straightening, graveling, filling and installing culverts. Also, a maintenance program was initiated that included grading and winter snow removal.

The mail route was extended so that the mail was delivered within a quarter of a mile from our house. In addition to upgrading, many of the other less-traveled roads were abandoned, at least for county maintenance. The road improvement program was probably one of the most beneficial developments on the Flat.

Along with the improvements to the roads, a higher percentage of the families now had cars. Although we did not get a new car, we did purchase a secondhand 1934 Chevrolet, a tremendous improvement over the old Oakland. Most of the Flat families now had cars that were newer and better. Other improvements were in tires and batteries.

Horse drawn vehicles were mainly phased out by the mid 1940s. However, horseback riding was still popular and was still needed for off-road travel. Such riding was probably best epitomized by the Stowe family. Two brothers, one of the brother's wives and the brother's dad all lived on the same ranch. This ranch was located about a mile and a half south of our house. These brothers, Ed and Burt Stowe, and their dad were perfect examples of the all around cowboy that was often portrayed in the history books on the Wild West. They were expert riders, horse breakers, excellent ropers and as tough as nails.

Ed, a tall, sinewy man of about 150 pounds, had a hawk-like nose, piercing brown eyes and black, straight hair. Ed was well-known for talking loud and using profanity with every other word. He and Burt would often communicate by using a whistling code that both seemed to understand well.

Ed would often win bets with strangers to the community by loading a 120-pound sack of grain on a truck by using only his teeth. Burt, a small, medium-built man of about 130 pounds and about five feet four inches in height, had a balding head and twinkling brown eyes. A bachelor, except for a short period of married life; Burt lived with Ed and Ed's wife, Edna.

Both Ed and Burt would occasionally get in fights at some of the local dances around the Elgin area. They were both exceptionally tough men in a fight and seldom lost. Burt once whipped a 300-pound man that lived on the Flat, using a painful hold that made the man give up in a hurry.

The Stowes always had a large string of saddle horses that they kept around their barn, and a much larger herd of semi-wild saddle horses that roamed the Flat area. The Stowes spent a lot of time rounding up and moving cattle and horses. They would often invite other residents of the Flat to join them on horseback rides. They would ride down and cross the Wallowa River and ride clear up its east side before returning home.

My folks occasionally joined these riding groups and would generally ride the Stowes' horses, since we did not have any horses that could keep up. My mother recalled how Ed and Burt would communicate with each other with their whistling on these rides, and how their dad would continually give riding instructions to the other members of the riding group. The length of the rides nearly killed my mother and she had to quit participating in these events.

As I grew older, Ed and Burt would occasionally take me along on one of their horses during their range and cattle checkups. They tried unsuccessfully to teach me to rope and one time convinced me to jump from a horse on to the back of a fleeing calf. Ed and Burt were roping calves from their horses, tying up their feet and earmarking and castrating them. They had given me a rope and let me try roping the fleeing calves. Although I tried several times, I did not have the experience to succeed.

Both of them told me that if I could not catch one with a rope, I should try to bulldog one from my horse. Finally, after some good-natured persuading, I gathered up enough nerve to launch my rigid body from the back of the speeding horse to the back of the running calf that was sandwiched between my horse and Burt's horse.

Following the Stowes' instructions, I dove for the front shoulders and locked my arms around the calf's neck. For a few yards, the 200 pound calf carried my body at a stumbling gallop. We then both went into a tumbling roll in which I lost all bearings on what was up or down.

All I could concentrate on was clinging tightly to the calf's neck as our bodies took turns being ground and scraped by the rocks, dirt and sticks. Finally we ended up with the calf on top of my stomach, its kicking feet pointed towards the sky.

It was the next few moments that really worried me. Ed and Burt scared me to death when they pretended as though they thought I was the calf and started tying my feet together. It was only after my desperate yelling that they, with a great deal of laughter, let me go and took care of the calf.

The Stowes loved horses and loved to work with them. They even organized a few polo games on their ranch. These games were eventually discontinued when some of the participants got hurt. The Stowes probably best preserved the old way of life on the Flat with their continued use of horses.

I acquired my first car when I was sixteen years old. The car, a 1934 Chevrolet, was the one that had belonged to my folks. It was not my first choice for a car, but funding for a newer and better one was not available at that time. Once I had made up my mind that this old car that had been abandoned by my father could be restored to running again, I was a lot more exuberant about my new ownership.

Many plans rushed through my head as I vigorously brushed and scrubbed the old Chevy. that was parked on my folks' ranch. It had only been a few days earlier that I had helped my dad tow the old car with his tractor to this resting spot, after its motor had quit, down on the county road. My dad had not made any major effort to start it, as he had purchased another car and the old Chevy, much like a terminal patient, had been growing progressively worse during the last two years.

Years of dirt and oil accumulations on the car's motor and numerous leaks in the exhaust system resulted in large emissions of black and blue smoke whenever the car was driven. Even in the coldest weather, the family rode with all windows rolled down, everyone's eyes red and dripping tears from the fumes.

It was not unusual to be hailed down by other drivers thinking that the old Chev was on fire. Lack of power from a coughing, sputtering motor and an occasional loud backfire characterized the engine as we would shift to the lowest gear to climb any slight hill.

Starting and keeping the motor running was another major problem. Loose and corroded battery cables, a weak worn-out battery and old spark plugs and points made the car hard to start. If the car did not start immediately, the battery would quit turning the motor over and an old hand crank would have to be used.

Apparently the designers of this car did not ever try to use the hand crank, as the support for the bumper left just barely enough room for the crank to turn. These supports were all known as knuckle busters as skinned knuckles were common place when cranking was required. They were especially dangerous when the engine backfired. Also the hand throttle, which regulated the engine speed, had to be set at a high idle or the engine would die. This resulted in jack-rabbit starts and squealing tires.

My sister and I finally refused to ride down the main street of Elgin in this car with my folks because some of our school friends had called us "The Gas House Gang." The jack-rabbit starts and the clouds of black smoke belching out like a locomotive provided an entertaining spectacle for the town residents during our drives into Elgin.

One might have asked what I was doing pampering this car, which only a few weeks earlier had been the shame of my life. It had all started shortly after Dad had purchased his other car. I incorrectly surmised that if Dad had enough money to buy another car, he might have some extra cash for a car for me. When I asked him for some money to buy another car, he told me that the best he could do was buy spark plugs for the old Chev; adding that he thought that the plugs were what caused it to quit.

I had put my dad's proposal on the back burner and probably would have forgotten it if I had not happened to discuss the proposal with George Kennedy. George, who was a fair mechanic and had helped Dad repair the old Chev a few times, casually mentioned that probably the main thing the old car needed was a change of oil, which had not been done for about three years. He added that the engine should also be flushed with some type of a cleaner.

George's statement kindled a fire of hope that seemed to gain momentum as I had more detailed ideas on restoring the old car. A few days later I drained the old oil and refilled the crankcase with sheep-dip. With the aid of new spark plugs and a secondhand battery, I finally got the car started. After following George's instructions on allowing the car to run for thirty minutes on the sheep-dip mixture, I drained out a solution of crud that looked like a sheep herder's dishwater. After I had refilled the crankcase with new oil, replaced the oil filter and made several other minor adjustments, I got the old car running better than it had for several years. As I cleaned and polished, I found myself imprinting on the old car like a cow to a newborn calf.

Despite some continued but reduced engine smoking, I was on cloud nine as I proudly drove the old Chev along the twelve mile route from our ranch to Elgin High School. My popularity was immediately enhanced as I dragged the main street of Elgin with a carload of animated high school students. Unlike today, when a large percentage of high school students have cars, very few of the Elgin students had cars. I soon learned to prioritize an overwhelming number of requests by fellow students to drive them to their various destinations. I found this necessary in order to live within my limited weekly ration of fuel for my car.

Previously, I had been required to ride the school bus home to the ranch after classes were over, and was unable to participate in after-school activities, such as sports, plays and dances. The availability of a car opened up many new opportunities and probably had one of the greatest impacts on my young life.

Numerous stories could be told of the old car's trips to dances throughout Union and Wallowa Counties, trips to football and basketball games, trips to the Cove swimming pool and many others. Probably the most memorable occasion occurred when the engine quit on a side street entrance to La Grande's main street. After the battery refused to turn the motor over, I got out the hand crank and started cranking.

By this time a large number of cars were backed up and added to my embarrassment and distress by a noise-brigade of honking. In my rush to get the stubborn motor started again, I had forgotten to take the car out of gear before cranking. My first spin of the crank launched the old car into a forward leap that sent me tumbling to one side, scrambling for my life.

Quickly regaining my feet, I desperately tried to catch the runaway Chev as it raced through a mass of honking cars with screeching brakes. Somehow the car reached the far side of the street and impaled itself on a metal light post. I quickly and quietly nursed the old car out of town through a back street after a group of college students helped me push the old car back away from the pole and on to the street. I did not feel secure until I had parked the car deep in the woods of our Cricket Flat Ranch.

The most satisfying moment of my car's history was the time I had to use it to tow my dad's car to La Grande when his car broke down about five miles from our house on the county road. He traded his car in on another one shortly after that. He did not think it was too funny when I offered to sell the old Chev back to him after the tow job.

Having made numerous trips driving the old car through roads covered with snow and deep drifts, I became well-known for my driving skills on roads that were impassable to most other cars. I nearly scared my Uncle Virgil and his wife, Winn, to death one time when I drove them from my folk's house to the town of Elgin during a raging snow storm.

The old car, with its sixteen inch knobby tires, was put to the test as it plowed through three feet deep snow drifts. As we approached the drifts at a high rate of speed, the car's windshield took on a blinding blanket of snow before it broke through. Hanging my head out the window for visibility, I would struggle to hold the swerving car on the road as I tried to gain speed for breaking through the next drift.

During all this time, spraying snow was showering my aunt and uncle from the open window. By this time, my passengers were in a state of shock as we braved drift after drift all the way to the plowed highway leading into Elgin. It was an impressive ride that stuck in all our memories.

I proudly continued to drive the old Chev from 1946 through 1952, although it did have several rest periods from minor malfunctions that depended on my accumulating adequate funds for repairs.

Breakdowns and malfunctions seemed to increase with time. A leaking radiator that I could not afford to replace and increasing smoke leaking up through the interior of the car required that I limit my driving to summer months during the last two years of the car's life. Driving with all the windows rolled down and refilling the radiator with water every twenty miles was a bothersome necessity.

Finally, in 1952—for the second time—the old Chev, which had left me with many youthful memories, was towed to its retirement site on my folks' ranch when the engine got too hot and would not start again.

Today, roads on the north part of the Flat are all graveled, but most are still unpaved and can be in pretty rough condition during certain times of the year. Logging trucks, recreational vehicles and trucks hauling gravel for improvement of private driveways now dominate the once primitive paths that helped settle the Flat.

Chapter 9

Child Discipline and Motivation

Raising children that were obedient and responsible seemed to be achieved more successfully by the parents of the 1930s than by parents today. Several factors seemed to contribute to this success. Probably the leading factor was including the children in the work force at an earlier age and giving them responsibilities for performing their assigned duties.

In my family, we learned that we had to perform daily chores at a specified time and place. These chores were done without reminders on a daily or weekly basis, and if we forgot, some type of punishment was administered. Also, repeated punishments for the same offense progressively got move severe.

The severity of the offense and the number of warnings I received usually dictated the type of punishment that I could expect. Usually the first step for a mediocre offense, was a mild scolding accompanied by a detailed explanation of how I had broken the rule and why the rule had to be followed. On the second offense I was generally denied some privilege or pleasure that was dear to my heart.

One of the rare treats that I was regularly denied, as part of my punishment, was a piece of candy that, on rare occasions, would be doled out to my sisters and me after the evening meal. This simple act by my parents was enhanced in its effectiveness by my sister, Rosalie.

During my candy punishment sessions, Rosalie would ceremoniously tantalize me unmercifully. She would position herself where I could observe every lick and bite that she would slowly take of her candy. She would manage to drag these sessions out as long as possible with slurping and sighing moans of pleasure. On some occasions, I could not stand her tormenting actions any longer and would grab the candy from her careless grasp and devour it. This act would always increase my punishment and was generally only carried out when my revenge and the yearning for the candy overcame my better judgment.

Taking away a promised fishing trip or a trip to the movies was generally a punishment used for a more severe offense. Denying fishing trips, which was my favorite pastime, was a very effective tool in adjusting my attitude. I was left at home while my dad and Jack Halsey took a planned fishing trip into the high Wallowa Lakes after I had neglected my milking chores one evening. To me, this was one of the worst punishments I can remember. It certainly branded itself in my memory when I was tempted to break a rule.

Adding extra chores to my work schedule was another popular method of discipline. This was an effective tool, especially when the chore was one that was regularly performed by my sister, Rosalie. I often found myself washing separator parts and peeling potatoes, while Rosalie gave me gloating smiles of delight when my mother was not watching.

Sometimes these distasteful chores seemed to coincidentally be assigned when a dreaded task was reaching its deadline to be performed. One of Dad's favorite punishments was the removal of a large pile of cow manure that accumulated at the back end of our cow barn.

Shoveling this large vile smelling pile into the back of the truck and hauling it to our garden was a hated chore. I got to the point where I was a perfect angel when this pile was reaching the removal point, so that dad would have no excuse to use it as a discipline chore.

My parents did not hesitate to use corporal punishment on the more severe offenses. Corporal punishment during the 1930s and 40s was a widely accepted method for disciplining children. Parents, babysitters, relatives and teachers were all given the green light in administering different degrees of corporal punishment. Slapping of the face, hair-pulling and twisting, twisting of ears, slapping the hands with a ruler and using various types of paddles on the buttocks were all used. My folks, as well as most of the parents on the Flat, used the fear of a good old-fashioned spanking to keep their children in line.

In my case, spankings were administered by my father on a regular basis, starting when I was at a fairly young age. Frequency of occurrences peaked about the age of ten. Apparently I had learned to abide by most of my parent's rules at that age, or other forms of punishment seemed more appropriate, as my spankings stopped when I was about fifteen years old.

My dad's main tool for dressing down my backside was a thirty-inch-long razor strap, which he folded in half and used to deliver up to fifteen whacks. On one occasion, when my dad did not have access to his strap, he used a flexible willow stick. Dad never spanked me in front of anyone outside the family. If I messed up at someone else's house, my whipping would be postponed until I got home, or when he could find the time.

Sometimes it would be several days before he found the appropriate time and place for these lashings. In a few cases I had more than one whipping waiting on the back burner. One thing Dad was consistent on was never forgetting about these postponed punishments. Also, if I had several lashings to be administered, I received the exact amount that was due. He never combined several whippings into one.

Sometimes when I was receiving one of my floggings, Rosalie would crack open the door of the adjoining room and gleefully watch my punishment. It was a joyous moment one time when Dad, who somehow must have seen her through the back of his head, told her, after he had finished with me, that it would then be her turn. He then gave her a good whipping while I got to watch.

My mother rarely administered spankings. Her main control over my sister and me was by threatening to have our dad spank us when he got home. However, when that failed, she would give us a sharp slap along the side of our face.

When other adults were around, she would grab the lobe of an ear or a lock of our hair between her forefinger and thumb, and with a simultaneous lifting and twisting motion would march us out of the room on our tip-toes. I imagine I resembled a ballet dancer as she would steer me through the crowd.

During my eight years of attending a one-room rural schoolhouse where one teacher taught eight grades, I saw a wide range of corporal punishment used by six different teachers. One teacher used a heavy duty yardstick, which she repeatedly broke over the kids' backsides. Another used a foot-long ruler. She would require the students to hold out their hands with their palms up and then dealt the hand a number of stinging blows.

The most severe punishment came from a teacher that used a two-and-one-half-foot-long board split out from a hardwood desk. This was the only teacher that raised the concern of some of the parents. This board tapered from one and one-half inches at the handle to about four inches at the spanking end.

Another teacher used a two foot long, one-half inch wide paddle with several holes drilled in the spanking end. One teacher used only the palm of her hand on the buttocks. Only one teacher did not use corporal punishment. She used the threat of a large burley school board director being called in to spank us as a highly successful deterrent.

When I entered Elgin High School in 1945, corporal punishment was still used. However, it was not used as frequently as in my grade school years. During my Freshman year, the rumor was started, perhaps by school administrators, that the superintendent employed a spanking machine to deliver his discipline spankings.

This machine was described in many different, terrifying forms by various students that were supposed to have been nearly killed by its use. In later years the truth was ferreted out that spankings were delivered by the superintendent using a two-foot-long wooden paddle with holes drilled in the spanking end.

The superintendent, a small slender man, commanded a great deal more respect and fear when it was learned that he had easily manhandled and flogged a tough ruffian student who had bragged that no school administrator could whip him.

Behavior that resulted in corporal punishment by parents and teachers naturally varied with the individual family and school official. In our home, lying to my parents, disobeying orders and using profanity were the big three that created most of my spankings. The use of a sexual four-letter word and a four-letter word describing body wastes, were words that would instantly generate a painful strapping by my father. In school, physical fighting was the main behavior that would result in spankings. Expulsion from school was rare, with spanking usually being the last and highest form of punishment.

Having been raised in an era of conservative discipline when spankings were usually the final and ultimate deterrent to ill behavior, I may be prejudicial in my opinions on the subject.

However, it is my honest opinion that the pendulum has swung much too far to the left in today's views on child discipline. I do not believe that one teacher could have controlled eight different classes of students if she did not have the threat of the paddle as a deterrent. I believe that school officials and some families have lost all control of children because of insufficient forms of discipline.

Probably the most important key to my folks' success in controlling their children was using consistency and follow-through on whatever type of discipline was used. Once I was told that I was going to be disciplined in a specific manner, I was never able to persuade my folks to use a lesser degree of punishment. I found out at an early age that it did not do much good to argue unless the folks had made a mistake in judging me guilty. In these cases, my persistent pleading of my case usually prevailed.

The youth of the 1930s and 40s were much like today's youth in that they did not enjoy hard, repetitious work. Incentives, such as work ethics, bribery, fear and the need to be responsible all helped.

However, obtaining maximum work effort out of the young workers of the community was pretty difficult to do. Most of the youngsters received very little pay for their work at home and not too much more pay when they hired out to a neighbor. Despite their reluctance, most of the kids had to work whether they liked it or not, and it was up to the adults to keep them working in a productive manner.

Keeping the kids motivated and accepting of work responsibilities was a challenge to parents, especially when monetary incentives were low or non-existent. In my case the promise of a fishing trip or trips to town to enjoy a movie or coke was an added bonus for doing my chores in a satisfactory manner.

Generally speaking, after children reached the early teens, work opportunities for pay would open up around the neighboring farms. These paying jobs included picking up rocks in the fields, haying jobs, sewing sacks on combines and many other ranching type jobs. Most of these jobs required hard physical labor and long hours for very low pay. Employers all had their favorite tactics that they used to get the most out of their workers.

Obe Scott was perhaps the master of them all in obtaining maximum work efforts out of his employees. Using a mixture of all the motivation tactics known to man, he was able to capture all the employees' available energy and direct it towards the job. My first experience in working for Obe occurred when I was about 13 years old.

My dad had sent me on foot to Obe's house after he had received a phone call asking if he could hire me to do some haying work. Not having many opportunities to earn money, the offer of fifty cents per hour motivated me to race over the three-fourths mile of wooded lane to Obe's house.

Obe, a large, heavyset man with a slow drawl that had a southern or mid-western accent, immediately started laying the foundation for his motivation tactics. When I arrived, he walked up to me, and with a pretense of amazement and shock said, "Gee, Harlan, I can't believe how much you have grown since I saw you last."

He then remarked that he bet that there were not many kids that could handle me in a fight. He added that probably all the hard work that I had done for my dad had put those bulging muscles on my arms. Just those few little words had me flexing my muscles under my blue linen shirt and feeling like a world beater.

Obe's next step was to explain the job we had to do that day. The project involved hand-pitching loose hay onto a flat-bed truck, hauling it to a barn, and transferring it into the barn by a set of hay nets.

A younger boy was to drive the truck in the field, one person would pitch the hay on the truck bed and the other person would stay on the bed of the truck where he would spread and tromp the hay. Pitching the hay onto the truck was the hardest job of the three and required a good amount of strength and endurance.

After a bumpy ride to the field in the old flat-bed truck, Obe and I each grabbed a pitchfork and I waited for Obe to tell me which job he wanted me to take. He promptly drawled that pitching the hay on the truck was the hardest job and that very few kids my age could handle it. Then, almost as an after thought, he mentioned that one of the other kids in the neighborhood, who just happened to be about my age, had pitched for him in another field. He then added that this kid was exceptionally tough for his age and that he doubted if I could handle the pitching job.

A loaded gun held to my head could not have done a more effective job than Obe's well-chosen words in intensifying my desire to grab the fork and start loading. It had just so happened that I could whip this kid that Obe mentioned in any sport that existed and the idea that this youth could pitch better then me made me want to prove myself.

Grabbing the bait like a hungry trout, I pleaded with Obe to let me pitch. Putting on an act like a Hollywood star, Obe reluctantly climbed to the bed of the truck, while grumbling that he would let me try pitching for awhile. However, he added that he was reasonably sure that I would not last too long.

It was with the resolve of a pit bull in a fight that I attacked the piles of hay on that hot July day. For the next few hours, while Obe kept up a continual barrage of statements that were as effective as a bull whip on a horse, I tore into the piles of hay like there was no tomorrow.

On numerous occasions Obe expressed amazement at my endurance and speed and kept mentioning that there were not many boys my age that could equal my work. Several times he said that I was throwing hay up so fast that he would soon have to take a rest because I was tiring him out. After each of these statements, I speeded up so I could force him into a rest, which by this time was needed much more for me than for Obe.

By lunch break, I was like an endurance runner that had used up all of his energy reserves. I had to drag myself to the excellent meal prepared by Obe's wife, Gladys. Normally I would have porked down one of these gourmet meals in five minutes.

However, I was so tired that I fell asleep halfway through my meal and woke up only momentarily when Gladys removed my head from my pillow of potatoes and gravy and guided my numb body to a couch. Obe, feeling compassion for my exhausted body, extended our lunch break an extra half hour before waking me up and heading back to the field.

Although the nap had refreshed me considerably, my work efforts waned as the hot dusty afternoon wore on. Time seemed to be suspended in space as my tired body gradually wound down like a rundown clock. Obe's repeated verbal stimulations that had worked like an electric prod on a stubborn pig during the pre-noon period were now having fewer results as we labored beneath the hot sun.

Obe, seeing that his motivational speeches were becoming less effective, decided that it was time to change his tactics. Like a great basketball coach responding to a new defense by the opposing team, Obe changed his offense. As my increasingly sore muscles slowed my movements, Obe said, "If you keep up this fast pace, we could haul more hay than when my son-in-law and I hauled on this same field last year."

He added that the rest of the men around the neighborhood would really be shocked if they heard that a 13 year-old boy had pitched more hay than a grown man. The mental picture of myself suddenly thrust into the community limelight as a youthful superman was all it took to temporarily rejuvenate my tired and spent muscles, and I again increased my efforts.

However, as the hot sun inched its way agonizingly towards its western-most setting point, my mind, which had dictated my work effort, rapidly surrendered its control of the physical parts of my body. My arms and shoulders, which were getting increasingly sore and stiff, felt like they were made of lead.

Despite thick gloves provided by Obe, blisters were forming on my hands and fingers. I was physically exhausted, much like a gasoline engine that has run out of fuel and was running on fumes.

Obe, sensing my physical condition, had now given me the easier job of spreading the hay on the truck while he pitched. This helped, but instinctive thoughts, perhaps designed for the self-preservation of my body, had begun to flash across my mind. I was now desperately grasping for a face-saving excuse that would allow me to gracefully exit this torture chamber and still maintain my credibility and reputation in the neighborhood.

Inasmuch as great minds work best under pressure, I suddenly had an inspirational idea. I would pretend that I was sick and, with a little luck, I could induce myself to vomit. I then pictured how Obe would drop everything and drive me home to my parents. I pictured how he would tell how hard I worked until the time I had fallen violently ill.

As the idea framed itself in my mind, I started searching for the right moment to initiate the most important acting job in my young life. My chance for an early career in Hollywood was short-circuited however, when Obe casually mentioned that a couple of years ago he had had a town kid out pitching for him and that this kid didn't have the guts to finish out the day and had pretended to be sick.

Then, saving his best shot for last, he added, "Boy, I am glad you are a tough country kid and not one of those town wimps."

It was at this point that I realized that any idea of quitting early had been shot down like a jet plane with a heat seeking missile. Now, a town kid, in a country kid's eyes, was about the most despicable, low-down, weak-kneed type of sissy that ever walked the face of the earth.

Country parents seemed to imprint their kids at an early age with how much better off they were and how much better they were than the town kids. This was probably done to quell any envy that kids living in a rural setting might feel when seeing the easy access that youngsters in town had to the soda fountains, theaters, ball parks and other city-associated activities. I now knew that I had to finish the job, even if it killed me.

It was about an hour later when we hauled the last load to the barn and Obe handed me four dollars for my work. The money and the continuous laudatory comments on my work seemed at least to halt the outward flow of strength from my exhausted body, which by this time seemed to be functioning independently from my brain. My legs felt like a pair of stilts as I staggered down the wooded lane towards my house.

I was about halfway home when a resting spot of fir needles beneath a large fir tree beckoned my weary body for a rest. It was at this location that I was awakened by my mother's worried call, and together we reached the house just as it was growing dark.

As the years passed, I had several other jobs on the neighboring farms, but none are as vividly remembered as that first job with Obe. Even though these jobs were difficult and boring, they seemed to be a valuable training experience for the youth. These jobs taught kids how to work hard, they made kids mentally tough, and all and all seemed to better prepare them for some of life's later challenges.

CHAPTER 10

THE COUNTRY SCHOOL

As with most young children, school played a major role in my rural farm life. It probably played a much greater role in the youth at that time than it does today. Lack of transportation, the greater distance between families, and children's part in the work force all seemed to make school a major focal point.

We all looked forward to the increased socializing and to, a lesser extent, a partial relief from farm chores during the winter months. I generally got out of the morning milking chores and many other daytime chores that I would have had to perform if I had been home.

Our schoolhouse was located on a bare open ridge surrounded by farm fields. Nearby, isolated farm dwellings nestled near north-south running strips of timber. These timber strips broke up the pattern of farm lands that had been laboriously carved out of the virgin timber stands during the late 1800s.

Stubblefield Mountain could be viewed from the south, Smith Mountain gave us an east view and Swaggart Butte could be seen to the north. The main county road leading to Elgin ran in a north-south direction directly in front of the schoolhouse.

The single-room school, which was approximately 40 by 50 feet in size, was accompanied by a small attached entry way, a nearby woodshed, two small outhouses and a 20 by 50 foot shed serving as a horse barn. Each side of the schoolhouse contained three vertical-placed, rectangular three by eight foot windows that had to withstand all the flying objects tossed by the students.

A huge pot-bellied stove with a half-moon shaped lid that opened from the top was located in the center of the room. An eight-inch diameter stovepipe climbed vertically from the back of the stove to a point about five feet below the 18-foot ceiling. This pipe, secured by numerous support wires fastened to the ceiling, ran horizontally along the ceiling for another 20 feet, where it entered a brick flue at the back of the building.

The wood-eating stove, which consumed ten to twelve cords of wood each school season, played an important role in our school life. Heating was a problem, especially when temperatures plunged to near sub zero temperatures. The uninsulated building with its high ceilings and single pane windows was located on one of the wind prone areas of the Flat. During these cold days, the ritual of opening the heavy stove door lid and chucking seven to eight large-sized chunks of wood through a mixture of belching smoke and flames occurred several times a day.

These cold days in the old schoolhouse provided an atmosphere of learning that will never be observed again in American schools. Desks that were normally distributed by class throughout the school building, were concentrated closer to the stove. The younger students were seated closest to the heat in the maze of concentrated desks.

The one teacher, responsible for teaching eight different grades of 15 to 20 students, had a difficult time weaving her way through the closely-spaced desks. The never ending task for the teacher included tending to the different students, handing out assignments and occasionally admonishing an older student that had left his desk to take a heat-blocking stance by the stove.

Oral instruction prepared for one class or student was heard by all, as each student struggled to concentrate on his assignment. Stationary blackboards were commonly used in instruction, but were largely abandoned during these cold spells, since it was simply too cold in that part of the room.

On a few occasions, the five gallon cream can used for drinking water and located at the far end of the room would develop a thin layer of ice during the day.

Students seldom left the school building, except for restroom breaks, during recesses and noon hours on these cold days. They occupied themselves by playing blackboard games, listening to stories read by the teacher or just visiting with each other. The teachers were generally quite strict about rough-housing or running activities inside the building. It did not take the students long to brave the outdoor elements once temperatures hit freezing level or above.

Some of the teachers initiated a hot lunch program during the winter months. Our homemade lunches were supplemented by a stew mixture that was prepared by the teacher. Each family would generally contribute some meat or vegetables for this stew, which they would send along with the student's lunch with a tin cup and spoon.

Illegally poached venison was not an uncommon ingredient and it was rumored that horse meat, said to be beef, was occasionally used. The teachers, who at first let the older students individually dump their ingredients in the pot, took full charge when it was rumored that someone had slipped in some coyote meat. The teacher would place this mixture on the flat top of the large wood burning stove. Here it would boil and simmer giving off appetizing aromas throughout the morning. This stew was certainly a welcome treat on these cold days, especially when some families could not afford to send much food for their children.

The suspended stovepipe that ran horizontally from above the stove to the back of the room was the weak link in the heating system. When the main brick flue would start to plug up, this horizontal pipe would send blue and black smoke halos from each pipe joint until the entire upper section of the room was filled with smoke. On a few occasions the pipe soot ignited and sent a loud, roaring sound along the red glowing horizontal pipe. As the flames flared out of each pipe joint and the pipe began to turn a dull red, the concerned teacher would herd her wild-eyed charges out of the schoolhouse door until danger had passed.

In addition to teaching the basics, teachers spent a lot of time involving the students in learning poems, songs and short plays. All students participated in these activities. Parents and other adults faithfully attended these performances just before Christmas and Thanksgiving, on Valentines Day, on Halloween and the Friday before Easter Sunday.

These programs were quite long and each student had to recite at least one poem, be involved in a play and participate in a song. Every program would have several plays and songs. Teachers and students would spend quite a bit of time rehearsing and making costumes for these events. Sometimes some of the parents would help in making the costumes. In my case, my parents spent a lot of time in the evening hours making me practice for these performances. These events were well-attended and enjoyed by just about every member of the community.

Students' birthdays were always celebrated with adult participation. School was let out about two hours early on a birthday and all parents usually attended. Cake would be brought by the parents and if ice or snow was available, ice-cream would be made at the school. Parents and students would both gorge themselves on ice-cream and cake. Students always looked forward to the birthdays and the accompanying parties.

Although most of the students were fairly well-behaved, as in any group of youngsters, there were always a few that dealt the teachers a lot of misery. One of the favorite pastimes was chewing paper spit wads and launching them to the ceiling with the aid of a ruler. Wads with the right moisture and consistency would stick on impact and some, after drying, would fall. As the wads accumulated, the smoke-colored ceiling closely resembled the wart-covered back of a toad.

Another diversion was using soda straws as blowguns to launch Austrian peas at fellow students. These miniature cannon balls could be shot the full length of the school room, hitting an unsuspecting student in the back of the head. These straws would make a hissing sound when the peas were launched like a cruise missile. This sound would generally pin-point the launching site and it would not take the teacher long to locate and identify the sender.

A few of the boys, including myself, would play a game we called, "Pin the Tail on the Teacher." In this game we would try to paste a funny face drawn on a sheet of paper on the back of the teacher's dress. This was usually attempted when the teacher was assisting another student. It was a risky game, especially after it had been played on the teacher a few times.

Live garter snakes or mice were often captured and left in the top drawer of the teacher's desk. One teacher turned the tables on her students after someone had left a mouse in her desk. After we had all had our hot lunch stew, she told us that she had put the mouse in the stew because we did not have enough meat in it.

She added that she had put the main part of the mouse in the lunch cup of one of the suspects. She went on to say that any other tricks of that nature would result in a gathering of several mice and snakes for the purpose of making a stew. She then said that all the students would have to eat this stew until it was gone. This ended the mouse and snake planting tricks on this particular teacher.

One student scared all the other kids and the teacher when he dumped live ammunition in the woodstove.

We would often advance the school clock so that we would get out of school early. When we did this, someone would have to beat the teacher back to school the next morning and turn the clock back to the right time. Another favorite trick often played on new teachers was to put a rotten egg in their overshoes. This was a pretty nasty trick and usually resulted in some severe punishments.

Outdoor activities during lunch hours and recesses varied. Playing tag, hide and seek, Anne-over, playing on home made swing sets and teeter-totters and foot races were the primary outdoor activities during good weather. In winter, making snow figures, sledding and skiing, digging snow caves and snowball fights were common. Snowballs made out of wet slush and allowed to freeze were quite dangerous to the kids and hazardous to the large school windows. They were eventually banned, with the threat of a severe penalty.

Occasionally, some less desirable activities took place in the large horse barn where the teacher could not observe our actions from the large schoolhouse windows. Smoking homemade cigarettes, inducing dog fights, fist fighting and telling dirty jokes were some of the pastimes that eventually prompted the teachers to ban the horse barn for all uses except taking care of the horses.

Student discipline, unlike today, was primarily dictated by the teacher, and what the teacher did was usually backed up by the parents. As mentioned in another chapter on corporal punishment, the teacher had full rein in spanking students. Students, including me, usually got an additional spanking from their parents when they got spanked at school. One teacher used a 30-inch slab from an old hardwood desk to deliver her spankings.

This teacher quickly put an end to fist fighting, which had been commonplace before her arrival, with the use of the slab. Two students incorrectly assumed that, by throwing this paddle down one of the toilet holes, her spankings would have to come to an end, or she would obtain a less painful paddle. However, after finding the paddle, she forced one of the guilty students to hold the other one's feet, while he retrieved the paddle. Then, hardly letting the paddle dry, she whipped them both with it.

Most of the school discipline amounted to penalties less severe than corporal punishment. Restricting recess privileges, assigning janitorial duties around the school, assigning extra schoolwork and the teacher writing notes to the offending student's parents were some of the punishments used.

Packing wood from the woodshed to a large pile inside the school room was a popular punishment. Technically, packing the wood was the teacher's job. However, teachers seldom touched the wood because there was generally a waiting line of offending students ready to assume this chore.

The teachers were also responsible for the janitorial duties around the school and did not hesitate to assign these duties as punishment. One of the dreaded assignments was cleaning out the outhouses. We would have to sweep the floors and then scrub them down. All the walls would have to be wiped clean or painted if we could not get them clean with soap and water. Cleaning windows and sweeping the schoolroom floor was also a common punishment

The main subjects that I can remember taking were math, spelling, writing, reading, English, geography and science. In math there was a lot of emphasis on repetition of multiplication tables, addition, long division and subtraction. In the later grades we had to work quite a few story problems, especially those containing questions on computing interest income. One teacher had the whole school sing the multiplication tables the first thing every morning.

Spelling was a subject that commanded a lot of the student's time. Most of the classes had spelling tests about every day. Spelling contests were often held on special occasions when the parents were present. Spelling was always my weakest class and I had to spend much more time on this subject. Penmanship was practiced almost daily, with a lot of emphasis placed on form. Students all had to compose short stories and poems.

A considerable amount of time was spent in memorization. Learning poems and reciting them was a common assignment from most of the teachers. One teacher insisted that we memorize all the states and their capitals. When this challenge was first presented to me in the form of a test I tried to devise a method to cheat on the examination, since I figured that there was no way that I could successfully memorize and correctly spell the states and their capitals.

To cheat the system, I prepared a miniature-sized list of the test items and carefully hid it at the base of a hand-cranked pencil sharpener, which was mounted on the side of the wall some thirty feet away. When I got stumped on the test, I would deliberately break off the end of my pencil and take an allowable trip to the sharpener to sharpen my pencil. There I would slip a quick peek at the list and return to my desk.

I was on about my tenth state and about my sixth trip to the pencil sharpener, when I felt someone's hot breath down my neck. As I slowly turned around, I came eye-to-eye with the stern-faced teacher. I desperately searched the floor for a crack or knothole that I could disappear into. However, there was no escape and I ended up on the outhouse cleaning crew, as well as honestly learning and passing the test.

The test in Figure 1 gives an example of some of the types of subjects and the degree of difficulty of our tests. Although this test, which is from the book, "Schools Of Wallowa County," was administered during 1912, it is quite comparable to the exams we had at our school.

Thinking back to how it was, I believe it would be a real challenge for today's teachers to take on the job of teaching fifteen to twenty students ranging from the first to the eighth grades. In addition to teaching, they also had to carry out all the disciplinary measures on the students, as well as be the school custodian.

Teachers presenting oral instruction on one side of the room would often be interrupted by another student from another class needing assistance or discipline. With her attention focused on a certain section of the room, it was difficult for her to observe disruptive behavior and to pinpoint its source. Lack of copying machines prompted much more work for the teachers. They were required to spend many hours standing up while tending to individual students or writing on the blackboards. They had a pretty tough job.

Figure 1.
STATE OF OREGON
Questions for Eighth Grade Diplomas

May, 1912

TO THE APPLICANT: Select any eight of the following questions.

TO THE EXAMINER: Grade the first eight answers only.

ARITHMETIC—A

1. W. B. Lewis borrowed $800 from the First National Bank of Portland, Oregon on January 14, 1909, due in three years with Interest at 8%, payable semi-annually. Write a note showing the above transaction.

2. The volume of a box whose interior dimensions are 2.4 inches, 5 inches, 1.7 inches is how many times as great as that of one whose interior dimensions are 3 inches, 1.6 inches, and .85 inches?

3. What will it cost to plaster a school room 32 feet long, 18 feet wide and 12 feet high, at 32 cents a square yard, deducting 50% of the area of the walls on account of blackboards, baseboards and openings?

4. A pile of wood contains 21 cords. The pile is 100 feet long. How high is it, the wood being two feet long.

5. What is the interest on $654 from June 1, 1910 to September 15, 1914 at 7%?

6. A city is assessed for $1,250. They wish to raise $31,450. How much must one pay who is assessed upon $7,750?

7. A ladder 75 feet long just reaches the top of a 50 ft. pole. How far is the foot of the ladder from the foot of the pole?

8. What is the area of a circle whose radius is 36 feet?

9. A man received $675 as his commission at 5% for buying land at $25 per acre. How many acres did he buy?

10. Add the following: 8,467; 9,376; 4,753; 8;472; 9,762; 9,321; 77,356; 87,253; 87,676.

SPELLING

To be orally asked by instructor.

1. Forcible 2. Sensible 3. Quarrel 4. Agreeable 5. Mileage 6. Judgment . 7. Advantageous 8. Peaceably 9. Grocery 10. Attorney 11. Embargo 12. Innuendo

13. Proviso 14. Science 15. Decimal 16. Currency 17. Creditor 18. Physician

19. Excellent 20. Diligent 21. Altogether 22. Welfare 23. Crystallize 24. Angel

25. Athlete 26. Coercion 27. Dissipate 28. Endurance 29. License 30. Mutilate 31. Orthodox 32. Pestilence 33. Spurious 34. Circumference 35. Measure 36. Discount

37. Consignee 38. Endorsement 39. Alternative 40. Comparison 41. Synopsis 42. Imperative 43. Antecedent 44. Anesthesia 45. Auspices 46. Deodorize 47. Emanate 48. Necessary 49. Preparation 50. Invincible.

TO THE APPLICANT: Select any ten of the following questions.

TO THE EXAMINER: Grade the first ten answers only.

GRAMMAR.

1. Write a letter to the county superintendent describing a famous picture you have studied during the past year, or on some other subject.

2. Write a sentence using a clause as the subject.

3. Name the three classes of complements. Give illustration of each.

4. Insert the proper form (I or me) in each blank and give the reason for your choice:

(1). She invited you and_____to go driving.
(2). The kite was made for Harry and_____.
(3). If you were ______would you go?

5. Insert appropriate relative pronouns in the blanks in the following sentences and give the reason for your choice:

(1). This is the man_______spoke to us yesterday.
(2). This is the man_______you saw.
(3). The cat______you despise is a very useful animal.

6. Write a letter ordering a year's subscriptions to some magazine.

7. Insert the proper form of lie or lay in each blank in the following sentences.

(1). Let him______there.
(2). I found it _______on the floor.
(3). You had better______down for a while.
(4). I was so weary I ______down in my clothes.
(5). I_____the book down.

8. Write the possessive case singular and plural of the following nouns:

Child, lady, boy, man, fairy.

9. In the following sentences underscore the phrases, and tell how they are used.

(1). A man should learn to govern himself.
(2). To break a promise is a breach of honor.
(3). Your writing that letter so neatly secured the position for you.

10. Insert the proper auxiliary (shall or will) in each blank in the following sentences.

(1). I______be glad to see you.
(2). How______will I send the package.
(3). I______do as I please.
(4). I______not be gone long.
(5). He_______never enter my door.

11. Write five sentences using the past tense of one of the following verbs in each:

Drink, eat, fly, draw, go.

12. Tell which of the italicized words is correct and give the rea-

son:

(1). She plays very (good) (well).
(2). The door shut (easy) (easily).
(3). Deal (gentle) (gently) with him.
(4). He stood (firmly) (firm) in spite of opposition.
(5). She looks (beautifully) (beautiful) in a pink gown.

TO THE APPLICANT: Select any ten of the following questions.
TO THE EXAMINER: Grade the first ten answers only.
GEOGRAPHY

1. Draw an outline map of North America and put in three mountain ranges.
2. Mention four things that make the climate of Baker City different from Portland in December and tell what the difference is.
3. Name three important products exported from Brazil, from China.
4. Give the race, color, distinguishing features and occupation of the people of Mexico.
5. Tell what direction you would sail and what waters in going from New York to Manila. How will this route be shortened?
6. Draw an outline map of your county, putting in the rivers, mountains, largest cities, and give the population.
7. What is the cause of the Belt of Calms?
8. What and where are the following: Edinburgh, Hanover, Tientsin, Korea, Shasta?
9. What is the cause of the Gulf Stream? Tell what countries are affected by it, and what the effect is.
10. Name three national parks in the United States and tell which one is in Oregon.
11. Name five articles of importance that Oregon Exports and tell in what part of the state each is produced.
12. Name four of the provinces of Canada that border the United States.

(Courtesy of Dale Johnson)

One of the major hardships in attending school was traveling to and from the school-house, especially during inclement weather. Distances of travel ranged from just over one-fourth mile to almost three miles. With a few exceptions, parents did not generally pick up or deliver their kids from the school. The students either walked or rode horses. During exceptionally cold weather, George Kennedy, who lived near our house, would equip his horse-drawn sled with hay and blankets and would deliver his kids, as well as other students along the route, to the schoolgrounds.

Walking or riding a horse over the one and one-half miles that my sister and I had to travel, was cold and tiring, especially during cold weather and periods of deep snow. A mid-way stop at my Great Aunt and Uncle Obe's place, where my aunt would replenish my energy with a cookie and a cup of hot chocolate, was always a welcome respite on my long trips to school.

When I was in the first grade, a large tom turkey belonging to Obe and Gladys proved to be a major challenge to my arriving at school on time. This gobbler ruled over Obe's barnyard with an iron fist and would immediately challenge my presence when I attempted passage through the barnyard. Detouring around the yard created a major problem because I had to leave the open path through the yard and climb over three fences in deep snow drifts. This detour would sometimes delay my school arrival up to an hour.

When my dad heard about the turkey problem, he gave me a willow stick and told me to walk through the barnyard or he would use the stick on me. With courage bolstered by this threat, I squared off with the gobbler; we faced each other like a couple of gun fighters at the old corral. After about a one-minute confrontation, in which the gobbler lost his pride and a bunch of feathers and I received a good thumping from the tom's wings, the gobbler surrendered his kingdom and ran.

School would sometimes be closed for short periods of time until trails and roads could be opened by horse travel or plowed out. Snow accumulations sometimes exceeded four feet in depth and could not easily be removed. During these periods, trails would simply be packed down on top of the snow until it was packed hard enough for easier travel. Horses were the main tool used for tramping these roads and trails out. Horses would often have quite a struggle breaking the first path through the snow.

Rosalie and I had some frightening experiences traveling along the wooded path between the school and our house. One time we observed the tracks of a large cougar that had followed our tracks in the snow. Another time I was nearly hit by lightning when a bolt struck a tree about 100 feet from where I was walking. Rosalie was afraid to walk home alone, and would go into a real panic when I was sick and didn't go to school. She used to shut her eyes and run down the trail, bumping into trees and stumps.

Unsupervised trips home from school seemed to provide the most opportunities for the students to get into trouble or dangerous situations. Rosalie and I were supposed to take the short route home, which followed a private road through our Uncle Obe's property and the George Kennedy farm. This private road was not maintained by the county, and was not our favorite route to take.

We would often go against the wishes of our parents and take the longer county road route that was used by the majority of the students. This county road was the one where we were most apt to get into trouble. We would often race our horses along the road when it was slick with ice or packed snow, or we would tow kids on sleds and skis with our running horses. My horse, Snip, once ran out of control for almost a mile while towing two sled-loads of kids. Fortunately, he wore himself out traveling up a long hill and I was able to bring him under my control.

On one occasion, an old single horse cart that had been rigged to steer by hand almost caused serious injury or death. The kids had laboriously dragged it up the long steep hill leading to the school during the morning, and then decided to ride it down the steep incline on the way home. Lawrence Scott, the boy in charge of steering, lost control of the cart near the bottom of the hill and the cart, along with its load of children, ran off into the ditch. Several students sustained cuts and bruises when they were thrown out of the rolling cart.

We would often have mock wars with sling-shots; slinging rocks at each other from partially fortified positions in ditches, or behind trees.

We were rarely hit as the two foot long rawhide strings with their attached pocket, which launched the rock, were not very accurate. However, their range of close to 200 yards made them a dangerous weapon when someone did happen to get hit. Some of the kids sustained painful bruises from these weapons. One student came home displaying a golf ball sized lump on his head, prompting the parents and teacher to ban the slingshots.

Fist fights were common on the way home from school. Teachers who clamped down on fighting on the schoolgrounds often unwittingly moved these fights to the unsupervised home route. These fights, which usually started as fist fights, usually ended up as glorified wrestling matches. Weapons were seldom used, and if they were, they were usually confined to what sticks or rocks that could be found along the road. Knives or guns were never used.

I once brought on the full wrath of my mother when I returned home after one of these fights. As usual, I had decided to take the forbidden path home from school that followed the county road. During the walk home, Lawrence Scott and I decided that we would adjust each other's attitude.

Our fight, which started in the middle of the road, soon ended up as a mud wrestling match in the bottom of the wet, muddy borrow pit. We were so covered with mud that Jack Scott, Lawrence's brother, could not assist his brother in the fight, because he could not tell which one he was. My clothes were torn and covered with mud, my entire upper body looked like a pig that had just got up from a mud bath and my geography workbook looked like it had been dropped into a mix-master.

It was this scene that greeted my mother as I entered the yard gate outside our house. My mother had been forewarned about my appearance by Rosalie, who had raced by me some 100 yards from the house. She had managed to fill my mother in on every graphic detail of the fight before I arrived.

I can't remember all the things that my mother said to me as I walked into the yard, but it was one of the strongest lectures I ever received without actual physical punishment. I do remember her last few words, mentioning that she could hardly wait until Dad got home so that he could administer the whipping that I deserved. Dad did not disappoint her, as my body received its second thumping for the day.

Once, a group of students swiped some penned-up chickens for a chicken feed while returning home from school. Swiping chickens and then having a chicken feed was kind of like stealing watermelons out of a farmer's field and then having a watermelon feed. After they had eaten the chickens, they learned that their owner had separated these chickens out from the rest of the flock because they were sick and had to be destroyed.

We had six different teachers at our school—all women—during my eight years of attending Fairview Grade School. Their tenures were short, probably due to the isolated conditions and low pay. All but one boarded at the Obe Scott residence. Our last teacher, Lillian Glasson, was a resident of the Flat and had four children of her own.

I do not remember the chain of command in our school system. However, I do remember the teacher enlisting the support of the students in preparing for the visit of the County School Superintendent. For about two days before his arrival, we would vigorously clean the entire building and would neatly arrange the school facilities like a group of soldiers preparing for an inspection by a General.

When he arrived, we would fearfully sit at our desks as quiet as church mice until he left about two hours later. I do not know if it was the general rule at that time or just a coincidental visit, but the superintendent made a trip out to our school to administer my eighth grade test for my diploma. It was quite an honor for me as I was the only one in my class at that time.

Like schools today, considerable controversy was generated when community members had to make decisions on school policy. School board directors' meetings were well-attended and vociferous arguments would erupt. Some of the arguments would even lead to fist fights on some of the hotly-contested issues. Most of the arguments were generated over what and how much improvement was needed in school facilities and teachers' pay.

Miscellaneous expenses for the school were often raised by fundraising pie and basket socials. These auctions would be held at night at the school house and would be well attended by the community. I remember that, on a few occasions, volunteers made emergency repairs to the school facilities.

The Fairview Grade School was officially closed following my graduation from the eighth grade in the summer of 1945. All or most of the small country schools in Union County were consolidated into the larger schools at that time. The advent of a large school bus, which transported the students to the town of Elgin, ended an era of rural country education that was probably one of the last of its kind in Oregon public schools.

STUDENTS ATTENDING FAIRVIEW SCHOOL SPRING OF 1944
Left to right, bottom row: Tobey Thompson, Ruth Glasson, Dixie Lee Thompson, Betty Halsey, Marie Glasson Mary Glasson, Barbara Halsey, Rosalie Scott, Richard Scott, Wesley Scott, Larry Thompson.
Left to right, top row: Warren Scott, Florence Scott, Ardith Thompson, Beulah Kennedy, Grace Kennedy, Racheal Thompson, Lawrence Scott, Jack Scott, Harlan Scott

TEACHERS TEACHING AT FAIRVIEW LISTED BELOW:
Matilda Niggle: 1937-38, 1938-39, 1939-40
Martha Wurgler: 1940-41 Thelma Barnhart: 1941-42
Elma Cusick: 1942-43 Lillian Glasson 1943-44, 1944-45

CHAPTER 11

DEFYING GRAVITY

There have probably never been many young boys that have not dreamed about soaring high in the clouds without a care in the world. I was no different. From an early age I had a preoccupation with defying the laws of gravity. One of my favorite pastimes was to lie on my back in the shade of a tree and watch a hawk effortlessly ride the thermal wind currents into an upward flight until it disappeared into the clouds. At times, I would imagine that my eyes were in the hawk's head and would try to visualize the tremendous view and elation that one would have flying from that height.

My first attempt at defying gravity occurred after my folks and I had attended an air show near La Grande. During the show, several persons had parachuted out of planes and landed in a nearby field. The sight of their gentle descent to the ground produced a flood of new ideas on ways that I could foil Newton's laws of gravity. It took a couple of days of brainstorming to conclude that my mother's umbrella closely resembled a parachute, and that it would make a good substitute in my planned jump.

Fortunately, I did not have access to a plane or a high cliff, so I had to come up with an alternate jumping site. After ruling out trees because of the their impeding limbs, I settled on the large opening to the barn loft that was used for receiving hay. This 15-foot by 12-foot opening, which was about 18 feet above the ground, in my opinion, offered an excellent launch site for my first jump. Its only drawback was that it was not high enough to give me a good view of the countryside as I would gently float to the ground.

I secretly borrowed my mother's umbrella from the bedroom closet and climbed up the laddered passageway to my jumping site. As I fearfully gazed from the barn opening to the ground below, I realized for the first time that the distance to the ground appeared to be closer to 100 feet rather than 18 feet.

However, as I remembered the parachutists at the air show floating gracefully to the ground, I gradually overcome my fears. As I prepared myself for the jump, I imagined myself gently floating to the ground like a thistledown. I even tried to gauge the wind so that I would not drift too far from the barn.

Having made all the last moment preparations, I was at last ready for what I figured would be my first of many jumps. Firmly grasping the handle of the umbrella, I gave a final barn-clearing jump into space. The only thing I recall before my quick reunion with the ground was the snapping sound of the umbrella braces as they transformed the umbrella into a shape resembling a badminton bird. My planned slow drift to mother earth was, instead, more like a speeding car hitting a brick wall at 100 miles per hour.

My first memory after hitting the ground was of the sound of my jaw as it gave my knees a resounding whack. My knees and jaw smarted with pain, and I had to extract my feet from their four-inch burial site in the barnyard soil.

I quickly looked around to see if anyone had witnessed my pile-driving jump and was relieved to find that there were no witnesses to this solo flight failure. I next looked at my mother's umbrella, which now looked like it had been dragged by the handle through a two-inch knothole. Praying that it would not rain for a while, I buried the convoluted rain protector in a remote part of the forest and licked my wounds.

My next attempt to free myself from the ground was prompted by one of my mother's childhood memories related to flying. She had recalled how one of her cousins had attempted to fly in an apple box when it was launched from a tree. His crashing failure did not discourage me because his attempt, in my opinion, had failed to incorporate all the principal aerodynamics necessary for flight.

My dad had explained, after many of my questions, how the forward motion of a plane's wings created an upward lifting action. It was my opinion that my mother's cousin failed in his flight because he had lacked the forward motion to create lift.

After reviewing my mother's story, I carefully started crafting a flight plan that would rival that of the Wright Brothers. As with my parachute plan, I had to select a launching site that would give me both some elevation and also some floor space to launch and build my aircraft.

Perhaps my jarring fall from the barn opening had prejudiced me against using it again as a launch site. Instead, I settled on a treehouse with a small front deck that my friends and I had constructed. I am sure that my selection of this latter site was mainly determined by its lower height of ten feet, as opposed to the 18-foot height of the barn opening.

It did not take me very long to nail an eight-foot long board to the bottom of a large wooden box. After assembling this air-worthy craft on the treehouse deck, I tied a twenty-foot rope to the box and gave my sister, Rosalie, detailed instructions on how to handle her end of the flight plan.

She was told to start running with the other end of the rope at the same time I launched myself from the deck so that the forward motion would create air lift on the wings of the plane. I further instructed her to slow down if the plane started going too high and pulling her off the ground.

Here I was, getting ready for my second attempt at flight. I envisioned myself floating in my craft some twenty feet above the ground and shouting instructions to my envious sister below. It even entered my mind that I would keep my promise to let Rosalie take a turn in my plane after I had enjoyed several trips in the craft. Entrepreneurship even entered my mind as I planned how I could charge my friends a nickel per ride, and perhaps make a two-seater for larger profits.

With all kinds of dreams floating through my head, I shouted for my sister to start running with the rope as I launched my aircraft. Like a duck shot out of the sky, my dream craft and I crashed to the ground amidst the sounds of breaking boards and a couple of squawking hens that apparently thought a giant hawk was after a chicken dinner.

My posterior received the brunt of this fall as my cockpit failed to cushion my brutal collision with old Mother Earth. Luckily, Rosalie—running as she was—had been able to escape being hit.

As I sat amidst a pile of broken boards trying to catch my breath, my sister casually said, "I have changed my mind. I don't *want* a turn in your plane."

My flying aspirations—although dampened for a couple of years—again surfaced after watching a ski jumping movie. After seeing this movie my everyday thoughts dwelled on the jumpers gliding through the air like giant eagles. It was not long before I had formulated a plan designed to launch me skyward in my third attempt to foil gravity.

My plan involved fastening a box with an attached foot board for a wing to the top of my sled. I would then construct a ski jump at the bottom of a steep hill that overlooked our family orchard. I calculated that my sled would have considerably greater lift than skis and would carry me over a cluster of fruit trees, fences and buildings to an open field some 300 feet away.

For the next week, I diligently spent all of my spare time constructing a jump ramp by rolling up large balls of snow and shaping and tramping them down until I had formed a crude ramp. I built the ramp so that it would point skyward at an angle designed to launch me safely over the nearby fruit trees.

It was about three days later on a clear beautiful Saturday afternoon that two neighbor boys from a nearby ranch helped me attach my self-made plane to my sled. They dubiously watched as I pulled my craft up some 100 yards to the crest of the hill and prepared to launch my creation. Memories of the pain and bruises caused by my previous two flight attempts surfaced as I focused in on the ramp.

The ramp, which was pretty good-sized, looked only about six inches wide as I gazed from my vantage point some 300 feet away and 150 feet above my jump site. Probably the main thing that made me go through with my jump was my expectant friends below. With my heart in my mouth, I sat down on the sled with my legs on each side of the attached box. Then, using my feet for steering, I launched my sled craft down the steep, slick incline.

My trip down the steep trail to the ramp was difficult but fast. My top-heavy sled careened from one side of the trail to the other as tears caused by the cold air hitting my face partially blinded me. With my sled gaining speed at every moment, my body felt like it was coming out of a power dive in a plane as I hit the ramp and was propelled into space.

The upward tilt of my ramp, instead of directing my craft into a forward gliding pattern, shot my sled into more of an upward flight that peaked about three feet above a thickly-limbed apple tree. As I hung in space with my arms firmly grasping the attached wing on the sled, the craft made a slow backward role and deposited us both in the middle of the apple tree. My bulky sled did not follow the path of broken limbs made by my body, and I landed on my back beneath the tree.

By this time my two friends seemed to be in shock as they stared down at my motionless body. Other than having the wind knocked out of me and a few scratches, I was not hurt. However, most of my new coat was generally scattered on several tree limbs. Torn strips of draped red material on the limbs of the apple tree made the it look like we had started decorating it for Christmas. My sled, which had separated from its box and wing, had to be retrieved out of the top of the tree. Although I did survive a plane crash later on in my life, this was my last boyhood attempt to fly.

Chapter 12

Outdoor Recreation on the Flat

Fishing and hunting were the primary recreational pursuits of the majority of the Cricket Flat residents. These two sports were popular because they could be enjoyed without traveling long distances. Good fishing and hunting were available within five miles of most of the Flat residents. They helped supplement our diets with a nutritional and varied meat supply. Several of the residents depended on deer meat as one of their main food supplies. Hunting and fishing were cheap sports to pursue, as well.

Very few of the residents purchased licenses and most of them already owned cheap rifles and fishing equipment. The need for the meat seemed to overcome their good judgment in obeying the game and fish laws.

Some of the other recreational activities were skiing, sledding, picking mushrooms, horseback riding, picnicking, camping, swimming, huckleberry picking and a limited amount of horse polo. Most of the sledding and skiing activities were done by the younger persons, although some middle-aged men used skis and snowshoes for winter travel when the snow was too deep for horses.

Most of the horseback riding was done for work purposes or required transportation. The Stowe family, mentioned in an earlier chapter, were among the adults that most liked to ride horses for recreation.

Almost everyone on the Flat liked to hunt mushrooms for both the food and the recreation it afforded. The morel mushroom, which grew during a short period in the spring, was the main mushroom pursued by the Flat residents. Since the morels seemed to come in thick after fall burns, residents kept close track of the forest fires and would canvass them thoroughly for mushrooms the following spring. It was not unusual to collect several gunny sacks of these delicious fungi on a good burn.

Huckleberry picking was another popular sport. Flat residents would migrate to the higher elevations five to ten miles north of the Flat. Here they would combine berry picking, camping, fishing and hunting, with the women doing most of the berry picking and the men supplying their households with deer, elk, grouse, and fish.

Deer were the main game animals hunted on the Flat, since they were a good meat source and lived on most of the ranches where they were fairly easy to harvest. Early on, Flat residents did not pay much attention to the game laws. Most of the residents could not afford the license fees. They liked to hunt out of season and game law enforcement personnel were nearly non-existent.

Unlike today, elk were seldom seen on the Flat. Hunters had to cross the Grande Ronde River and hunt the timbered flats, some two to five miles north of the river to find elk. Hunters illegally hunted elk occasionally in this location. However, game law enforcement personnel patrolled the public Forest Service lands in this area much harder than the private lands on the Flat, thus discouraging illegal hunting.

Flat residents had several effective methods for harvesting deer. The most effective and common methods were deer drives. This method involved the placement of hunters in key locations where deer were known to travel when frightened. The rest of the hunters would then drive through the thick timber where deer commonly hid. If the drive was successful, deer would spook out ahead of the drivers and run right past the hunters on the stands, where they would be shot.

Another successful method was to carefully sneak up to fields, either early in the morning or just before dark, and catch the animals feeding. Dogs were also used successfully. The use of dogs was mostly for tracking down wounded animals. Uncle Jack had a small terrier breed that he often used on deer. When this dog would get after a deer, it would emit a high-pitched bark that pinpointed the animal's location. It was a very fast running dog and would eventually run the deer back by the hunters.

Spotlighting was another highly successful method for taking deer. This method was frowned on by most of the residents, including my dad. It was a distasteful method to most because they did not feel it gave the deer a sporting chance and too many wounded animals would escape and die without being found. It was also felt that this method would lead to the depletion of the deer herds if used by everyone. There were a small minority of the residents that spotlighted and either gave the meat away or sold it because they killed more than they could use for their families.

Unlike day when most private land is posted with "NO TRESPASSING" signs, landowners on the Flat kept their lands open to all hunters. Hunters never requested permission to hunt on another's property. However, in most cases, if a hunter killed a deer on someone else's property he would look up the landowner and share the meat with him.

Harvested meat was also equally shared with those taking part in the hunt. In the off season or during periods of hot weather, a single hunter who killed a deer would generally look up his nearest neighbors and split the meat with them. This was mainly done because lack of refrigeration required using up the meat before it spoiled. During hot weather, meat either had to be smoked, canned or partially cooked and put in salted down crocks.

I did not enjoy the hunting as much as I did the fishing trips. Perhaps my role as driver and not being allowed to pack a deer rifle until I was twelve years old dampened my spirit for hunting deer. Since deer liked to keg up in the thickest brush, in the most inaccessible spots known to man, these places were where the drivers had to go.

I can remember my dad sending me over the steep brushy breaks of the Wallowa River Canyon, with other youngsters, to contour the side of the canyon for two to three miles to where Dad and other adults would be positioned on stands. I once told my son that I had never even *seen* a deer until I was twelve years old because I was always crawling in thick brush on my hands and knees where all I could see was the ground.

Grouse hunting was another activity that many of the Flat residents took advantage of, especially during the 1930s. After about 1942, some disease seemed to severely reduce the blue grouse population, and hunters had to depend more on the ruffed grouse for hunting after that time. Since the ruffed grouse populations had always been much smaller than blue grouse numbers and the ruffs were much smaller in size, overall hunting pressure on grouse tapered off rapidly after the 1940s.

When we first moved to the Flat, blue grouse seemed to be everywhere we looked. We would generally see over 100 every day when we would mow our hay fields. The grouse would be scattered along all the roads leading to our fields and in our timber. After the young had reached three fourths of their adult size, we would start harvesting them for the table.

Shotguns were generally not used, as the birds would trustingly fly up into a tree, where they would be shot in the head at short range with a .22 rifle. We would harvest these birds for eating purposes from mid-summer clear through the fall. Today, blue grouse are very scarce on the Flat, while ruffed grouse populations are only slightly smaller than they were in the 1930s.

Since we generally had a lot of snow during the winter months, snow sports were extremely popular, especially for the younger residents. Riding our sleds and skis down some of the steep county roads was a favorite activity of all the youngsters. Sometimes the snow would develop a heavy enough crust to support our thin-runnered sleds. When this condition occurred, all the kids would rush to the steepest open hills and sled until they were physically exhausted or until the warm sun melted the crust so that it no longer supported the sleds.

It was an exhilarating experience to brave the cold morning air and listen to the sharp crunch of our feet as we trailed our sleds across the rock-hard snow. The bright morning sun would nearly blind us as its light was reflected across the sparkling white terrain.

Our wind-exposed faces would turn bright red in the crisp cold air and our breath would vaporize into miniature columns of smoky steam as we would race to the top of the hill. When we reached the top, we would take a running start and belly flop our bodies down on the three foot sled. It would not take long before we would be racing along at over 30 miles per hour, with the cold wind chilling our faces and bringing tears to our eyes. The slicing sound of the sled runners seemed to harmonize with the creaking sounds of the sled as it would hit slight bumps in the snow.

The thrill of our ride would be heightened by feelings bordering on fear as our speed increased dramatically towards the middle of the hill. Sounds and the chill of the wind would simultaneously increase as our speeding sled raced down the steep part of the run.

Our faces would now be numb from the cold air. Stationary objects in the snow would flash by our tear-filled eyes like flitting shadows. Then, almost in relief, we would gradually start slowing down and finally end our ride at the bottom of the hill. After a few minutes of blowing on our hands and rubbing the circulation back into our faces we would be ready for the long trudge back up the hill for another ride.

Skiing was also popular. We could ski on the open hills without needing the crust required for sledding. Skiing equipment was much more primitive than what is used today. My first pair of skis were home made by my dad. He took some thin boards and shaped and bent the tips up by putting them in boiling hot water and keeping a constant bending pressure on the tips. He put a single leather strap around the middle of the board to secure my feet. I never did use ski poles nor have the benefit of a ski lift. We often used a horse or car to tow us like a boat tows a water skier. We also towed sleds this way.

On occasion, if weather conditions were right, we would ice skate on the small ponds around the community. Only a small percentage of the kids had ice skates, but those that did not would use their sleds or just slick shoes to have fun skidding around on the ice. Fortunately, I had inherited a pair of skates from one of my uncles and was one of the lucky few.

Once I got tired of skating, I would generally share my skates with some of the ones that were less fortunate. I remember a girl that had much smaller feet than myself putting on five pairs of socks so that she could wear my skates.

Some of our ice skating outings proved to be quite dangerous because of thin ice. We sometimes pushed our luck in our eagerness to skate. Usually, if the ice was thin we would skate close to the edge of the pond where the water was shallow, so that if we did break through we could easily get out. I, as well as some of my friends, did break through the ice on several occasions. However, other than getting an ice-cold bath, we were never in any serious danger.

Of all my recreational opportunities, fishing was my favorite. It did not matter if I fished with someone else or by myself, it was a sport that I constantly looked forward to and would do on a full-time basis if I had been given my choice. Perhaps my love for fishing was due to my dad and Uncle Jack taking the time and showing me fishing methods when I was about six years old.

My interest and skill in angling were much greater than most of the other Flat youngsters. There was another boy in the neighborhood however, that was always able to catch more and bigger fish then I. It did not matter if I used the same type of equipment or fished in exactly the same way, this boy—Ken Miller was his name—would always come out the best on our fishing outings.

Besting Ken on a fishing trip became one of the major goals in my young life, and I would jump at any opportunity to fish with him with the hope that I could catch more fish or the biggest fish. To the best of my memory, I don't think this ever happened.

I had four fishing spots where I liked to fish. Three of these locations were in the Flat area and the other was in the high lakes of the Wallowas. Most of my earliest fishing was done on a small drainage called Rysdam's Creek, about a mile back of our house.

As I grew older, I would hike down to a section of the Wallowa River called the Long Point area. In my later teens I spent considerable time fishing for steelhead and Coho Salmon in a short section of the Grande Ronde River below its confluence with the Wallowa River.

My fishing of the high Wallowa lakes was mainly confined to a number of years in my pre-teens when Lloyd and Eunice Gray would take me on week-long camping trips on the Lostine River. From this camping spot, Lloyd and I would hike in and fish many of these high, pristine lakes.

Little old Rysdam's Creek, where I spent most of my earlier fishing years, was a small creek that would go partially dry during the late summer months. Trout would concentrate in the creek's larger pools, except during the early spring when flows were greater. I would usually walk or ride a horse over to this creek with my old telescoping steel fishing rod equipped with its antiquated automatic fly reel. I would either use angle worms dug out of our garden or periwinkles that I would find in the creek for bait.

Regardless of how many fish I would catch, it was always a thrill to feel the sharp tug of a hungry trout as my worm-covered hook would drift along the bottom of the pool. I was always filled with apprehension that I would lose the fat eight-inch trout as I would hoist its wiggling slick body to the steep grassy bank. After catching the fish, it would not take me long, in following my dad's training, to clean the trout and store it in a gunnysack containing freshly-picked green grass dampened with water.

After I had picked my way for about a mile along the narrow stream bed where large slick boulders formed an interrupted pathway for the small discharge of water, I would generally have ten to thirty plump rainbow-colored trout stored away in my burlap sack. I would then take a refreshing swim in one of the larger pools in the creek that we called the "Big Hole." This large pool, approximately twenty feet in diameter and about five feet deep, was the largest pool in the creek. Besides being a good fishing hole, it offered an excellent place to take a refreshing swim in clean cool water.

After I had finished fishing, I would drag my tired body out of the steep canyon and walk the mile and a half stretch back to the house. I would always beam when my mom praised my catch. The fact that I had caught the fish always seemed to make these pan-sized trout rolled in flour and fried in butter seem that much better to eat. Of course, the trout complemented the other dishes in Mom's state-of-the-art meals.

Spending a week away from the ranch camping and fishing with Lloyd and Eunice and family on the Lostine river was always like a visit to heaven. I would always make sure that I didn't do anything at home that would jeopardize this trip, especially about two months before going. I would carefully save my money so that I could buy dry flies and other fishing tackle that might be needed. I would carefully listen to and try to follow my folks' advice in making myself a welcome guest while on this trip.

Driving over the 17 miles of steep winding road from the town of Lostine to our campsite nestled along the head of the Lostine River never ceased to impress me as the most beautiful spot in the world. In sharp contrast to the more level terrain and smaller canyons of the Flat, the Lostine canyon could have been described as God's carpeted stairway to heaven. Only the primitive road closely following the river gave any clue of man's presence. The awesome beauty of the river and canyon seemed to sharpen my sense of sight, smell and hearing and heighten my awareness of nature's diversity.

Rugged cliffs, varying in color from gray, brown and off white, rose from different levels along the steep canyon walls to dizzying heights. These cliffs seemed to be fighting for space with huge granite slides composed of truck-sized boulders and narrow vertical green ribbons of deciduous shrubs and trees.

Occasional green meadows guarded by alpine fir and an occasional patch of snow followed the rocky slopes down to where they gradually merged into thickening patches of lodgepole pine and spruce. As we followed the rough Forest Service road, we would catch occasional glimpses of the crystal clear Lostine river weaving its way through lush green meadows and stands of lodgepole pine and spruce.

It was this type of scenery that kept me spellbound until we reached our destination near the end of the road. As we would park the car at our campground nestled in under several large spruce trees, I would longingly gaze at the slow, meandering waters of the Lostine—deep clear waters, revealing even the smallest bottom-dwelling rock with a deceiving clarity.

I could hardly wait until I could grab my fly rod and test these beautiful waters for trout. However, I was soon to learn that Lloyd was a dedicated camper who first had to set up two tents with an accompanying outdoor kitchen and cooking facilities that would have put a Forest Service firefighting cook camp to shame. Every piece of camping equipment from frying pans to gas lanterns had its own special place.

It would seem like an eternity before we would get our camp set up to perfection and I would get the signal from Lloyd to grab our fishing gear and catch some fish for supper. I would be like a hog racing for a milk trough as I rushed to the clear water's edge with my fly rod. I would usually be rewarded during the next few hours with a mess of plump Eastern Brook Trout. During the darkening evening hours the aroma of frying trout and fried potatoes skillfully cooked by Aunt Eunice over the gas-fired cooking stove, would stimulate my hunger to its highest degree.

I soon found that the pink, firm-fleshed brook trout were the best tasting fish that I had ever eaten. After gorging ourselves on fried fish, pork and beans and fried potatoes, we would top our meal off with marshmallows roasted over the open campfire.

As we would group ourselves closely around the bright campfire, our minds and bodies would seem to be mesmerized by the dancing flames and an occasional light breeze that would spread the pleasant aroma of smoke around us. Darkening skies would gradually cause the outline of the trees and mountains to fade so that our whole world seemed to be reduced to a small circle around the camp fire.

Fireside conversation, which was frequent during the early part of the evening, would gradually fade out as if we were afraid of breaking the sanctity of the moment. As the chill of the night would gradually overcome the warmth of the fire, we would retreat to the warmth of our sleeping bags and quickly fall asleep under the soothing soft murmur of the river.

Our stay at the campground was like moving in on the first floor of a mansion. The trip to the second floor would take place when Lloyd would lead me over the steep scenic paths to some of the high lakes nestled in glacier dug basins. Since these trips would run to six or more miles in distance, we would leave our camp before first light in the morning. After carefully packing our lunches and fishing tackle into light packs, we would start climbing the primitive, poorly-maintained trail just as the still hidden sun was starting to brighten the skies.

The chill of the early August morning would soon be forgotten as we would start the long upward climb to our destination. Although we went to several different lakes over the years when I camped with the Grays, my first trip, which was a four and a half mile hike into

Francis Lake, was the most memorable. It seemed like an eternity of steep climbing on the dusty switchback trail.

We had probably gone about a mile when the glaring bright sun started peeking over the east horizon and spreading its transitional light over the jagged snow capped peaks to the east. These snow-capped peaks, with their lower reaches of gray and black granite slides, would hurl back the morning pioneers of sunlight in blinding displays. As we would look to the other side of the Lostine River, the crystal clear air made it appear that we could almost touch the rough terrain several miles to the west.

As we climbed in elevation, the zone of lodgepole pine and spruce gradually started to change to alpine fir and species of pine that I was not familiar with. The fine soils of volcanic dust were beginning to change to coarser granite sands. Huge granite slides with house-sized boulders began to dominate the hillsides. Cascading waterfalls on distant mountainsides, not visible before, now started displaying vertical white lines in the belts of lowering sunlight. Some of these cascades seemed to be making suicidal dives to oblivion as their white spray plumes seemed to disappear into wind-swirled mists.

Short, knurled, and bent pine were soon the only trees left as we reached the highest part of the climb. These few scattered trees, clinging to life in the rocky outcrops, reminded me of hunch-backed old men leaning into a strong wind, precariously clinging to life in this soil-barren site. The young, granular soils of the High Wallowas were now restricting their welcome to all but the hardiest of plant life as we reached the crest of a narrow hog-back shaped saddle.

I have never forgotten the view that commanded my attention as I looked down from this saddle. At last, we had reached the objective of our arduous two-hour climb: a quarter mile below us, nestled in a dead-end valley, was Francis Lake. This beautiful, forty-acre lake was surrounded by a mixture of open meadows, huge granite boulders and alpine fir.

A silver stream fed by a large snowfield took a snake-shaped course as it slowly wound its way through a beautiful, green meadow. This snow-fed stream, which ran into the sparkling clear lake, reappeared at the mouth of the lake and exited into a stream bed of car-sized boulders.

My weary legs and sore feet seemed reborn and the anticipation of reaching the lake rejuvenated my entire body. Slipping and sliding down the steep treacherous trail, we wasted little time reaching the lake's shore and unloading our gear. As we raced to assemble our fishing gear, we could see huge, 20-inch eastern brook and rainbow trout patrolling the waters along the shoreline. These large fish resembled miniature torpedoes as they would occasionally break the water's surface for insects.

It seemed like an eternity before my trembling hands could assemble my fly rod and tie on one of my favorite gray hackle flies. After a few false casts, I was able to cast my fly in front of a large, cruising trout. In a slow deliberate charge this huge rainbow gently sucked my fly from the water's surface as I simultaneously set the hook.

The calm water was suddenly transformed into a churning froth as the big trout made repeated jumps and attempted charges towards the middle of the lake. Finally the fish began to tire and I carefully led this slab-sided fish to a shallow cove for landing. After a few futile runs I was able to gently slide this beauty out onto the beach.

In the excitement of landing my fish, I had completely forgotten about Lloyd. It was only after I had proudly packed my fish over to show Lloyd that I noticed he was having problems with his reel. He had just recently purchased a new spinning reel, one which had just come out on the market, and had tangled his line on his first cast. He was impatiently pulling the last tangle out of his line when I showed him my fish. After congratulating me on my catch, Lloyd promptly got ready to make another cast with his new reel.

In the meantime, I put my fish in my packsack and quickly hooked an even larger fish on my next cast.

"I've got another one!" I hollered.

"I see you do," replied Lloyd, sounding disgusted.

As I was playing my fish, I could see that Lloyd was having trouble with his reel again. There was a huge ball of tangled monofilament line, that looked like a barbed wire entanglement surrounding a military fort, dangling from his reel.

Lloyd, who was a large, tall dark-complexioned man with a great sense of humor, now seemed about ready to explode. He looked like a traffic cop directing traffic as one arm would lash out with a handful of line, and then his other arm would shoot out to the other side with another tangle.

It seemed like the more I played my fish the madder Lloyd got in his frenzied attempt to untangle his line. He was not the only one to feel disappointment; my large fish, in an eye popping jump, threw my hook and escaped. I decided that it would probably be good manners to help Lloyd untangle his line before I did any more fishing. However, I soon saw that I was too late to save his line. Looking like a karate knife fighter, Lloyd was slicing off three foot sections of line with his pocket knife in much the same manner that my dad would try to start his Fordson tractor.

"I am through trying to use this blank, blank reel. I'm going to use my fly reel like I should have done in the first place," Lloyd shouted angrily.

It was only after a thorough search of both packs that Lloyd found that he had forgotten to bring his dependable fly reel. Then I found out how much Lloyd resembled Dad in his vocabulary during stressful moments. The only real difference was that instead of taking his vengeance out on his hat, Lloyd decided that he would fill Francis Lake with rocks. A couple of his angry throws almost sailed across the lake, as he rapidly depleted the rock supply in our area.

Lloyd soon calmed down, and, after we had built a fire and boiled up some strong coffee, he even began to laugh about his predicament. It was not long before we were splicing three foot sections of monofilament line together and rigging his pole so that he could fish without a reel. I don't know if the rock throwing scared the fish or if they just decided not to bite, as Lloyd and I spent the rest of the morning fishing the lake without getting a bite. However, we did manage to catch quite a few smaller fish in the stream below the lake.

I had many more enjoyable trips with Lloyd and Eunice and their children, Doris Jean, Barbara and Don, in the Lostine River area. Doris, Jean and I even tried swimming in the frigid snow-fed waters of the Lostine. Our swim was brief to say the least. I really appreciated the Grays' patience and willingness to include me on these outings.

When I grew older, I would spend quite a bit of time fishing the Wallowa River in the Long Point area. This was a stretch of river where access was limited on the west side to a steep trail winding down a long point. During the late summer, after I had completed my chores, I would ride my horse down this point in the evening and enjoy the fishing. I would then spend the night and come home after a couple of hours of fishing in the early morning hours.

This was a therapeutic trip for me in that it would give me some solitude for thoughts and dreams that often could not be concentrated on when I was around others or when I was busy with my routine chores. No matter how many times I made this trip, the first sight of this river, as I started my horse down the steep winding trail, would erase any concerns or guilt that might be burdening my soul. The long point that I rode my horse down dropped about a 1,000 feet over its three-fourths mile course to the river. Part of the trail passed through an old burn where a thick stand of deciduous shrubs and young conifers sheltered the path. The trail then led along an open grass-covered ridge until it reached the river.

The stretch of river that wound around this protruding point was a fisherman's dream. A series of deep, swift riffles, alternating with deep holes and churning eddies made excellent habitat for rainbow trout and large silver-colored whitefish. Most of the bigger trout would run around 15 inches in length, but once in a while a 20-inch fish would take my fly. It was always a thrill to see the dark shadow of a trout come charging out from a submerged rock or overhanging bank and see the telltale white flash of his underside just before he hit my fly.

I would usually fish until almost dark before unrolling my sleeping bag and mattress pad out onto an exposed grassy flat overlooking the river. After seeing that my horse was tied securely, I would build a fire in an old rock fire pit and fry some trout in an old frying pan that I kept in my pack. It would not take me long after eating fried trout and a sandwich brought from home to crawl in my sleeping bag and watch the reflection of the dancing firelight on the nearby water.

It was during these moments of solitude that the stillness of the night and the flickering firelight began to open up channels of understanding that had previously eluded me. Despite living a structured and disciplined life with two loving parents, I would frequently feel sorry for myself.

I would envy the kids that lived in town with their easy access to the movie theater, the soda fountain and the school sports. I always wanted to own a bicycle and have a place to ride it. Dating a girl was something I was beginning to dream about. The worry of ending up on a farm, milking a bunch of cows preyed on my thoughts. Seeing other boys that didn't have scheduled daily chores was always a sore spot. I often resented my meager allowance for the work that I did. These were just a few of the thoughts that would often pass through my mind.

It was during these periods in the sleeping bag, when the flickering glow of the fire would send dancing reflections across the rippling surface of the river, that I would experience a type of spiritual event. My senses would seem to leave my body and give me the sensation that I was floating in space, hovering in a stationary position over the middle of the river. I could look back and see myself and the fire and look down and see the reflection of the firelight on the water below me.

It was during these periods that I would see my problems through the eyes of an objective bystander. These meditations seemed to last until I fell into a deep, refreshing sleep without a memory of my senses floating back into my body.

I was always much happier after I had experienced one of these out-of-body experiences. Although I have never experienced anything of that nature since those days, the magic moments left some lasting memories that have served me well whenever I became despondent and felt sorry for myself. One of the thoughts that has always served me well was to be grateful for the good things that I had and to not be in a hurry to look on the other side of the fence for greener pastures.

During my middle and late teens, Ken Miller and I discovered an untapped fishery of steelhead and salmon just below the confluence of the Wallowa and Grande Ronde rivers. We undoubtedly experienced some of the best fishing in the state for these two species for a period of about four years.

However, the word eventually got out and the site was ruined by over fishing. We would drive a car down a steep primitive road located on Ken's family property to where the road dead-ended about one-half mile above the fishing sites. We then hiked down and waded the Grande Ronde to gain access to our favorite spots. Our fishing for steelhead would usually start about the middle of August and the Coho would usually start in October.

It was a great thrill to cast a Colorado spinner baited with a grasshopper on my old bamboo fly rod and feel the solid strike of a bright fresh steelhead. It was always a challenge to land these acrobatic jumping fish with my old, automatic fly reel and flexible bamboo rod.

These fish would sometimes fight for thirty minutes before they could be landed. The Coho Salmon, which are now extinct in the drainage, were terrific fighters. They would often roll up in my line and cut it with their gill plate. It was not unusual to hook six or eight of these fish in one day. Ken and I spent many hours fishing these holes without being pressured by other anglers.

It was only after I had moved away from the ranch for several years that I realized how many good recreational opportunities I had had in my own back yard. I truly believe that today's youth would be much better off if they were given the opportunity to fish the little brook, or slide down a steep hill on a sled. The following poem, " A River So Old," was written to express my appreciation for the great times that I had on the Wallowa River.

As I looked at the view some 1,000 feet below,
I back-tracked in time to a point long ago.
A ribbon of blue-green with rapids showing white,
With long gentle curves, until it disappeared from sight.
It divided the hills that ascended to its edge,
Hills on each side that seemed to make a pledge,
That they would never cross this barrier of time.
Hills that were clothed with scattered fir and pine,
Intermingled with grasses that seemed to combine,
With occasional rimrocks, often in a line.
Steep narrow ravines laced with shrub and tree,
All shown together they seemed to agree,
That the scene was meant to soothe whatever eye,
That bathed its vision from the river to the sky.
It was from this river that I caught my first fish,
A plump silver trout that was fit for the dish.
My dad and myself had ridden down the steep trail,
Through the top of the canyon through the brush and rock shale,

Through the Eyes of a Boy

To the edge of the river where we tied the white mare,
That ascended the trail to deliver us there.
My father rigged up two telescope poles,
And we quickly headed for two good looking holes.
I will never forget my first look at the river so near,
A cascading torrent so bubbly and clear,
Water racing through stretches like a runaway train,
And building in crescendo like a jet engine plane;
Then to gradually fade in noise and speed,
As if all the water had suddenly agreed,
To slow to a stand-still and suddenly get deep,
Near rock-covered banks that were so high and so steep.
Thousands of white bubbles below the surface everywhere,
Looking like pearls cascading down a stair.
They seemed to give fleeting glances of the bottom now and then,
With the current changing directions again and again.
Occasionally the bottom sparkled as if it were gold,
In this beautiful river, a river so old.

It was in this setting that I was imprinted within,
To angle for fish from mother nature's inn.
Was it nature's fancy linen and a table set fine,
That hooked me on fishing, like a tasty red wine?
Now as I look at this river there is never any doubt,
That it was the fancy setting that hooked me on trout.
If only this river could tell its story from birth,
It would be a story of very great worth.

It could tell of the Indian that had given it a name,
The mighty Wallowa, a name it would claim.
It could tell of the Grizzly, the Wolf and many more,
That no longer roam its rocky steep shore.
It could tell of the Coho that not long ago,
Swam in its waters to its upper flow,
Or the mighty Sockeye that went to Wallowa Lake,
So thick in the river it was an unending wake.
It would tell of the Indians that roamed its shore,
Thousands and thousands of years before,
The first white man to ever set an eye,
Upon this great river that never went dry;

Indians that lived and never made great change
To the river or upon its range;
Indians that lost their homes and their life,
To ice jams, floods and moments of strife.
It could tell of the white men who first came to trap,
And opened it to others by the use of a map.
Hardy pioneers that carved out from the land,
Fields and cabins and some gold from the sand;
Independent souls, resourceful and loyal,
They harvested trees and worked the soil.
They built railroads and highways, ditches and a dam,
And made Wallowa Valley a place for white man.
They used the river, they used it bold,
This beautiful river, a river so old.

As I gazed at the Wallowa like a painting on the wall,
I contemplated its future, its use overall.
Could man continue its use and still hold it in awe?
Could he protect its beauty and obey nature's law?
Could he protect its source in its mountains so high?
Rugged rocky peaks reaching for the sky,
Snow-covered basins with their crystal clear streams,
Gray granite rock slides bursting their seams,
Blue-colored lakes with waters so clear,
That at first glance it would appear,
That you could touch the bottom with no effort at all,
But you find them deeper than twenty feet tall.
Air so clear that one's eyes can readily see,
Alpine fir and the lodgepole tree,
A mile away on a mountain side,
Objects so clear they can not hide.
Many small streams and springs all combine,
Mixing their juices like grapes in a wine,
Gathering forces in an awesome display,
Leaping off cliffs like mountain goats at play,
White foaming falls of a hundred feet or more,
Pounding rocks below with a spray and a roar,
Resting in deep pools at the base of the fall,
Deep bubbling water waiting for its call,
To go racing over rocks and brush covered banks,

Past A-Frame cabins and small bridges of planks,
Past roads and lodges and many a campground,
It reaches a spot that leaves one spell-bound:
A deep blue lake five miles or more,
With long steep ridges cradling each shore.
A beautiful setting that seemed to flush the soul,
Of one's worries that he can't control—
Worries of the future and regrets from the past,
For a while are forgotten; please make it last.
A setting that opens a new channel to the brain,
Of new understandings that we suddenly gain.
Are these communications that are being told,
From this beautiful river, a river so old?

Still admiring its beauty from my view from afar,
I had several thoughts before going to my car.
Compared to other rivers the Wallowa is still sound.
It still has its beauty and its water from the ground.
Its waters are clear and they still maintain their flow,
Perhaps even better than a century ago.
The Wallowa's only dam at the foot of Wallowa Lake,
Helped water storage so the farmers could take,
Water for their crops and many other use,
And maintain fall flows without the abuse.
I still catch trout from Rondowa to Wallowa Lake;
Fish of good size that one would want to take.
Salmon are in trouble, that I will agree,
But mainly from dams closer to the sea.
Its source in the mountains is a treasure to preserve,
A labyrinth of beauty that touches every nerve.
Yet as I leave and drive towards my place,
I realize our acquaintance is only a trace,
Of this great river and the time it has spent,
Flowing its course with the earth's consent.
Comparing our ages is like the blink of its eye,
From the time I was born to the time I will die.
The Wallowa will be active many a year from today,
Outlasting generations that have long gone away.
Will it be able to maintain its true face,
A million years from now to perhaps a different race?

Of this question no one can tell:
Will it be peace or will it be hell?
Second guessing the future, the Wallowa I would take,
To dominate man when its body is at stake.
Like a beautiful maiden with an alluring eye,
It creates a passion, it makes men cry.
Surely mankind with his knowledge to spare,
Will maintain this river with its spirit and flare,
A river whose value far exceeds gold,
A beautiful river, a river so old.

The Wallowa River

Chapter 13

Indoor Recreation and Socializing

Events that entailed some type of socializing with other members of the community were commonly attended by most of the Flat's residents. Attendance of these events and others were much more prevalent than they are today. I am sure that the isolation of the rural setting, the lack of other types of home entertainment that we have today, and the financial constraints of the residents made socializing popular.

Unlike today, when most working people are on tight schedules and visiting is usually reserved for after-work hours, folks of the earlier times seemed always to take time to visit with their neighbors when they had occasion to meet.

Neighbors traveling the county roads in their cars or trucks frequently stopped their cars in the middle of the county road when they met another vehicle and talk for several minutes. Sometimes another resident would arrive at one of these road-blocking visits. Instead of being impatient to get by, they would usually get out and join the conversation. These visitations would generally be carried on regardless of how busy everyone's work schedule was at the time.

Unlike today, when unannounced visits, especially just before meal time, are somewhat socially unacceptable, drop-in visits were common events on the Flat. It was a generally-accepted social obligation at that time to drop whatever one was doing and visit for a while.

If it was close to meal time, the host would invite the visitors to stay and eat with the family. The host would sometimes have to do some real scrambling to come up enough food to divide amongst the visitors and her own family. In some cases these hastily-arranged meals offered slim pickings for everyone, especially since they did not have easy access to a convenience store or refrigeration.

My mother was well known around the community for her ability to put together a quick and appealing meal on short notice. With one exception, she followed the gracious host custom to the fullest degree. However, there was one elderly gentleman by the name of Gene Carver who tested her graciousness to its breaking point.

Gene was an elderly man that lived in a small cabin near the Joe Scott residence. I do not know what type of arrangements he had with Joe's family, but I know he did eat most of his meals there. He was a stoutly-built man of medium height and probably had not had a bath in ten years. An old worn-out cowboy hat covered his bald head in a manner that attempted to cover a large bump located high on his forehead.

Gene, who had a collection of sayings and a unique humorous method of delivering them, always answered questions about the bump on his head in a slow raspy drawl: "I sent off for some hair growth cream and they sent me a breast growth hormone by mistake."

Now Gene, who did not work, was one of several people on the Flat who spent most of their time traveling around the neighborhood visiting their neighbors. Gene, who did not have a car, would slowly trudge around the community in a manner that would place his arrival at someone's house just before meal time.

He would usually distribute his visits on a rotational basis, knowing that his welcome was limited to about two visits in a row. However, if Gene found a new family in the neighborhood or someone that went out of her way to fix a good meal, he would keep coming back until she could figure out some way to discourage his meal time visits.

My mother, being a very kindhearted person, was at first a very gracious host to Gene. She actually invited him to come back again some time after his first visit. However, after about the sixth meal in a row, Mom and the rest of our family were getting fed up with him, so to speak.

Gene, who was a pretty fast eater, would finish his main course before the rest of the family and then hog down most of the dessert. Also he got to the point where he was telling my mother what kind of food he liked and how he liked it cooked. The last and most important drawback to the whole family was his body odor. Rosalie and I got so we would take our plates outside because we could not stand the odor and the folks wanted to do the same.

My mother was at her wit's end on how she could end or slow down Gene's visits without being rude or hurting his feelings. Finally, she developed a plan. My sister was assigned to watch out our back bedroom window for Gene's arrival, which was generally just before noon. When she saw him slowly trudging up the road, she was to alert my mother. At that point my mother, Rosalie and I were to all go into the back bedroom and hide; thus giving the impression that we were not at home.

My mother's plan was carried out like a well-organized army attack. My sister sounded the alarm as instructed and we all retreated to the bedroom. My sister and I were elated to see our adult mother lowering herself to playing a child's game of hide and seek as we quickly scrambled for a place to hide in the small bedroom.

We soon heard Gene's slow deliberate knock as he stood on our front porch. Then a moment of silence was followed by Gene's voice shouting, "Is anyone home?" With Rosalie and me thoroughly enjoying this game, and with our suppressed giggles and mother holding her finger over her lips in a sign to be quiet, we waited for what seemed to be an eternity.

It was with a hushed voice that my mother finally told me to carefully creep out and see if I could see anything of Gene. Skillfully keeping a low profile and scanning the front porch from one of the living room windows, I satisfied myself that Gene was not around the outside of the house. I gave a reassuring all clear sign to Rosalie and Mom and we all resumed our normal composure. As my mother started towards the kitchen door she sighed in a relieved voice, "Well, it looks like the old coot is gone; we can go ahead and eat now." As I trailed Mom into the kitchen, I saw her gasp and put her hand to her mouth.

There, sitting at our kitchen table with a defiant look on his face, was Gene. This was one of the few times that I saw Mom speechless. It took her several minutes of fumbling around the room preparing the meal before she started talking in a restrained voice. Gene, undoubtedly having this trick played on him before, won the battle that day.

However, Mom, summoning all the courage in her soul, finally got up enough nerve after our meal to tell Gene that it might be best to wait a month or more before he came back again. Gene did come back, but his visits were not nearly as regular as before.

Staying all night after a daily visit was another common custom, especially during the winter months. One would have thought that since houses were small and beds were already being used to their maximum capacity, that overnight guests would have created a problem to the host.

However, couches, extra blankets, sofa chairs and bare floors were all used without second thoughts. The hosts' children often gave up their beds to the guests during these nightly visits. Even during the Summer months, daily trips to both sets of my grandparents who lived in Wallowa and Joseph were usually followed by overnight stays.

Just as Gene Carver abused the open welcome for meals tradition, another neighborhood man abused the overnight stay custom. This man would usually time his unannounced visits so that he would arrive just before the evening meal. After the meal was over he would start dropping hints that he hoped would lead to an invitation to stay overnight. If the host did not take the bait and give him an invitation, he would then come right out and ask if he could be put up for the night, knowing that there were not many Flat residents that would turn his request down.

This unabashed gentleman had another quality that often made his overnight stays less than welcome. He would never offer to assist in any of the daily routine chores that often followed the evening meal. While other members of the family would be busy doing their chores, he would find other things to occupy his time, such as talking to one of the family members who didn't happen to be busy, listening to the radio or talking on the party line telephone. He also seemed to ignore or pretend that he didn't hear when members of the family would give tactful hints to him for help.

This guest, like Gene Carver, was really beginning to wear his welcome out at our house. He had increased his overnight stays from one a month to two to three times per week during one particular long, cold winter.

My mother complained regularly to my father about how this man was cutting into our food rations. I did not realize it at the time, but the regularity of his visits and the constant pressure on my dad from my mother had apparently prompted Dad to come up with a solution that would diplomatically resolve the problem.

Our regular guest had just finished eating, fired up his old stinking pipe and was taking a relaxing stance by our radio when my father, calling him by name, requested in a rather forceful manner that he assist him and me with the firewood. This chore consisted of splitting up wood in our woodshed into stove-sized chunks for both our cookstove and heating stove. Wood was hauled to a large wood box in our kitchen for the cookstove and the larger heating stove chunks were stacked on the outside front porch.

Dad's request surprised me because the wood packing was my chore and I had already packed in my normal amount of wood to its designated locations during the day. However, I did not argue as dad had a firmness in his voice that commanded instant silence and obedience.

It did not take long before we were splitting and packing wood in the dim light of a kerosene lantern like there was no tomorrow. Much to my delight, since this was my job, we made walls of wood under the open sided porch until we only had a small passageway into the front door to the house.

We piled wood from the already-filled wood box in the kitchen clear to the ceiling. After about an hour of wood hauling, we had filled every available bit of space with wood and made our way into the house. All three of us were tired, especially our guest. He was breathing hard and searching for a good easy chair to flop his weary body in. He was looking quite relieved that this hard work, which he certainly was not used to, was finally over.

However, we soon found that the three of us still had work to do. Dad, still using his forceful voice and catching our guest just before he could sit down, said, "It looks like its going to snow tonight. We had better feed the livestock now, rather then waiting until the morning."

I was amazed at Dad's statement since we had never fed our cows in the dark. before. We normally fed our cows in the morning. This meant crawling up in the dark hay loft of our barn and pitchforking the loose hay out a side window of the barn loft. Then, after the hay was pitched out on the ground, it had to be scattered out so that our animals would have equal opportunities to eat the hay.

As we walked out to the barnyard, Dad said that he would crawl up in the barn loft and pitch out the hay. He then added that I could hold the lantern while our guest spread out the hay. Our cows, shocked and happy that they were getting fed for the second time this day, eagerly followed our guest around as he slowly dragged his now exhausted body around the barnyard spreading the hay. After about an hour and a half of feeding cows, we all slowly left the cold dark confines of the barnyard and gathered our tired and aching bodies around the welcome heat of the stove.

It was during our hand warming session around the stove that Dad casually mentioned that we were all going to have to get up a little earlier in the morning because he needed our guest's help in cutting down a tree with an old cross-cut falling saw.

After Dad talked about the tree, it did not take our guest long to nervously start looking for his coat and hat, mentioning that he was sorry that he couldn't stay. He had suddenly remembered that he had forgotten some important chores at his home that should be taken care of tonight. He then rode off into the night on his old brown horse. Much to my mother's relief, this man never spent the night at our house again.

Talking on the party-line phone that served the Flat residents was one of the major forms of socializing. This antiquated system consisted of a light gauge single-strand wire strung on a support system of trees, rotted-out poles, fence posts and any other device that would hold the wire off the ground.

At each house the wire was connected to the old-style hand-cranked telephones. Each house was assigned a calling code based on the number and length of the rings. Our code was three short rings. An emergency number used for fires or some other life-threatening situation was seven short rings.

There was no assigned work crew to make needed repairs, so maintenance, which was nearly nonexistent, was usually done on a volunteer basis by whomever had the most urgent need to call.

There were usually from twelve to thirteen homes connected to this party line. Marathon conversations kept the line tied up most of the time. It was not unusual for four or five different parties to be on all at once. Nowadays, they would be called conference calls.

Butting in on a conversation to say that you had an important call to make was generally accepted with no hard feelings. Eavesdropping was done by most of the parties so it was not a good idea to say anything that you didn't want the whole neighborhood to hear.

The party line phone system was not tied in with any line to the outside. However, the Emil Miller family, who lived in closer to the town of Elgin, had both a party line system and a regular phone to the outside. The Millers were very public-spirited in relaying messages from the Flat residents to persons on the regular phone system. This was a real important service that helped resolve some crisis situations on the Flat.

Social events, in which two or more families would pool their food resources and would meet either at a residence or public meeting hall such as a church, a schoolhouse, a grange hall or a clubhouse, were common. During the 1940s my folks were associated with about five families that would regularly get together for potluck dinners on Sunday afternoons. They would rotate these dinners between the residences. Each family would bring a generous food supply, thus making the meals a few notches in quality above the average meal served at home.

Great camaraderie occurred at these get-togethers. Families would generally start arriving at the selected host residence shortly after noon. The men would visit while the women put together a pre-cooked meal. After a delicious feast, accompanied by visiting and good-natured humor, a card game called "Hearts" would be played. The game's losers would then have the honor of washing and drying the dishes. After the dishes were completed the families would generally separate off in fours and play pinochle during the rest of the afternoon.

Participants in these events always looked forward to visiting the Francis Miller family. Francis, who happened to be the most renowned prankster in all of Union County, always kept his guests rolling in laughter with his carefully planned and executed pranks. He would canvass the whole state for the purpose of obtaining gag tricks. He probably invented the whoopee cushion.

He had water glasses that would slowly drip out of a small hole near their top when one took a drink. He had fake worms or other horrible-looking insects that he would put in some of the table dishes. One of his favorite props was fake baby manure that he would slyly drop behind one of the guest's small children. Then he would sometimes have to make dramatic rescues of this fake item when the child's mother would grab it in some paper and rush to dispose of it. He would always manage to plant a loud "whoopee cushion" where some unsuspecting, bashful female guest would sit on it.

Probably one of the most used of his pranks was a hardbound book that he would casually leave on a piece of furniture. This book's cover had a sexy, provocative title accompanied by a picture of a voluptuous, half-dressed woman. When one opened the book's cover a mousetrap-triggering device would detonate an enlarged pistol cap. The resulting very loud bang would both severely startle the book's opener and would embarrass him in front of the rest of the guests.

The children had good times at these potluck events. While the parents were playing card games, the children would usually retreat to the woods or the out-buildings for varied types of entertainment. Activities included hide and seek, Anne over, building tree houses, rotten egg fights, snow sports during the winter time, throwing green apples at hornet's nests and others.

Many of the children's activities were not too well-chaperoned by the adults and we would sometimes get ourselves into dangerous situations. One time we formed up sides and had a B-B gun war. Taking up positions behind trees, logs and buildings, we would take pot shots at each other as we ran from one fortified position to another. This game was quickly stopped by the adults when one of the kids nearly lost an eye from an unlucky hit.

Another time, two boys and I put our lives in peril when we climbed to the top of some rather flexible trees during a moderate wind storm. Although we did not get caught by our parents, the fright from the more-than-expected sway of the trees during the wind storm was ample incentive not to repeat the performance.

We had another dangerous game that we played. We would screw a metal cap onto the end of a three-fourths-inch pipe, pour some water in the pipe and then wrap a thin layer of cloth around a steel bolt. We would then forcibly drive the bolt into the end of the pipe and heat the pipe over an open fire that we would build out of tree limbs.

When the pipe would heat up to a certain degree the steam formed inside the pipe would suddenly send the bolt out, accompanied by a hissing head of steam, with the velocity of a speeding bullet. We would aim the business end of the pipe out over an open field, bordered by the county road, so that we might be lucky enough to see where our missile lit.

This dangerous pipe game, like most of our most exciting sports, soon had to come to an end. We had carefully driven a tight fitting three inch bolt into our pipe and were listening to the small amounts of steam starting to escape around the bolt as the hot fire progressively increased the water temperature in the pipe. Knowing that the hissing sound of the steam was a warning that the pipe was about to launch its speeding projectile, we started putting distance between ourselves and the fire. As we geared ourselves for the firing of the pipe and the accompanying shower of ashes and steam, a new concern suddenly appeared on the scene.

An opening in a grove of trees that screened our view of the county road to the north suddenly revealed an unexpected traveler. Vern Stowe, a neighbor who lived on the north end of the Flat, suddenly entered our field of view. Riding his fast-walking horse; he was rapidly approaching a collision course with the projected direction of our makeshift cannonball. We seemed to be locked into our positions like stone statues as the pipe hissed angrily and Vern slowly moved toward the expected trajectory of the bolt.

Suddenly, the angry voice of my father jolted us out of stupor as he asked what was going on. All I could do was jump up and down excitedly and point to the steaming pipe in the fire with one hand and then point at Vern with the other. Rube Witty, a cousin of my dad's, saved the day. Rube run up and gently rolled the pipe out of the fire with his foot and at the same time pointed the bolt end of the pipe so that it pointed away from everyone. The pipe never went off after it left the fire.

I received quite a lecture from my dad over this incident. He went to great lengths to tell me how dangerous it was and how we could have killed Vern Stowe if it had gone off and hit him. The ironic part of his lecture was that I later learned that he and some other boys had done the same thing during their youth. However, in Dad's case the pipe *had* gone off and nearly hit an unsuspecting adult.

Housewarmings for newcomers and going away parties for those moving from the community attracted a large attendance by Flat residents. Those attending would usually bring both food and presents to the hosts. On occasion, some of the guests would also bring hard liquor or home brew to liven up the party.

Shivarees for newlyweds also gave an excuse for gatherings. These events often came as a surprise to the young couple. Again, those attending would bring gifts, food and sometimes drinks. Some of these events could turn into some really wild parties. The newly married couple would usually be subjected to a variety of pranks before the evening was over.

Shorting the bed sheets, putting cracker crumbs in the bed, putting sugar in the salt shakers, tying their clothes in hard knots, hiding their shoes, throwing the groom in the pond or watering trough, jacking their car off the ground and placing it on blocks of wood were a few of the more common tricks.

Sometimes the newly-wedded couple could ward off some of the tricks if they had stocked up with a large supply of beer and cigars beforehand. Before the night was over everyone, including the youngsters, would have access to the cigars. One of the sickest moments of my life occurred when I attempted to smoke two cigars at one of these events.

During the 1940s my folks joined the Grange. This organization met on Saturdays at the Cricket Flat Grange Hall, located approximately three miles out of Elgin. The Grange offered an opportunity for socializing with residents living in closer to Elgin, known only on a limited basis before.

The Grange would hold a business meeting followed by a potluck dinner. During the afternoon, some type of entertaining program would be held, which would include a short skit, or a children's program. Sometimes a guest speaker would attend. Since my sister and I had attended the Fairview Grade School, this was our first opportunity to meet some of the students attending the Elgin Schools.

One of the highlights of the Grange was the Christmas program. Francis Miller, a Flat resident and Grange member, would play the part of Santa Claus. He loved his role as Santa and played the part with much more enthusiasm and loudness than anyone I have ever seen. Grange members and their young children would set the stage for his arrival by all seating themselves in the Grange meeting room. The parents prepped the children for Santa's arrival by telling them to listen for Santa ringing his bell as he entered the outside hallway.

Santa's arrival into the meeting room was not for the weak-hearted. He would burst through the door loudly ringing a large bell and shouting ho, ho, ho, at the top of his voice. Little children up to six years old would often panicked and jump into their mother's laps for security.

Francis would then pass out bags of candy and popcorn balls to all the kids that had enough nerve to take them. He would also try and hold every kid that would let him and discuss how good they had been that year. His hugs and kisses were not confined to the kids, as he would pick out four or five of the pretty girls in the room for a generous kiss and hug.

During the 1930s and 40s it was not uncommon to have evening parties at someone's house. If the house was large enough and someone was in attendance who could play a musical instrument, a room would be cleared out for dancing. Violins, pianos, and guitars were the main instruments used for these affairs. The dancing and music would not have taken any prizes for performance ability. Usually there were not too many that knew how to dance at these parties.

I remember one party held in our small house where there were about thirty people in attendance. Most of the men and boys segregated themselves in our fourteen-by-twelve foot kitchen where they visited and participated in contests of physical strength.

Arm wrestling, Indian leg wresting, handgrip contests using a broom handle, pulling contests with a shovel handle from a sitting position, thumb wrestling and many other strength contests were engaged in. It seemed like everyone had to challenge everyone else.

The women and young girls separated themselves off in our living room, which was only slightly larger than our kitchen. There they played parlor games, such as pin-the-tail-on-the-donkey, feeling another's face while blind-folded and trying to guess their identity, spelling contests and other games.

I remember another party at the Obe and Gladys Scott home where many of the same types of games were played. However they did some different things there. As the guests arrived, four men would have the woman sit in a chair They would then blindfold her and tell her that they were going to lift the chair up with her in it. She would then be instructed to put her hands on their shoulders as they lifted her up.

However, instead of lifting her and the chair they would simply kneel down on the floor, thus giving her the sensation that she was being lifted up. After kneeling down, they would then ask the women to jump out of the chair. The main thrust of the joke was to watch the woman's reaction when she reached the floor sooner than expected.

Another feat of strength that the men tried was to reach down and grab the leg of a chair with one hand and see if they could lift it up while keeping it in a vertical position.

One trick played on the men involved announcing a contest. After getting three volunteers, they would have the men get down on their hands and knees next to a wall. They would then be told that the object of the contest was to see which one could place his knee the highest on the wall. Then, after the men were all straining in an effort to raise their knee as high as possible, they would be asked to bark like a dog. Of course everyone in the house would erupt in laughter.

One of the jokes they played was on the cruel side. Two chairs were placed approximately four feet apart. A blanket was stretched over the two chairs so that it would appear that there was a board beneath the blanket bridging the two chairs. The next step was to conceal a half-filled tub of water beneath the blanket. Two people were then recruited to sit on each of the chairs, leaving what appeared to be a seating place between the two. The pranksters then patiently waited until someone from another room or some fresh arriving guests would take the bait and soak their bottoms in the tub.

This tub joke created some hard feelings on one occasion. A large overweight woman and her husband arrived at one of these parties just after they had set up the blanket-tub trick. Although they had intended for the man to sit on the blanket, his wife reached it first. Water flew in all directions as her lower anatomy wedged itself in the wet tub. After a round of good-natured laughing, the two men pulled her to her feet, with the mistaken belief that the joke was over.

However, their troubles were just beginning. As they pulled the woman up, the tub stuck to her bottom and the remaining water ran down her legs and into her shoes. The resulting spectacle of this large woman soaking wet from the waist down and sporting a tub and a blanket on her rear end was more than those in attendance could take. As the two men tried to yank the tub from her posterior, everyone was rolling on the floor in laughter. However, her husband did not think this incident was funny and abruptly left the party with his wife after she was freed from the tub.

Although most of the parties exhibited good-natured laughter and fun, a few tilted more towards barroom brawls. One party ended up with two large men being knocked out and taking beauty rests in a snowbank, another man was hit in the eye and yet another was hammered on the head with a high-heeled shoe.

Dances were another social event attended by about half of the Flat residents. My folks would occasionally attend dances in Elgin and during the late 40s they started going more often, when some of the Flat residents started holding dances in a clubhouse. This clubhouse, which used to be the Pine Grove District School House, was purchased by twelve families living in the Flat area. They pooled their labor and money to upgrade the facility so that it had electricity and cooking facilities.

This clubhouse was heavily used by many of the Flat's residents for potluck dinners, pinochle parties and dances. The dances, geared for both the adults and the youth of the community, always stuck in my mind as a salvation for the Flat's youngsters.

This clubhouse offered a place for the young to learn how to dance. Although some dancing occurred at some of the house parties, they did not provide the opportunities available at the clubhouse. I will never forget the melodic sound of the old piano coupled with the high-pitched plaintive cry of the violin playing the Red River Valley. The rhythmic beat of the piano would seem to lock the shuffling feet of the dancers into a unified step that only good music can produce.

It was on this dance floor that I first summoned up enough courage to ask a girl to dance. She was a girl that only a few years before I had regarded as a nuisance tom-boy type that had no business even trying to look like a girl. I was not even flattered when this girl acted like she had a crush on me.

Watching her from across the room, I suddenly decided that this girl, in her pretty red dress and long brown hair, was not so bad. Then as the music began to strengthen my courage and I saw other kids my age or younger out dancing on the floor, I decided that I would give this eager, young girl an opportunity to teach me how to dance.

Many thoughts rushed through my head as I wove my way through the dancers to approach this girl. What crazy impulse had caused me to actually go through the motions of holding a girl in my arms and making a fool out of myself on the floor? What would my peers and the adults think when they saw I could not dance? Would they think I had a crush on this girl? I probably would have turned back, but the thought of showing my peers how eagerly this girl would jump into my arms when I asked her to dance gave me the courage to go through with my mission.

Finally, I reached the far end of the bench from where this girl was sitting and started walking past a number of other girls to reach my destination. Marching grim-faced like a soldier heading into a death march, I suddenly did a military right-face and stopped directly in front of the girl.

Avoiding looking directly into her eyes, I summoned my carefully-planned words for a self-confident delivery. Feeling a sensation like having the wind knocked out of me, I found that I was as speechless as a fence post. All I could do was move my lips in a sucking motion that resembled a gasping sucker freshly removed from the water.

It seemed like an eternity before I finally weaseled out in a course whisper, "Would you like to dance?" The girl looked somewhat surprised and then stabbed me with a negative shake of her head. I have been humiliated several times in my life but nothing before or since can compare with my feelings at that moment.

I was sure that everyone in the building, including the piano player who had her back to me, had witnessed my humbling moment. I would have given anything at that time to be able to make myself invisible. My walk across the room to ask her to dance was nothing compared to my crushed feelings as I retreated to a lonely position in the kitchen portion of the hall.

It was about an hour later when I felt a light tap on my shoulder and an older girl that I hardly knew asked me to dance. Suddenly, I seemed to have a new lease on life as I walked back to the dance floor. Only an hour before I had made a vow that the floor would never again be honored with my presence. The girl must have felt sorry for me as she dodged my clumsy feet for the rest of the night. Although I never saw my rescuer again, I will never forget her kindness. In later years, I attended many dances at the clubhouse and danced many times with the girl that turned me down.

It was during the winter months, when daylight hours were short, that we had the most idle time to spend inside the house. Many forms of entertainment would occupy our time during these cold winter evenings. Playing games of all kind, reading books, playing with toys, sewing for my mother and listening to the radio were some of the main ones.

Listening to the radio was probably our favorite family pastime. Our old radio was nothing like radios today. It was a bulky black rectangular-shaped beast weighing about thirty pounds. Its bulk was mainly caused by a high number of large-sized tubes and two large speakers on each side of the tubes.

The radio was powered by a car battery that was attached to the radio by two wires running from each battery pole. The radio antenna consisted of a wire running from the back of the radio and through a hole in our living room wall. From the outside wall of the house the wire climbed to the top of a sixty-foot tree. Then from the top of the tree it spanned a 150-foot space to the top of another tree.

Despite all the wire for the antenna and the huge radio, we only received two to three stations and the volume was often so low that we would almost have to place our head next to the radio to hear. The large car battery would not last too long and had to be charged up fairly well for sufficient volume. To recharge the battery, Dad would switch batteries with the one on the car on a regular basis.

Some of our favorite programs besides the news were the Red Skelton Program, the Jack Kirkwood Show, Amos and Andy, and the Whistler. Political speeches by the President and Oregon State College football games were always big events for Dad. He would often change the battery just before these events to get sufficient volume.

During the evening hours the family's interest in the radio was comparable to families today watching their favorite television program. To accommodate the large radio, its large battery and the antenna wire running to the outside, the radio had to be placed against the house wall farthest away from our wood stove. This meant that in order to hear we all had to place ourselves in the coldest part of the room.

I remember my mother sitting in a rocking chair with a large heavy blanket wrapped around her body from the waist down. A long thick shawl would be covering her shoulders and the upper parts of her arms. Only her head and hands would be free from a heavy cloth covering. Her hands were kept free so that she could sew or knit.

My dad, sitting in a straight-backed chair, would usually be wearing a heavy wool coat and an old fedora hat as he would tilt one side of his head towards the radio. My sister and I, since we did not dress as warm as the folks, would spend more time moving between two straight backed chairs seated near the radio and the woodstove where we warmed our back sides.

During the early 1940s, Dad purchased a better radio at an auction. It was much smaller, produced much more volume, and could receive more stations. It improved our lot considerably as we could hear it from anywhere in the room. This allowed us to sit on our couch near the stove where we were much more comfortable and a lot warmer during the cold weather.

Reading books occupied plenty of our time during the cold winter nights. There were many times when bad weather would blank out radio reception or there was nothing on the radio but music. When this would occur, reading was our next choice. The biggest drawback to reading was poor lighting.

During the 1930s kerosene lamps were our major lighting source. Their light was barely good enough for night reading. The lamp glass seemed to always be sooting up so that light was greatly reduced. It was not uncommon to have to clean the glass two to three times a night.

During the 1940s we switched from the kerosene lamps to white gas lanterns. These lanterns provided much better light, especially for reading. The first ones we had were not perfect. They were always plugging up and causing the light to go dim, or were hard to light. Some would create a small explosion when lit and nearly set the house afire on a few occasions.

My most memorable moments in reading were when my father would read aloud to the rest of the family. My father would position himself in an old rocking chair with his feet near the warm crackling stove and with his back towards the kerosene light. My mother, sister and I would generally start out seated on an old couch located on the other side of the stove. After Dad had read a while, Rosalie and I would soon park ourselves on the floor near Dad's feet.

From our location we would silently strain our ears to catch every word that Dad read. At times we would be in a spellbound state listening to the soft murmur of Dad's voice as our feet absorbed the warm radiation of the stove. These moments were like no other time in my life; I would visualize the characters, objects and the scenes described in the book as the flickering light of the lamp sent dancing shadows across the smoke-colored ceiling.

Dad's announcement that it was time to go to bed would always come too soon for Rosalie and me. We would always beg him to read just a little bit more as he placed the book marker in the book and put it away. We must have been desperate for reading material as there were several books that Dad read to us more than three times. He read most of the O. Henry and Jack London books. He read "White Fang" and "Call of The Wild" at least three times. I also read these books myself more than twice when I was older.

My sister and I read a lot to ourselves. My favorites were dog books and western novels. Zane Grey books were all family favorites. Grey's books were a favorite trading book among the Flat residents. About a month after Christmas, neighbors would start quizzing each other on which Zane Grey book they got for a Christmas gift so they could negotiate a trade.

The folks subscribed to two magazines that we all looked forward to reading. "Colliers" and "Life Magazine" seemed to hold the interest of both the children and the adults. My mother had pretty strict standards on what books and magazines she would allow Rosalie and I to read. One time my dad came home from an auction with a box full of "True Magazine " and "True Confession" magazines. It did not take my mother long to get rid of the "True Confessions" and she would have thrown the "True Magazines " away too if Dad had not rescued them.

I remember my parents having quite an argument over allowing these magazines to be kept in the house. It was finally agreed that Dad could keep the "True Magazines" as long they would be kept in a place where Rosalie and I couldn't find them. We were not even allowed to get close to Dad when he was reading one, as Mom would sternly warn us to keep our distance.

Seeing Dad read these forbidden magazines whetted my curiosity to its highest degree. Knowing that Dad was hiding these magazines some place in the house was like hiding a jar of honey in a room full of bears.

It did not take too long before I was afforded an opportunity to satisfy my curiosity. After giving me a list of chores, Dad drove my sister and Mom to La Grande to do some shopping. Working in a whirlwind fashion, I quickly completed my assigned chores and started my diligent search for the forbidden fruit. Carefully searching the house like a drug swat team, I finally found the treasures hidden beneath a bunch of old clothes in a box on the back porch.

After taking an observation point where I could see the folks' old car driving up the road, I breathlessly started scanning the pages of the magazine. However, my expectations of lustful photos of sex and naked women were not met. The only thing that I could find was a picture of a half-dressed woman that was roughly drawn in a cartoon. It was then I decided that there must be some real sexy stories that I had not taken the time to read. Not daring to risk being caught, I decided that I would hide a couple of the publications in my favorite hiding spot, thinking that my dad would not count the magazines in the box.

It was a couple of days later that I carefully retreated to my favorite hiding place in the barn to spend more time on my forbidden fruit. After reading several of the stories, I was still extremely disappointed. Even though the articles were real interesting, containing stories of combat and hunting dangerous, wild animals, I failed to find many regarding the juicy sex I was looking for.

However, there were a lot of words that I didn't understand. I finally decided that these words contained meanings that would probably throw an entirely different light on some of these far-fetched tales. I felt sure that there had to be some hidden meanings in some of these words or my mother would not have been concerned about my reading them.

It was then that I decided that I would take a different approach to ferreting out the secret code that had to be lurking in those magazines. Taking a pencil and paper to my secret cache, I copied down about twenty of the most mysterious words that I could find. I then laboriously looked each word up in the dictionary to see what it meant. This went on for about two weeks without my unlocking any titillating meanings.

I probably increased my vocabulary more in that time period than during any other time in my life, because, for each word I looked up, I also had to look up many of the words in the dictionary that described what the original word meant.

During the next several months I managed to read all the magazines that Dad had hidden in the box. I also estimated that more time was spent looking up words in the dictionary than reading the magazines. I was like a miner with gold fever. I would find just enough tantalizing words to keep me interested and there was always the hope that I was about to hit paydirt. Other than increasing my vocabulary, I never did hit paydirt or solve the mystery of why my mother was against these magazines.

There were several games that were popular with Flat residents. Pinochle, hearts, cribbage, Monopoly, checkers, Chinese checkers, anagrams, chess and poker were the most popular ones. When several families got together, Pinochle was the most popular game. Sometimes these games were more casual and other times there would be organized, with prizes given out for high and low scores.

The men sometimes got together and played poker. Most of these games took place at one of the Elgin taverns. My father, who was a pretty good poker player, loved to gamble and was able to play quite a bit with little money. During one spring he was able to get part of his ground cultivated by a neighbor in return for a gambling debt. My mother, who was totally against all types of gambling, eventually talked my father into quitting.

My father also loved to play chess. However, Obe Scott was about the only other person on the Flat that played. They both required a lot of time to make their moves and their games, much to the disgust of their wives, would go on most of the day.

Eventually, Dad taught me how to play. It would take Dad so long to move that I would read a Zane Grey book during the game. For this reason, I hated to play chess with him. About the only time I would play Dad was to get out of work. When I saw that he was about to take me out into the cold winter weather to cut wood or make posts I would suggest we play a game of chess. Although I hated the game, it was better than working in the snow and the cold.

My mother and dad spent quite a bit of time playing Anagrams. They used to argue over this game because their old dictionary had a lot of pages that were torn out or unreadable. The whole family would often play marathon games of Monopoly. Chinese checkers and regular checkers were also popular family games.

Fundraising pie socials were probably the best-attended social events on the Flat. These events, which would be held at the schoolhouse, were designed to raise money for school needs that were not budgeted. The women and their daughters would go all-out to bake their best pies and then wrap them up like a Christmas presents. Francis Miller would then auction off the pies to the highest bidder amongst the men and boys.

Once a man or boy had bought a pie, the maker of the pie come forward and they would eat the pie together. The women's pies would generally be separated and auctioned off separately from the younger girls' pies so a young boy would not have to eat with an adult woman.

Francis Miller would have a lot of fun trying to disguise the pies so that the bidders would not know whose pie they were bidding on. His favorite target was usually some young man who was attempting to buy a certain girl's pie. He would try his best to get the other bidders to bid the young man up, telling them what a nice pie it was. He would often take the decorative wrapper off one pie and put it on another to confuse the bidders.

I was quite bashful around the girls when I was in grade school and it always took all my courage to buy a girl's pie and help her eat it. The girl and I would often eat our pie without saying a word to each other.

Making home brew and root beer were other hobbies that many of the residents engaged in. Everyone had their own special recipe and loved to compare batches with their neighbors. Many stories were told about home brew and what could go wrong if it was not made right. My folks had their own little experience with home brew when they found themselves in an embarrassing position with my dad's folks.

It was mid-morning, once, when my parents' party line phone rang out with its three short jingles. The three short rings were the signal that the call was for our residence. After answering the phone, my mother, listening to the caller's message, seemed to be somewhat concerned . After hanging up the phone she immediately rushed outside and called out for my dad.

The urgency written on my mother's face and the speed in which she called for Dad immediately whetted my twelve-year-old curiosity. I was all ears when my dad entered the house. After a quick low-toned conference between my parents, my uninvited radar-like ears soon picked up enough of my mother's conversation to give me a piece meal picture of what the phone call was about.

Briefly, the phone call was from Emil Miller, a Cricket Flat resident who happened to have both a party line phone and a phone to the outside. (As mentioned in another chapter, this was the way that the Flat residents would place or receive their calls from the outside.)

Emil had relayed a call from my grandparents, Dave and Stella Scott, who lived approximately twenty miles away in the town of Wallowa. They had called to let the folks know that they would be arriving at our house around mid-afternoon to spend the night. Normally, it was a joyous occasion to have visitors, especially my grandparents, to our house where everyone was welcome.

This time, however, my young intuition soon sensed that a major crisis was brewing as far as my folks were concerned. You see, the "brewing crisis" was, in fact, home brew. It just so happened Dad had two crocks of home brew in the mash stage sitting behind our old wood cooking stove, where temperatures were ideal for fermentation. In a lot of families this would not have presented a problem, but in this case the gravity of the situation facing my parents was, in their eyes, a real crisis.

To further explain the drama, more background on my grandparents should be given. Like many of the families growing up in the early 1900s, my grandparents held strong religious beliefs and followed them rigorously. Neither one drank or smoked and they brought up all their children with a religious training prohibited drinking. They instilled such respect in their children that even as adults the women of the family would never smoke in front of my grandparents. My parents were always very careful not to drink or even have alcoholic beverages in their house when my grandparents were present.

Getting back to the crisis at hand, it was soon apparent that my parents differed as to what should be done before my grandparents' arrival. My mother, not being a drinker, wanted either to dump the mash out or hide it in the barn.

My dad, on the other hand, was too frugal to waste the brew by dumping it out and was afraid that the cool temperatures of the barn would ruin the brew in the crock. After a fairly heated discussion between my parents, it was decided that, even though the brew was not quite ready to bottle, we would bottle and cap it and then hide it in the barn.

A bottling and capping assembly line was soon formed. A chair was placed on our kitchen table and then the crock of brew put on the chair. A siphon hose was activated out of the crock to fill empty beer bottles, which were then capped by a hand capper located at the far end of the table.

Since my parents did not know exactly what time my grandparents would arrive, they were in a real hurry to get the bottles capped and hidden in the barn. My sister and I were recruited to help so as to speed up the project. My job was to control the flow out of the siphon hose into the bottle. My sister then handed the filled bottles to my dad at the end of the table where he would cap them. My mother, who spent a considerable amount of time glancing nervously at our clock, then took the capped bottles and placed them in two cardboard boxes.

My mother had just placed the last bottle in the box when the purr of a car motor penetrated the final assembly line noise of our capping operation. My mother, who was now a nervous wreck, rushed out on our back porch and shouted, "Oh my gosh! They are here!" My parents looked like a couple of moonshiners that were about to be raided by the law. For a few seconds they seemed too stunned to move as they desperately tried to think of a quick and easy place to hide the brew and capping equipment.

Suddenly gaining his composure, my dad grabbed the two boxes of brew and said to me in a loud whisper, "I am putting these under our bed; put the crocks and the capper in the cellar."

We had just barely gotten things put out of sight when my grandparents knocked on our door. My folks, acting as though they had just thrown a murdered body in the woodstove, graciously ushered my grandparents in. Gradually, they regained their composure during the afternoon of visiting.

Several hours later, after one of Mom's delicious evening meals and some more visiting, everyone went to bed. In our normal sleeping arrangements, my sister slept in her bedroom, which was adjacent to the room where my parents slept and I slept in a very small room adjacent to the kitchen.

When we had company, however, they would sleep in my sister's room, she would sleep in my room, and I would sleep on the living room couch. We had all drifted off to a restful sleep after our day's anxious moments when the peaceful quiet of the night was shattered by a loud bang coming from my parents' room.

This loud noise awakened everyone in the house, including my grandparents. We all converged on my folks' bedroom fearing the worst. I remember my granddad standing in the doorway between the two bedrooms with his flashlight, as we didn't have electric lights. "Did the bed fall down?" he asked. "No, I cracked my elbow against the wall," replied my dad in a subdued voice.

Dad's explanation seemed to satisfy everyone and I gradually drifted back to sleep. My sleep did not last too long, however, as another loud bang again rocked the house. This time I heard my grandmother say, "Are you all right, Noel?" thinking that he had again cracked his elbow against the wall. "Maybe you should switch sides in the bed with Ethel," she added.

After some light discussion, everyone quieted down again, only to be subjected to another noise. This time the popping sound was not as loud, but was followed by a swishing sound. Also I could now smell the distinct odor of home brew emanating from my folks' bedroom.

By now I knew that the noises we had heard were coming from exploding beer bottles or caps blowing off and the pressurized liquid squirting out like a freshly opened champagne bottle. We later learned that this was common when home brew was bottled too soon.

Shortly after the last explosion I heard my dad get up. I watched his silhouetted figure disappear through our outside doorway carrying the two boxes of home brew out of the house. Apparently the agitation of the bottles triggered another set of explosions as Dad's progress could be followed through the darkness of the night by the sound of exploding bottles. With the bangs growing progressively softer, the sound of Dad's retreat faded into the surrounding woods.

It was a few minutes later when my dad tiptoed back into the house smelling like a bum from Burnside Street. We learned later that as he was carrying the two pasteboard boxes, stacked one upon another, the bottom of the lower box gave away and the remaining bottles then fell out and exploded at the base of Dad's feet and legs, thus practically giving him a home brew shower.

By now the entire house smelled like a brewery. Dad was soaked in home brew and there were puddles of brew under and around the bed. It was probably a good half hour later before Dad had cleaned himself up and Mom had wiped the brew from around and under the bed.

Windows and doors were all left open to air out the house in hopes that the odor would disappear before morning. Mom was a basket case by this time, and I could tell, by catching occasional glimpses of her face in the dim glow of the flashlight, that if my grandparents had not been there my dad would have been in *big* trouble.

In the meantime, my grandparents in the adjoining room had not moved a muscle since the second explosion. I am sure that they were awake and now knew that Dad was not hitting the wall with his elbow. They were just being polite so as not to embarrass my folks. Nothing was mentioned about the incident the next morning and my grandparents left shortly after noon for their home back in Wallowa.

Chapter 14

All About Foods

During the 1930s and early 1940s Cricket Flat residents lived under a number of constraints that required them to prepare and handle foods differently from today's people. The absence of electricity and generating plants for refrigerators and freezer units, plus the distance to the nearest store, forced residents into a more self-sufficient lifestyle.

Long-term storage of perishable food supplies depended on methods other than freezing. Purchasing perishable foods at the nearest store was also impractical. Poor roads, which were sometimes impassable, and the lack of cars or the necessary funds for travel encouraged folks to be highly resourceful in regards to food.

One of the most important tools in food storage and preservation was the cellar. Just about every family had one. Cellars were vital in keeping foods and milk products cool during the hot summer months and were equally important in keeping vegetables, fruits and canned produce from freezing in winter. Two basic types of cellars were used on the Flat. One was the underground type, sometimes called the root cellar, and the other type was constructed above ground.

Underground cellars, if constructed correctly, were amazing storage units in their ability to maintain constant temperatures. This type of cellar, built into an excavated hole in a hillside, resembled a miniature log cabin without a roof. A layer of logs, placed on the top, would, in turn, be covered with a layer of two-inch planks. Next, the whole structure would be covered with a one-foot layer of straw and sawdust before being topped off with three to four feet of dirt.

A double-walled door approximately one foot thick and filled with sawdust would give access to the building. Most of the cellars would also have an inside screen door and a vent leading from the inside of the cellar clear to the outside.

Vents and screen doors were necessary to prevent odors and molds from building up in the nearly air-tight structure. During the summer months, the main door would be slightly opened and a small door on the vent would be slid open during the night for venting. Most cellars would have to be vented about once or twice a week during the summer months.

Numerous shelves for holding fruit jars would line the cellar's inside walls and two to three large bins constructed on the floor would be used for storing apples and potatoes. A two inch plank shelf located about two feet off the floor would be used for holding porcelain crocks of sauerkraut and salted meat.

The other type of cellar used was shaped like a small, single-room house. It had double-wallboard construction with its two-foot thick walls filled with sawdust. Its loft would be likewise filled with about a two-foot layer of sawdust. It also was vented and its doors were similar to the underground cellar.

The inside was similar, with the exception of a higher ceiling. When we first moved to the Flat, both types of cellars on the place. However, the underground one was quite old and we only used it a few years before the ceiling caved in. The other one, which was an above-the-ground cellar, was much newer and was quite close to the house.

The cellars had their bad points. In addition to problems with mold and odors, they were so dark that visibility was a problem. Burrowing rodents would come up under the floors, providing access for mice, gophers, snakes, frogs, toads and a variety of insects and spiders.

We would occasionally find black widow spiders in our cellar. This sent my mother into a panic and she pressured my dad into burning a sulfur candle overnight in the cellar. This would kill anything that happened to be living in the numerous cracks and other small hiding places.

We always kept the cellar's shelves lined with mousetraps and had to place poison-baited carrots in the bottom of our potato and apple bins to control gophers. One winter we noticed that one of our large apple bins was going down at a much higher rate than normal. After investigating, we found that gophers coming up from beneath the bin had eaten or destroyed about six bushels of apples.

On another occasion, some harmless garter snakes nearly gave my mother a heart attack. My father and I were milking the cows one early March morning when we heard a piercing scream coming from the cellar area. Thinking that something terrible was happening to my mother, we quickly rushed the 200 feet to the cellar. When we arrived, we found Mother in a near state of shock, proclaiming that she was never going into that cellar again.

After a few minutes of listening to her frantic description, we were able to learn what had happened. She had taken a small metal bucket out to the cellar to gather some potatoes out of the potato bin. Groping her way through the dark confines of the bin she filled the bucket with the few spuds that were located near the bin's bottom. As she walked from the dark cellar to the light of the outside she happened to look down in her bucket and see four or five sluggish garter snakes trying to squirm out to freedom from their bed of potatoes.

Of all of the wild critters that lived on the Flat, none could frighten my mother more than a snake. It didn't matter if it were a harmless variety no bigger than an angleworm, it would still send her into a hysterical panic. On this day, if neighbors living some distance away had reported seeing a flock of flying snakes overhead, they probably would have been just about right. It took Dad and I quite awhile just to find the potato bucket—which Mom had thrown some 200 feet away from where she had been standing.

It was some time before Mom could be convinced to enter the cellar again. Dad and I had to remove about thirty garter snakes that thought they had found the perfect place to hibernate at the bottom of the potato bin.

The orchard located to the west of our house provided us with a major food source. A number of apple, pear, plum and cherry trees gave us a variety of fruit for canning. We also had some trees that provided apples designed for winter storage. They would taste woody and bitter during the fall of the year, but as the winter passed, they would become progressively sweeter and more palatable. They kept very well in the large cellar bins.

Most of our other apples were for summer canning or eating fresh off the tree in the fall. Besides filling a couple of large cellar bins with apples, my mother would can about 300 quarts of fruit from our orchard each year. Almost every evening meal would include either canned fruit or a pie made from our stored fruit.

Several good stories could be told about the old orchard. My dad used the section of land fenced off with the orchard to contain our pigs. Since our pigs were always just one step away from starvation, they would patrol the orchard like traffic cops waiting for an apple to fall.

When we picked apples, the pigs would concentrate around the base of our ladder like a bunch of flies on a watermelon. This could prove to be quite dangerous as they would often bump up hard against the ladder in their attempt to beat another hog to a dislodged apple.

My granddad, Bill Halsey, had an expensive experience with our hogs. He was picking apples, perched on one of our flimsy ladders, and had been having quite a few problems with the hogs nearly knocking the ladder over. In a fit of anger he directed a forceful stream of profanity at one of pigs.

Apparently his newly-acquired false teeth had got caught in the eruption of cuss words and were spit out, landing like an apple in the midst of about thirty hungry hogs where they were damaged beyond repair. Granddad, who had a great sense of humor, said, "One of those darned hogs caught my teeth before they hit the ground and ran out of the orchard going thirty miles an hour with my teeth in his mouth. If I ever see that hog again, I am going to give him my dental bill."

During certain years the orchard would be plagued with yellow jackets and bald-faced hornets. The hornets, which had a very painful sting, would build huge, paper nests that hung down from the large, lateral orchard limbs. Since the hornets posed a major problem when picking fruit, the nests would have to be destroyed. Dad would generally do this by tying a rag on the end of a long pole, setting the rag on fire and then burning the nest. He would generally do this at night when the hornets were all in the nest and were not active.

These hornet nests would often provide a challenge when I had company. We had a risk-taking game that we loved to play, even though we often got stung. We would attempt to knock the nests off the apple tree limbs with the throw of a green apple.

The main thrill of this game was watching the hornets attack the pigs when the pigs mistook the falling nest for an apple. The strange irony of this game was that even though the hogs would squeal and run when first stung, they would eventually come back and eat the nest.

Once, I had a scary experience while picking apples. I was near the top of our old wooden fourteen-foot ladder when I noticed a group of hogs that had been watching my every move from the base of my ladder suddenly retreat to the far end of the orchard. Their retreat was shortly followed by the appearance of a large black bear that casually walked beneath me. Not daring to move, I breathlessly watched the bear amble to the far end of the orchard. I then raced down the ladder and fled like a deer to our house some 300 feet away. I told my mother about the bear, but it had disappeared by the time she looked for it.

We had a huge garden with most of the space taken up by corn and potatoes. The rest of the garden would be planted to turnips, beets, carrots, radishes, cabbage, lettuce and green beans. Most of the produce would be canned.

The cabbage would be sliced up and salted down in crocks where it would turn into sauerkraut. The turnips and onions would be put in gunny sacks and stored in the cellar and the lettuce and radishes would be used mainly for green salads during the spring and summer. My mother would end up canning 200 to 300 jars of vegetables each year.

In looking back at my mother's busy schedule, it never ceases to amaze me how much canning she did. During our early years, before we had easier access to stores, she would annually can 200-300 jars of fruit, the same number for vegetables, around 100 quart jars of meat, and would put up around 50 to 60 jars of jam and jelly.

The canning process was a time-consuming and arduous job. After cleaning and packing the produce in quart jars, eight of them would be placed in a non-pressurized canning kettle. Then the produce would be boiled for 90 to 180 minutes, depending on what type of produce it was.

My mother would sometimes have three to five canning kettles going at once. During the early years, when she only had the old wood cookstove, she could only handle three kettles at one time. Later on, when she used a Coleman white gas stove, in conjunction with the wood stove, she would have as many as five canning kettles going at one time.

The most miserable part of the canning job probably was working in warm temperatures. Since canning was mostly done during the summer months, my mother would have to withstand the warm temperatures from the wood cookstove on top of the heat of a typically-hot, late summer day. The temperature in the kitchen would often exceed 100 degrees.

Deer provided a major portion of our meat supply. When deer were killed during the summer months, most of the meat was preserved by canning. It would be cut into two-inch chunks, mixed with salt and water and packed in jars for canning. Most meats and string beans were generally boiled in the jars for about three hours.

During the 1940s Mom's canning was greatly facilitated when she was able to replace most of the canning kettles with large pressure cookers. The first ones she had were frightening to work with. Their pressure regulators would often malfunction, creating excessive pressure on the canning unit.

The old kitchen ceiling had several holes in it from the lead safety plugs that would blow out from the top of the cooker. It was a frightening and dangerous moment when one of the plugs would blow out. We would hear a loud bang, immediately followed by a loud shrill hissing sound of escaping steam.

It was quite dangerous to be within four feet of these units when they blew. I am sure that my mother would never have attempted to master the art of pressure cooking if it had not saved her so much time. The pressure cookers reduced the cooking time to about one third of the time required for open canning.

Smoke curing was another common method for preserving foods. My folks mainly used it for pork. However, they did smoke-cure deer meat and fish on a limited basis. Most of the Flat residents had smoke houses for curing meat.

Most of these houses were constructed from one-by-twelve inch boards and resembled small houses without ceilings. Large beams that supported the ceiling boards were strong enough for heavy twine or meat hooks to hang pieces of meat.

In the bigger smoke houses, a small fire box with a short section of stove pipe would be located inside the building. In the smaller houses the fire box often would be located on the down side of the building with the stove pipe running horizontally to where it came up through the floor of the smoke house.

One of the keys to the fire box working well was to have it and the connected pipe tight enough that the smoke would be drawn out into the building. A mix of green and dry apple or willow wood would be used for burning. When the proper mix of wood was put into the firewood and ignited, one had to be careful not to let the wood burn too fast, as a fast, hot burn resulted in less smoke. This was usually accomplished by some type of air intake control on the fire box. Once the system was operating correctly, the fire would burn very slowly and produce a large amount of smoke.

Preparing the meat for smoking was like making home brew. Every family had their own recipes. For pork, the main method was to inject the selected pieces of meat with a liquid solution of salts and sodium nitrates. This liquid was injected in various parts of the meat by the use of a large hypodermic needle. The amounts of liquid used, spacing in the meat, and age of the meat when injected were all important in doing a good job. Some would also hand-rub the outside of the meat with different mixtures. We always used smoking salt and brown sugar.

After the meat was hung in the smoke house for a couple of days, with the smoke flowing from every crack in the building, the wonderful aroma seemed to send a message about how good the meat was going to taste. Perhaps my memory has played tricks on my taste buds, or perhaps my sense of taste is not as sensitive as it used to be. In any case, I still believe that home-cured pork is a lost art today. I have a memory of the taste and smell of fried ham and bacon from these smoke houses being out of this world.

The Sadie and Ora Bechtel family were well-known on the Flat for their ability to cure pork. Everyone on the Flat would look forward to eating at the Bechtel home in hopes that they would get to eat one of Sadie Bechtel's fried ham dinners.

A few of the families, including ours, tried smoke-curing deer meat with varying degrees of success. Even in our best attempts, the meat never seemed to be as good as pork. We were told later by an expert on meat smoking that the deer meat did not have enough fat cells to sufficiently distribute the liquid preservatives.

We had much better luck making smoked deer jerky. This was done by cutting the meat into one-half inch strips, soaking it overnight in a salt brine, then hanging the strips in the smoke house.

Another method we sometimes used, usually with poor success, was called brining. We would cut deer meet into thick steaks, and alternate layers of salt and steaks in a crock stored in our cellar. This would preserve the meat but it was difficult to take enough of the salty taste out of the meat for eating. My mother would soak the meat in water for up to ten hours before cooking.

One of the most common methods we used and the one most preferred by my mother was called lard packing. Whenever we butchered a pig, we would take the meat that did not lend itself to smoking because of the high fat content and grind it up. If possible, we would harvest a deer at the same time and also grind it up. My mother would then blend the two meats together, shape them in two hamburger sized patties and partially cook them. She would then put a layer of the meat in a crock, pour hot lard over it, and alternate layers of hot lard and patties until she had filled the crock. She would also do the same with the straight pork sausage if deer meat was not available.

The lard packing method was a labor intensive project. I can remember spending many an evening with my folks preparing the meat. It was my job to feed the long strips of meat into the top of a hand turned meat grinder that would be attached to our kitchen table. Dad would work the hard turning handle of the grinder as the meat would slowly squirt out a number of small holes in the grinder's front assembly. I would alternate strips of deer and pork as my sister thoroughly hand mixed the meats together in a large dish pan.

It was my mother's job to fry the patties and cover them with hot lard in the crocks. She would generally have three frying pans cooking the patties and a bucket filled with chunks of hog fat simmering on the warming section of the old wood cookstove.

Although it required a lot of initial work to prepare these patties, it was my mother's favorite way to prepare meat. She favored this method because it allowed her to prepare a quick meal and it disguised the flavor of the deer meat, which she didn't like. Folks dining at our table always complimented her on how good these patties tasted.

Mom's deer and pork patties were sometimes the source of humor, and on one occasion some worry, in our routine farm life. My granddad, Dave Scott, thought that these patties were just about the most wonderful thing he had ever eaten. Whenever he came to visit he would always rave about how good this pork was. If my grandmother Stella was with him, he would generally ask her why she couldn't fix sausage that way.

As was already mentioned earlier, Dave was probably the most law-abiding man in the country. He would constantly remind Dad about how some acquaintances of his had recently been arrested for poaching deer and that he certainly hoped that Dad would never be tempted to break any law of the land. Dad would generally stare off into space, his Adam's apple moving up and down like a jumping jack during these lectures.

My parents would have contrasting facial expressions when Dave bragged about the patties. Dad would have a sly grin, while Mother wore a worried, guilty look on her face. My mother never did like my father to poach and lived in constant fear that he would get caught. She only put up with his poaching because it was a means of surviving and he would justify his actions by reminding her that he fed a lot more deer on his crops than he ever harvested.

I always suspected that my grandmother knew a lot more about Dad's poaching activities than she let on. Dave and Stella had just finished one of Mom's meals featuring her famous patties and Dave had come up with his routine comment about why couldn't Stella make her sausages taste that way. Stella, perhaps getting tired of this repeated statement, replied, "Well if you want to go butcher a pig and mix whatever they mix in with it, maybe I can make mine taste like that, too." We never heard Dave make that statement in front of Stella again.

Mom's deer and pig patties caused her some real worries on another occasion. It was shortly before the noon meal on a warm August day when the Union County sheriff drove up to our house in his patrol car. After speaking awhile with my dad, who was out in our shop, it was determined that his mission was to ask if we might have heard or seen anything of a plane that was missing.

As was customary in those days, Dad and the sheriff's conversation lasted about a half an hour. Not knowing that the sheriff was out there, my mother called out that dinner was ready. Being polite, Dad asked the sheriff to dinner, and being hungry, the sheriff accepted.

My mother looked like she had seen a ghost when Dad walked in the house with his guest and announced that he was staying for dinner. The fact that a neighbor to the south of us had recently been arrested for poaching, I am sure, was foremost in her mind as she quickly put on another plate and gave Dad a worried look. Her main fear at the moment was what was on the dinner menu. As the reader has probably already guessed, deer and pork patties were the main course.

The sheriff was very talkative all during the meal with a lot of his comments directed towards the excellence of the meal. He was especially complimentary in regards to the patties. As the meal was drawing to an end, Mom asked him if he cared for anything else.

Mom just about had a heart attack when he mentioned that if we had any patties left he would take one more. After finishing off the last patty with great relish, our guest, after raving again about the meal and the patties, thanked mother for the meal and mentioned something about knowing where to stop for good sausage as he walked out the door.

Dad and Mom had quite an argument after the sheriff had left. Mom was sure that the sheriff's real reason for being there was to look for venison and she was furious at Dad for inviting him in when we were having all the evidence he needed at dinner. Dad then mentioned that he did not know what she was having for dinner and that our guest was looking for some evidence on the lost plane.

Despite all of Dad's reasoning, Mom was firmly convinced that it would be just a matter of hours before the sheriff returned with handcuffs and leg irons and hauled them both off to jail. She even admitted that she had almost confessed when our guest had asked for his second patty. She did not rest until she had us haul all the crocks and jars of venison out of our cellar and hide them in our barn. We never heard from the sheriff again so her fears were unfounded.

Butchering hogs was always quite a project. Since it required quite a bit of heavy lifting by several men, a number of families would usually go together and butcher the hogs at one place.

Since Obe Scott had most of the facilities required for butchering, a good share of the families in the lower Flat area would take their hogs to Obe's place. After the hogs were stuck in the neck and bled, they were lowered into a vat of boiling water that had been heated by an open fire built beneath the vat. Several men would lift them out with the aid of ropes and lay them on a slatted bench. The men would then scrape the hair off with sharp knives before gutting them out and cutting them into quarters.

The hog butchering operation had to depend on a fast-moving, coordinated effort by everyone involved. Since scalding the hog would raise body temperatures at a time when meat should be cooling for good flavor, it was essential that the scraping of the hair and removal of the entrails be done as rapidly as possible.

Also, the hog's hair would become progressively harder to scrape off the longer one waited, after lifting the body out of the hot steaming vat. The men's scraping motions, with their long razor-sharp knives, seemed like a blur, as their long shaving strokes removed the hair from the hog's hide and they scraped the hair off their knives in the slatted openings of the bench.

They had barely finished cutting up one hog when another would be ready for dipping in the vat. When several families were involved, eight to ten hogs would be butchered in one day. The men would be exhausted by the end of the operation with their only rest being the noon meal.

The men were not the only ones kept busy during these sessions. Besides cooking the noon meal, the women had their own specific duties. After removing the hog's brains, tongue and eyes, the hog's heads would be boiled in large pots until all of the meat could be easily removed from the bones.

This meat was then made into a pulp and mixed with vinegar, black pepper, sage and salt. After cooling, this mixture was called head cheese, a favorite among most of the residents. The brains would often be fried with a mixture of eggs and served on the same day that the hog was butchered.

The women would also vigorously scrub and clean the pig's feet and put them in a pickling solution for later eating. The tongues would be done the same way. Some of the families also saved the pig's blood and made what was called a blood pudding. I am not sure just how this was made since our family did not care for it.

Another form of food preservation was fermentation. My mother would slice up cabbage heads into long shreds using a metal slicer. She then put alternating layers of cabbage and salt in a large crock. After the crock was full, she placed a weighted plate on top. After a while, the juices of the cabbage would mix with the salt to form a juicy brine. The resulting sauerkraut always seemed to be much tastier than when it was canned in jars.

The folks used a limited amount of drying to preserve food. Most of this was done by placing drying racks behind our wood cookstove. Strips of deer meat that had been socked in brine would be placed on these racks to make jerky. We never liked this jerky nearly as well as the type—described earlier—made in our smoke house.

We also did a limited amount of drying prunes and pears after slicing them into thin strips. Although this fruit was tasty, it did not seem to keep very long. Some of the residents had good success with drying fruit in the sun. However, our few attempts were unsuccessful because this method attracted hornets and yellow jackets during the drying process.

After port and venison, chicken was used most on the Flat. Young fryers reaching eating size between July and October were our primary meat source during the summer months. The whole family looked forward to a change from our winter diet of venison and pork.

During the middle and late 1940s, elk began to replace deer as our secondary meat source. My father started hunting elk, legally, north of the Grande Ronde River. He was generally quite successful during these hunts. Also, elk populations suddenly started increasing on the Flat, which presented more poaching opportunities.

We used elk in the patties with the pork in much the same way we did the deer meat. However, since we now had a kerosene refrigerator and rented a freezer locker in Elgin, we had a higher percentage of the elk made into steaks and roasts.

Some of the other wild meats that we used occasionally were salmon, steelhead, trout, whitefish, grouse and snowshoe hares. We tried jackrabbits a few times but did not like the meat. Probably the ones we enjoyed the most were the Coho salmon and steelhead that we caught out of the Grande Ronde River during the fall. We would soak these large fish in a brine and smoke them. These fish were also excellent fried in butter.

In addition to the wild meats, the woods provided other foods. The family would usually spend three to four days picking huckleberries. These picking trips, which involved camping out in mountain ranges five to ten miles north of the Flat, offered a real vacation from our routine farm work. The women would usually do most of the picking while the men hunted and fished. My mother would, in addition to making fresh pies, can the berries for future pie making and would make huckleberry jelly.

We also picked wild gooseberries, raspberries, serviceberries and thimbleberries. We made pies out of the gooseberries and jams and jellies from the rest. There was a woman on the Flat named Mary Miller who was well-known for her gooseberry pies. They had a custard type consistency that few other women could duplicate. Her gooseberry pies often brought the highest price at pie socials.

One of our favorite foods gathered in the woods was the morel mushroom, which grew primarily during the month of May. It favored burned areas and east-facing slopes. We would soak them in salt water after picking and then roll them in flour or cracker crumbs before frying them in butter. I used to get mad at my mother because of she would usually keep only those mushrooms for eating that were absolutely free of insects or worms. If she saw one bug on the mushroom, it was thrown away.

Since these mushrooms were usually scarce and relished by all, I would set up a second frying pan, for myself, and fry all of the mushrooms that Mom threw away. We did have a few other mushrooms that we ate, but none were liked as well as the morels.

Dairy products, made from the milk of our cows, were one of our most important food sources. Most of the family drank milk during every meal. We all used cream on pies and cereals, and in custards, ice cream, and many recipes. Butter was also used at every meal and was used in frying many different kinds of foods.

Making butter out of cream was something that children today may never experience. Rosalie and I had the job of making butter. We had a large butter churn consisting of a gallon jar with an enclosed paddle. This paddle was turned by an attached handle. I believe this was called a Daisy Churn.

We would fill this jar nearly full with our richest cream. After turning the churn handle for what seemed forever, the paddle would slow down and small pieces of butter would start forming in the cream. It would not take long before the paddle could not be turned any longer because the butter had formed into much larger chunks in the buttermilk.

At this stage we dumped the whole mixture into a large bowl. Then, using a large round wooden paddle, we would concentrate all the butter particles into one lump. After pouring the buttermilk off we would continue to massage the butter with the paddle until all the pockets of buttermilk had been worked out. Then, after working in a sprinkling of salt, our job would be done.

The by product of this process, buttermilk, was everyone's favorite. My mother would have to carefully watch my sister and me to prevent us from hogging down all the buttermilk before Dad had had his share. I have tried several brands of store-bought buttermilk after I left the ranch, but have never found any that tasted as good as the milk from our freshly-churned butter.

Another favorite dairy product was home-made ice cream. We had it quite often during the winter months when ice was available. The old ice cream makers were like the butter churns in that one had to turn a paddle assembly by a hand crank.

The container held a mix of milk, cream, eggs, sugar and a dash of real vanilla and was surrounded by chopped ice and salt to make it cold. The kids would take turns turning the hard-turning crank until it was too difficult to turn. We often argued over who would get to lick the paddle assembly as it was lifted out of the container of half-frozen ice cream.

We could hardly wait for the ice cream to harden up in its bed of melting ice. I could never get my fill of this treat. I would eat it so fast that it gave me temporary headaches. I usually kept eating until my mother stopped me.

I used to feel that I could eat about three times more than I was allowed. One time I was surprised to notice that my mother had borrowed Obe's ice cream maker and had set up to make two batches of ice cream. Thinking that we were having company, I vigorously helped make the two batches.

It was after the two batches of ice cream had hardened that I got the surprise of my young life. After telling everybody in the family that the ice cream was ready to eat, my mother dished out ice cream to everyone but me. Feeling slighted, I asked if I could dish up my own. My mother said I couldn't have any from the batch where she had been dipping from. Then she went on to say that the other batch was all mine. She gave me a large spoon and told me to start eating.

I thought I had died and gone to heaven. I had to be reassured several times that the gallon was all mine. The first three dishes went down like milk in a hog trough. I would hardly get one dish finished before I was making plans for the next.

I was on about my fifth dish when my headaches, which before had gone away rather quickly, began acting like they were going to be with me the rest of my life. My stomach was also beginning to ache and felt bloated. However, my eyes were still bigger than my stomach and I slowly downed two more dishes.

By this time my pain overwhelmed my greed. I told my mother, who looked at me with her knowing grin, that I thought I would go to my bedroom and rest awhile. As I walked into the room I felt I had to stand straight up or the ice cream would run out my mouth.

My head felt like all the ice in the ice cream maker was lodged behind each eye ball and my stomach felt like an over-inflated balloon. The next two hours were spent making promises to myself that I would never eat more than two bowls of ice cream again.

My lesson in gluttony was well taken, but it didn't spoil my taste for this wonderful dish. I still occasionally make a batch of homemade ice cream, although now its electrically turned. It still can't compare with the kind that's made out of real—rather than imitation—vanilla.

Despite our poverty during the 1930s and early 1940s, I can't remember ever not having enough food. I attribute this to my mother, who was well known for her ability to make the most out of the food resources she had. The many visitors that ate at our table always commented on her cooking. She had several specialties that she was famous for. She made a large bun that very few other women could duplicate. Her pie crusts were bragged on by everyone. Her chocolate cakes were well-known.

Our typical evening and noon meals would be a meat course of ham or patties, or canned venison, or venison steak or chicken. Our vegetables would almost always include mashed potatoes and string beans, or red beans, or sauerkraut, or beets or peas. These meals would also almost always include buns or slices of homemade bread.

During the summer months the meals would also include a green salad of lettuce and radishes. We generally had some type of dessert such as ice cream (in winter time only), cake, pie, some type of canned fruit or some type of pudding. If nothing else was available for dessert, Dad would break up a piece of bread and cover it with Karo syrup and cream. We used cream on all our desserts.

For breakfast we had a varied menu. We usually had hot cakes with fried eggs and ham or bacon about three days a week. Hot cakes were always our favorite. Mother would make a syrup out of brown sugar and cream that couldn't be beat.

We would usually have cold cereal with biscuits or toast two times a week and hot cereal with biscuits or toast two times per week. There was one breakfast we never looked forward to. Once a week, one of the hot cereals was called Cream of Wheat mush. Rosalie and I hated this mush with a passion and tried every excuse that we could think of to get out of eating it.

Besides being a superb cook and way ahead of her time in seeing that her family received a balanced diet on a poor man's budget, my mother was also a real disciplinarian when it came to eating. If we did not take what she thought was an adequate portion of every course served, she would quietly but firmly add the food to our plates.

Mother would never let us leave the table or have any dessert until we had eaten our main course. At first this led to marathon will-testing sessions in which my sister and I would try and outlast my mother with the remote chance that she might give in and let us go without cleaning our plates.

My folks soon put an end to these stalling sessions by putting a time limit on when we had to have our plates cleaned off. An old wind-up alarm clock was set at the end of our table and the alarm was set at a reasonable amount of time for us to complete our meal. If the alarm went off before we finished, our back sides were treated with a few well-delivered strokes from Dad's razor strap.

By and large, most of Mom's meals were so excellent that we readily cleaned our plates. However, about once a week we had that special preparation of Cream of Wheat mush. Mom's special talent for preparing culinary delights seemed to take a giant step backwards when it came to preparing this mush.

Perhaps Mom had been wrongly instructed at an early age by her mother or some other misguided culinary talent on preparing this particular dish. After a few minutes of stirring and hovering over the old wood cookstove, mother would carry to the table a kettle containing a boiling, churning gelatinous mush. For the first few minutes, this mush closely resembled the boiling, fuming mud caldrons of Yellowstone Park, with exploding bubbles at the surface of the mush emitting odors that prepared our palates for regurgitation.

If the mush was not immediately mixed with cream and sugar, which we usually did not do, it would form a hard pliable layer on its surface that could have been used for trampoline material. Beneath this trampoline surface, floating in the semi-liquid mush, were hard lumps varying from a marble to golf-ball size.

These lumps consisted of hard gelatinous gobs of half-cooked mush that seemed to absorb a lot of the worst-tasting parts of the mixture. Faced with the fact that we had twenty minutes to finish this churning compound, there were three distinct phases we went through in eating our breakfast.

First was the hoping stage. This stage, which usually lasted for about fifteen minutes, was a period in which we hoped that some emergency would come up that would save us from eating this mixture—emergencies such as a burning house, a sudden illness or any type of unusual situation that would cause the folks to leave the house.

We did get a reprieve one time when the neighbor's house caught fire and the party line phone ring of seven shorts alerted the folks that all help was needed. They both rushed out the door with Mom telling us to stay in the house and finish up our mush. After watching the folks disappear from view, we wasted little time in pouring our mush down a squirrel hole after our dog, Sug, refused to eat it.

We called the second stage our psyching stage. In this period, much like the great athletes before a big game, we would psyche ourselves up to an attack mode. This was usually done with half-closed eyes for better concentration and so we didn't have to see the mush.

We did, however, have to look frequently at the clock to make sure our time didn't run out. During these psyching periods, our train of thought was directed more towards gearing up for the dispatching of an enemy in as short a time as possible, rather than pretending that the mush was something that tasted good. With about a minute to go we launched into the attack or eating stage. Our main goal in this period was to eat the mush in the quickest time possible so that our taste buds exposure time was—if somewhat intense—at least short.

I actually had two separate rituals in my eating stage. First, with my hands moving like a blur, I would jerk the hard layer off my mush and place it in a saucer. I would then crumble my toast over this hard dish rag layer to help disguise the taste and then roll it up like a taco. After devouring this in a couple of bites, I would pour cream and a rationed one half teaspoon of sugar over the rest of the mush. I would then attack this mixture much like a hungry hog at a slop trough. Holding the dish within inches of my mouth, I would use my spoon like a canoe paddle to scoop the mush rapidly down my open throat, straight to my stomach.

The only delay in this operation would occur when I would encounter a large lump in my mush. These large lumps, which I never chewed, often bounced up and down in my throat passage like a yo-yo.

Our table manners left a lot to be desired in this operation and we were always under a verbal barrage from Mom. Watching our antics with an expression of shock and disgust, she would tell us how revolting we looked and how we should never eat that way outside the family or when we had company.

I am sure the only reason she tolerated our behavior was because she figured that this was the only way that she could get her vitamin packed food down our throats. She would also constantly remind us of the starving kids in China and how they would jump at the chance to eat some of her mush. For a long period of time it was my ambition to hold someone from China hostage at my mother's table and not let him leave until he had consumed a bowl of Mom's special cereal.

After finishing our breakfast, we did not have time to savor our victory over the mush. Immediately after we got up from the table, Mom would summon us to the west end of the kitchen and say, "Its time for your Castor Oil."

Now, castor oil, in our opinion, was a close second to the lumpy mush in its horrible taste—a thick clear liquid tasting like a mixture of rotten fish oil and sour milk. We would both close our eyes and grab our noses with one hand and slightly open our mouths. Mom would then shove a heaping tablespoon of this oil into each of our mouths and then not let us leave the kitchen until she was sure we had swallowed it.

Much like post victory celebrations by athletic teams, my sister and I would usually meet and compare notes after these breakfasts. Our negative comments on the mush and the castor oil seemed to reinforce and amplify our distaste. So instead of learning to like the mush as we did a lot of other foods, we seemed to progressively dread each mush breakfast more than the last. What would have eventually been the outcome of our dilemma will probably never be known as another set of circumstances came to our rescue.

It has often been said that a crisis must reach its worst point before it starts to improve. Well, this was the case with Mom's mush. It all started when our milk cows began eating scale weed. This particular weed, when eaten in large quantities by our cows, would cause the milk and its separated cream to gain a strong pungent taste and odor.

Our family had tolerated this taste in the past when the weed concentrations had been lower because our milk products were one of the main staples in our diet. However, due to the higher concentrations of the weed in the cow's food supply during this specific year, our tolerance was reaching the breaking point. We had just completed one of our Cream of Wheat breakfasts using the scale weed-tainted cream and our stomachs were churning like windmills. I might have been all right if I could have skipped my dose of castor oil.

When it reached my stomach, the oil seemed to act like a catalyst, converting my already churning stomach into a time bomb. Holding my hand over my mouth, I raced outside to the secluded back side of our barn and emptied my stomach. I had barely raised my head when I spotted my father at the far end of the barn holding his head in his hands. He sheepishly looked up and said that Mom's mush and the scale weed cream made him sick, too.

Coincidentally, after my father and I shared our experience behind the barn, Mother's Cream of Wheat breakfasts were gradually scaled down. Our daily castor oil dosage was also changed shortly later to cod liver oil, which was an improvement to our taste buds.

Fortunately for Rosalie and me, my father rarely prepared meals. During most of the occasions when my mother was too ill or was absent from the ranch, one of our grandmothers would do the cooking. On the few occasions when Dad did prepare a meal, he did not use any culinary imagination in his preparation.

His breakfasts would consist of coffee and cornflakes topped off with cream. His dinners and evening meals were generally made up of cream and Karo syrup poured over pieces of bread and some type of canned fruit. The only time I can remember his actually cooking anything was during a period of about seven days one winter. My mother was in the hospital and neither set of grandparents wanted to tackle the bad roads to get to our house.

It was during this period that we had a hind quarter of an elk that was hanging frozen in our woodshed. Dad went out in the morning after breakfast and cut enough steaks to last for a couple of days. He had to cut these steaks with a meat saw since the meat was frozen solid. Although my sister and I usually had some type of stew at school, the rest of our meals consisted of elk steak cooked by Dad.

Because of our limited financial resources, food purchases in town were limited to what could not be produced on the ranch. Mostly, the supplies we bought in town were salt, sugar, spices, hot cereals, dry cereals, coffee, tea, cocoa, vanilla, syrup, flour, eggs (during the winter months), brown sugar, meat-smoking solutions and a small amount of candy.

During certain periods of World War II when sugar was rationed, my mother found herself quite handicapped in a lot of her food preparation. Since she prepared a lot of desserts and canned plenty of fruit, she used more sugar than the average family. To make up for any shortage, several of the families on the Flat spent quite a bit of time searching for wild honey.

Most of the beehives we found were located in hollow trees on our ranch or on Forest Service land north of the Grande Ronde River. Once we found a bee tree, we would wait until late fall, when honey storage was the greatest and the bees were not quite so active, before we gathered the honey.

As soon as we felled the bee tree we would immediately use a rag to plug the bee's entrance to the inside of the tree. We would then cut into the tree with a crosscut saw, about two feet on each side of the plugged entrance. After cutting about half-way through the hollow trunk of the tree, wedges would be inserted so that a section of the trunk containing the entrance to the hive would be made ready to lift off.

The next step of the operation was the most important, if a person did not want to be stung. A slightly damp gunnysack would be set on fire, with the degree of dampness of the sack being such that the sack would smolder and smoke rather than burst into flame.

The rag would then be removed and the smoking sack would be placed in the entrance to the hive. After the smoldering sack was left in the hole for about three minutes, the wedges were driven in so that the slab of the tree containing the hive entrance would be lifted slightly to allow smoke to pass throughout the hive.

After the smoke was allowed to flow freely through the hive for about five minutes, the bees would become quite docile and the slab could be lifted off, thus exposing the honey for gathering. The bees in their docile condition could be easily brushed away from the honey. We would then mash up the combs, set the mashed-up combs in a cheese cloth in a warm location and allowed the honey to drain into a container.

Since Dad was generally quite busy with other farm work, it was my unofficial job to find the beehives. After a while I found the best method for locating hives with very little effort. I would place some syrup in a quart jar and leave it by the edge of our pond where the honey bees would concentrate for water. In about an hour, twenty to thirty bees would be flying in and out of the jar, gathering the syrup for their hive.

My next step was to put a loose-fitting lid on the jar, thus capturing a number of bees. Then I would release one bee and watch its direction of flight. Since bees take a relatively straight line to their hive, I would follow the bee until it went out of sight. A number of bees released this way eventually led me to the hive.

The art of collecting wild honey was one that had to be learned by experience and these experiences generated many different stories that residents often told with a great deal of humor. These stories often were not too funny at the time—at least for the individuals that were subjected to the consequences of angry bees.

One of my attempts to rob a hive by myself almost resulted in burning up a wheat crop of my Dad's and Uncle Jack's. I made several major errors in this attempt. First, I decided to make my folks proud of me by robbing a tree by myself without notifying them of my intentions. Second, I made my attempt in the warm, dry period of September rather than waiting until later in the year when the cooler weather had tempered the aggressiveness of the bees. Third, I had failed to consider the danger of my actions with regards to an uncontrolled fire.

My objective, which I had found using my jar method, was a large, fallen pine tree that contained a big colony of bees. The tree, which was located behind one of Uncle Jack's wheat fields, had split open upon falling and had left the hive in an exposed location that would have provided easy access to the honey. My plan was to put my smoking gunny sack directly below the combs of honey to subdue the bees and then gather the combs up in a large bucket.

It was mid-afternoon when I arrived at my destination riding Molly, the old dependable white horse. As I dismounted with my three-gallon bucket, a gunnysack and a water canteen, many thoughts raced through my head.

A mental picture of my walking into the house with my three gallon bucket heaped up with golden-colored combs of sweet, delicious honey heightened my anticipation as I assembled my gear. I could almost hear my mother's cry of joy and my dad's surprised words of praise complimenting me on accomplishing this difficult chore by myself.

My planned conquest of the bees and the confiscation of their honey was thus far right on schedule. Taking the cap off my water canteen, I carefully dampened the gunnysack to the right degree for producing smoke. Then carefully lighting a small dry section of the sack to start it smoldering, I took it and slowly advanced towards my destination. Unlike other trees that I had helped my dad rob for honey, these bees were actively going in and out of their hive.

With my smoking sack in hand, I was within about three feet of the hive when the bees decided that the kid with the smoking sack was up to no good. Perhaps they had learned to be overly aggressive in the past to protect their open vulnerable hive or perhaps they were a scout group of African Killer Bees. Whatever the reason, these bees attacked with the fury of a charging army. As they swiftly circled my head for their stinging attacks, I fought back with the only weapon at my disposal. This weapon happened to be my burning sack.

My smoldering sack quickly changed from a rolling smoke to a brightly burning blaze as I fanned the air like a Hawaiian fire dancer. All the time, burning pieces of sack were being thrown off into the tinder-dry grass like snowflakes from the sky. As I frantically fought the bees and scattered enough sparks to ignite a floating battleship, a strong westerly breeze fanned the many miniature grass fires into a roaring inferno.

Running for my life with the hot breath of the flames and the angry swarm of bees in pursuit, I reached my horse, tethered to a nearby tree, and untied and mounted her in one quick motion. I did not have to urge the normally slow-ambling horse to jump into a full-fledged gallop for both of our lives as we fled from the roaring flames.

As I raced towards our house on the panting, white mare, I looked back and saw a rapidly-advancing wall of thirty-foot flames and black smoke speeding through a sea of dry grass and logging debris.

I reached the house after a record-breaking run that would have put a pony express rider to shame and dismounted from Mollie screaming at the top of my voice. "Fire! Fire! Call for help," I shouted as I hurled myself into our house. It did not take my mother long to relay the message through our phone system to the Oregon Department of Forestry. Then she tried to gather more details from my excited babbling.

Fortunately, my uncontrolled fire—after consuming about fifty acres of dry grass and logging slash—ran up against a field of spring grain that was too green to burn. My dad and Uncle Jack, seeing the wall of flame in the distance, abandoned their harvesting job from a nearby field and raced over to try and save their grain fields. However, the green field saved the day as the fire died on its own.

Personnel from the Department of Forestry arrived soon after and mopped up the remaining hot spots. I felt quite intimidated when a large, uniformed Forestry official asked me a lot of questions about how the fire got started. After I timidly told my story and mentally prepared myself for a trip to the jail, the officer told me that he admired my honesty but thought my judgment could stand some refining.

One could say that my earlier expectations of making my parents proud of my honey gathering were shot down in flames. However, I did gather some notoriety out of the experience. My name was mentioned in the La Grande paper shortly afterwards when the paper described how a young boy set fire in his quest for honey. My friends and acquaintances continually make sure that I don't forget this incident.

The following poem is a true account of an incident that I wrote about my Uncle Ralph Scott and my dad. I titled the poem "The Quest for Honey" because it was Uncle Ralph's belief that honey would be his reward for his efforts.

Perhaps it was the thought of pancakes so golden and brown,
That initiated the thoughts of two men of renown.
Two men I heard conversing on that eventful day,
On the Noel Scott ranch near a barn full of hay.
Since I was only six, my memory of what they did say,
May not be exact, but it went something this way:
"There must be a wash-tub of honey in that old stump,
The one with the hole like the mouth of a pump."
Noel went on as I remembered long ago,
Speaking with thoughtful pauses measured and slow.

"From the number of bees coming out of that hole,
We should try and make it our goal,
To rob their honey as soon as we can;
There should be enough to fill every pot and pan."
Ralph said, "Won't they sting if we should try and rob,
And besides that, who will do the job?"
Noel looked at his brother and this is what he said:
"Ralph, there is a way to protect yourself, have no dread.
Two sets of pants, a hat and a veil,
All tied together around your legs and shirttail.
When I dress you up no bee will have a chance
To get under your veil or into your pants."
Ralph with an unsure voice answered his brother, Noel.
"Why should I be the one to fill your goal?"
Noel answered after some consuming thought.
"We will both share the honey and there will be a lot,
For Ethel's pancakes and the homemade bun,
That melts in your mouth and makes eating fun.
It would be better if I dress up you,
Because I have knowledge that you never knew,
On tying on veils and making pant legs snug,
And so bee proof that they will keep out a small bug."

Noel's convincing words were too hard to resist,
And Ralph was soon looking for Noel to assist,
Putting on loose-legged pants tied tight to his shoe,
Tied so tight that his foot almost turned blue.
One of Noel's shirts with sleeves very long,
Was put over Ralph to make protection strong.
Thick leather gloves tied over the shirt,
Plugged all the holes, even from the dirt.
Some of Ethel's cheesecloth draped over Ralph's hat,
And tied around his neck without any slack.
This completed the job of bee-proofing Uncle Ralph,
So that he was protected from the north to the south.
A final pep talk was given by Noel.
"If by some chance the bees find a hole,
A honey bee's sting does not hurt that bad,
And only one sting can be had,
While a yellow jacket or hornet can sting more than one time,
And brings up welts bigger than a dime.

Now take that ax and hit the stump several blows,
And keep on hitting until the swarm goes,
Far from the area where they won't bother us,
And we can collect the honey without any fuss.
The bees will first attack but will give up in a while,
So just keep hitting and keep up your style.
Keep a cool head and remember never fear,
For you're well-protected and I will be near."

Ralph approached the stump with a confident stride,
Like a veiled monster with an ax at his side.
And attack the stump, he did with a whack,
And the stump exploded with bees on the attack.
An increasing noise something like a rapid's roar.
The stump seemed to explode like a bomb from the war.
A twenty foot area all around the war zone,
Was a dark angry swirl with a moan and a groan.
The swirling black mass attacked with great force
Converging on Ralph with the speed of a horse.
Covering his veil so that he couldn't see,
A thousand angry insects not seeming to flee.
Perhaps the speed by which they hit the veil,
Formed a hole by which they could trail,
To the inside of the veil, next to the face,
Which was indeed, a very confined space.
It was not long before a warrior found the hole,
And it was then that Ralph lost control.
"I have been stung," Ralph cried with alarm.
"This one has stung once and he shows more harm.
He stung me again and another makes three.
It hurts like hell and I am ready to flee.
These are not honey bees, I know for sure.
Another sting I will not endure."
More stings were due as violent motions tore loose,
The protective veil that had been secured with a noose.

The next phase of the story was one of retreat,
For it was soon apparent that Ralph had quick feet.
Perhaps his football played at Wallowa High,
Gave him the moves that made him seem to fly.

Spinning and dodging with great bursts of speed,
Coupled with swatting at his face that was freed,
Of the veil now trailing like a giant kite tail,
Turning and flapping like a wind-driven sail.
The swatting actions of his arms made him look like a duck,
Trying to get air borne without any luck.
Just as it would seem that he had reached his top speed,
The sting of a bee would make him exceed,
His previous best by a record setting pace,
That if times could have been kept, it would be a record race.
The course of his flight was unsure at the start,
And his promise of help did soon depart.
His brother Noel was nowhere to be seen,
As he had taken refuge behind a log in the ravine.
Ralph's instincts now told him to look for his mother,
And since she was not there he would look for another.
Ethel, my mother, must have been his first thought,
Towards the house he sped faster than a trot.
Zigzagging and slapping with changing bursts of speed,
Ralph was approaching the place of his need.
The house was his goal with Ethel inside.
Maybe she could provide him a place to hide,
From these persistent insects that seemed like a cloud,
That was attached to his body like a giant shroud.
They were like fighter planes diving for the kill,
Angered by the raid on their nest on the hill.
They did not give up and stuck with Ralph like glue,
Driving him fast for the house straight and true.
Ralph reached the house with his guests by his side,
And plunged through the door with his hurt and his pride.

Now Ethel did not know about the event taking place,
For she was bathing Rosalie in the sink with a vase,
Filled clear full all ready to pour water,
Over the head of her three-year old daughter.
She was quite shocked to say the least,
For she could not tell, was this man or beast?
That burst through the door with a cry of fright,
With plenty of bees that were still hanging tight.
Ethel's first motion was to dump all the water,

Over the unsuspecting head of her naked daughter.
  She then grabbed Rosalie along with a broom,
And started swinging at everything in the room.
  Ralph soon saw that Ethel was not going to help out,
So he quickly made a quick turn about,
  And raced out of sight in the woods towards the south,
While Mom was wondering if that was really Ralph.
  The bees finally gave up and returned to their nest,
And another hour later Ralph returned from the west.
  No honey was had for breakfast the next day,
And no plans were made for a future replay,
  Of the events I have described and will never forget,
Of Ralph and the bees and the trouble he met.

As time edged towards the middle and late 1940s the folks become progressively less strict on enforcement of eating rules at the table. Cleaning up our plates before we left the table, eating prescribed amounts of foods that we didn't like and many other table rules, although still in force, did not seem to be enforced as rigorously as they had been. This seemed to be especially noticeable when it came to our two younger sisters, Marilyn and Anita. Rosalie and I were deeply troubled by this apparent shift in the enforcement of table rules. Although we welcomed the relief to ourselves, we were willing to sacrifice our taste buds in order to see our two younger sisters endure the same type of ordeals that we had experienced.

As time passed by and our two young sisters seemed to be getting away with murder, Rosalie and I were quite convinced that our folks played favorites. We would often try to enforce the old table rules on these two upstarts, only to be rebuked by our parents. Our two young precious darlings would often taunt us with "We don't have to mind you," after the folks would tell us that *they* would do the correcting. The old saying, "What goes around comes back around," finally came true in our case.

One day our folks made the announcement that they were taking a trip to Portland and were going to leave Rosalie and me in charge of the ranch. The news that we would also be in charge of our sisters was like music from heaven. Joyous visions of revenge were amplified when we heard the folks' parting words to Anita and Marilyn. "Now remember, you are to mind Harlan and Rosalie while were are away." Cries of distress filled the countryside as our two tearful sisters raced after the folks' departing car crying, "Please don't leave us."

The car had hardly pulled out of sight before Rosalie and I started setting up a work and eating schedule for our charges. Wild-eyed and tearful, they looked like two young lambs that had been thrown in with a den of wolves as they received a barrage of orders and rules that they had to follow. A new soldier's introduction to the rules of basic training by a hard-nosed sergeant could not have been much stricter than those given to our victims.

Planning what we were going to have them eat for the upcoming meals was the first order of the day. Since we were well aware of what they did not like, it did not take us long to come up with a good menu. For dinner and evening meals we would make them eat canned peas, stewed tomatoes and canned venison. We knew they both detested the stewed tomatoes, which Mom would top off with cream while cooking. If this mixture got too hot, the cream would curdle into flat lumps that were almost as bad as the Cream of Wheat mush. Then, of course, for breakfast we planned to have them eat that favorite, Cream of Wheat.

For their work schedule, they had to wash and dry the dishes after every meal. They had to wipe the tables down and sweep the floors. We also had them picking up trash out of our yard. They were to take a long afternoon nap and then, after finishing their after meal chores, they were put straight to bed.

Anita, who was quite young at the time, minded quite well. However, Marilyn was a different story. She was bound and determined that she was not going to eat our specially prepared meals. After a marathon waiting session at the table, I took her outside and threatened to throw her in a section of our pond that was inhabited by a generous supply of water snakes. This threat finally broke her spirit and she gagged her meal down much in the same fashion as we had done.

Now, while our younger sisters were eating our culinary specials, Rosalie and I were fixing ourselves dishes that we relished and very seldom got to eat while the folks were there. We fixed ourselves hotcakes and bacon every morning for breakfast and had homemade ice cream and other favorite foods for our evening and noon meals. Our young charges would only get their dessert if they finished eating a second helping of canned peas.

Rosalie was in charge of making sure the girls did a good job on the dishes. If she found one dish that was slightly wet or dirty she would make them take all the dishes out of the cupboard and do them over again. Besides all the work, I think both the girls got bed sores from taking such long naps and going to bed so early.

It was two relieved little sisters that ran down the road to meet our returning parents. It did not take them long to tell the folks about the tortures that had been inflicted upon them. However, the memories of their supervised stay with us apparently had an impact on their behavior, as they we a lot more respectful to Rosalie and me after their brief exposure to our basic training.

As time advanced through the middle and late 1940s our foods and methods of food storage and preparation gradually changed. Power plants and electrical lines allowed us to use refrigeration. Better roads and better cars provided quicker and easier access to grocery stores in town. More prosperous times allowed Mother to replace a lot of her home-canned foods with store-purchased goods. The old cellar was replaced by storage in the basement of our new house. Our huge garden was greatly reduced in size. These changes all contributed to a retreat from culinary ways of life that will never be forgotten.

Chapter 15

Running Away

It would be my guess that almost every child has either considered or actually has run away from home sometime during his life. I was no different from most children in this respect. I had considered running away from home at different times but had never received the final push that would actually make me carry out my thoughts.

Perhaps I would never have carried out the plan to run away if a certain set of circumstances had not surfaced in the right sequence. My parents had been under some stress because of the prospects of a poor crop year. For a two week period they had been rather cross with both my sister and me and had not tolerated any nonsense from either one of us. My dad had assigned me some extra chores, since he had been quite busy doing some exchange work for one of the neighbors. These extra chores had kept me so busy that I was beginning to feel quite sorry for myself.

The last and most important thing that put me over the edge was a hard and undeserved spanking from my dad. Rosalie and I had been bickering over some unimportant matter and she decided that she would get me in trouble with Dad by telling him that I had used a sexual four letter word in front of her. Without giving me a chance to defend myself, my father gave me a hard whipping. When he let me go I screamed loudly that he was not a fair father and that I was leaving the ranch. Then without looking back, I ran into the forest.

There were only a few times in my life that I have felt totally out of control with anger and this was one of those moments. Finally, after running blindly through the trees and downed logs, I fell down exhausted under a large tree. With anger and self pity pulsating through my entire body, I tearfully pounded the soft earth beneath the tree with my fists and screamed out a torrent of cuss words in defiance to the world. At that moment I hated my sister, I hated my dad, I hated my chores and I never wanted to see my family or the ranch again.

After about an hour of venting my anger, some control began slowly returning. Although I had become calm, the anger and self pity still had me convinced that I would never return to my family again. It was at this time that I started making plans for my departure. On a few other occasions I had contemplated what I would do if a reason did come up to leave my parents and some of these ideas started to take shape in my mind.

After about twenty minutes my mood of modified anger was now being replaced by ideas of how I was going to survive. The longer I thought the more ideas raced through my mind and I was beginning to get excited with anticipation of what I could do. Finally, I had part of my plan.

There was a small dug out cave that I had found when I was fishing in Rysdam's Creek. The cave was close to the creek and also near patches of wild raspberries and elderberries. I could live in the cave, I would have fish from the creek and I would have berries to supplement my diet.

Now that I had my basic plan many, other ideas started flooding my mind. I would take a couple of squirrel traps with me to catch ground squirrels. Since there was a bounty of five cents for every squirrel tail I could bring in to the Elgin Hardware, I could make a lot of money trapping squirrels. Also, there were mink and weasel that I could trap in the winter and sell the pelts.

I could visualize myself walking into the hardware store with a whole packsack full of pelts and squirrel tails and exchanging them for a whole bunch of money. I would even have enough for a motorcycle, which I could drive back to my cave.

My thoughts then shifted back to my parents. I could see them grieving my absence and thinking that I was dead. A mental picture of my dad tearfully telling my mother how sorry he was that he had treated me so bad really made me feel good. I could see my dad working himself to exhaustion trying to do all the work that had been assigned to me.

Perhaps my fondest thought was of Rosalie, with tears running from her eyes, confessing to my parents that she had not told the truth about me. Then I could see my parents punishing her severely for her crime.

As my thoughts raced wildly, I imagined coming back and visiting the folks after a few years. I would be much larger and at first they would not recognize me. They would throw themselves at me in happiness when they realized who I was and tell me how sorry they were for the way I was treated. They would beg me to come back, but I would firmly tell them no.

However, I would give them some money to help them out as I raced away on my motorcycle. Driving by the barn, I could see my work-bedraggled sister coming out, packing two buckets of milk and wondering who this big handsome guy on the motorcycle was.

I departed from my dreams long enough to start carrying out my plan. Coming back to where I could see the house, I waited until I saw my mother and Rosalie leave the house and go up to the garden. Then I sneaked into the house and filled an old packsack with a half loaf of bread, two squirrel traps, some fishing tackle and an old telescoping metal fishing pole.

It took me about an hour to reach my future home by Rysdam's Creek. The dirt cave, which was about two feet in diameter, had been dug by some animal into the side of a steep hill where it extended back into the hillside about six feet.

The lure of catching some trout made me forget everything for a while. It did not take me long to lay my pack down at the entrance to the cave and gear up for fishing. After catching a few trout and taking a refreshing swim in one of the bigger holes in the creek, hunger forced me to think about getting something to eat. I had not eaten since breakfast and the morning and mid-afternoon activities had heightened my appetite.

I had watched some cowboys in a movie run a stick through a fish and cook it over an open fire. This scene had made me decide that I would not need any cooking gear and I looked forward to cooking my fish over the open fire. My next step was to gather some firewood and scoop out a fire pit near my cave.

My mouth was watering with anticipation as I got ready to light my fire. It was then that I suffered my first major setback. I had forgotten to bring any matches.

I had watched my Granddad Dave build a fire with a bow that was designed to spin a round stick into a board. Even though I did not have such elaborate equipment, I thought I could probably start a fire by rubbing two sticks of wood together. For the next half hour, as my hunger increased, I vigorously rubbed the wood together until I had developed blisters on the side of my hands. Although the wood got warm it did not ignite.

Trying not to be discouraged, I came up with another idea. I would sun dry my fish. I had heard my mother tell how the Indians had sun dried their salmon. It did not take me long to lay my fish out on a flat rock where it could catch the last rays of the sun before it disappeared behind the hill.

It was about an hour later that my hunger made me decide that it was time to try my fish. It was a real struggle just to clear the flies and yellow jackets off a couple of the fish. I thought that since they did not look too appetizing, I would make a fish sandwich with the bread that I had brought in my pack.

Well, I seemed to be on a roll with disappointments. When I went to take the bread out of my pack, I found that the two squirrel traps had acted like an egg-beater on the bread during my long walk. The only thing that seemed to be left in a solid state was the outside crust of the bread. The rest of the bread was reduced to a pile of crumbs.

Still undaunted, I made a crude sandwich with a crusty section of the bread and one of the fish. I really can't give justice to describing how this sandwich tasted but I can truthfully state that it would not have made the number one list at Skipper's Restaurant. It did not take me long to give the rest of my sandwich back to the flies and yellow jackets and try to determine what I was going to eat.

After testing a few wild raspberries that lacked a good month before ripening, I decided that I would spend the night in my cave and sneak back to the house the next morning for some matches and salt.

The sun was just starting to disappear behind the west wall of the steep canyon when I crawled back in the dark cave to rest. Although I was tired and hungry my body did not seem to be ready for sleep.

Suddenly, a whole new train of thoughts that had not occurred to me before started to surface in my mind. My first thought was what had made this cave? As I started putting two and two together it suddenly dawned upon me that it must have been a pretty darn big animal to require a cave of this size. I had just barely analyzed that thought when the next question hit me even faster. Was the animal through with the cave?

It only took me a few seconds to make some new decisions on my running away plan. As I gathered up my gear I decided that our barn would be a better place to spend the night. In a matter of minutes I had climbed out of the dark shadows of the canyon to where I could see the sun nearing its setting point. The next mile to our ranch buildings was covered in record setting time as I tried to beat the fast-approaching darkness.

When I approached the barn, which was about 200 feet from our house, I met the recently-milked cows now returning to the fields to eat. This meant that Dad had left the barn and I would be free to enter without being detected. I had just started to open the back barn door where I couldn't be seen from the house when the delightful aroma of fried ham froze me in my tracks. This odor seemed to trigger a whole new set of ideas in my head.

It suddenly occurred to me that the folks were frantic with worry by this time. They were probably out searching for me now. They may have already organized a search party. Was it right to make them suffer any longer? Even though they would be glad to see me, would my dad greet me with a spanking? Many of these questions raced through my head as I edged up behind the shop, which was only about 100 feet from the house.

My stay behind the shop was interrupted by other odors. The aromas of Mom's homemade buns and ham gravy filled the air with a tantalizing intensity that wiped away the last lingering plans for running away. Yes, I had now fully decided that I was going back. However, how was I going to get back and save my pride at the same time?

Suddenly I had a plan that might work. I would walk up within hearing distance of where the folks were eating and cough. My mother could never stand to hear me cough very long before she would start worrying that I was coming down with the flu. It would not take my folks long to come running out when they heard my voice, thankful that I had returned home safely.

I quickly walked to the entrance to the back porch where I could see my dad sitting at his customary place at the end of the table. They had just lit a gas lantern and Dad was deeply engrossed in his newspaper, eating the meal that filled the air with wonderful aromas.

When I forced out my loud cough, I fully expected my folks and sister to come charging out of the house. However, my expectations were not met. Dad never flinched as he continued to read the paper and my mother did not appear. Thinking that possibly they didn't hear me, I walked up the steps of the back porch and coughed louder. Still there was no reaction.

My next step was to walk up and stand at the back kitchen door where I could see everyone at the table. Finally, after standing there for what seemed to be an eternity, my mother finally asked me to get a plate if I was hungry.

That was probably the longest meal that I had ever eaten in my life. My expectations of some type of reaction were unfulfilled. I was disappointed that my folks showed no relief on my return or any signs of worry.

On the other hand, I was relieved that I did not receive any punishment for running away and not showing up to help with my milking chores. Silence by my folks was the most effective punishment they could have given to deter me from a repeat performance.

Chapter 16

Religion and the Church

My parents were both raised in the Christian faith and regularly attended a small country church located on the north end of Cricket Flat. My mother was more dedicated to the church and its beliefs than my father. She did not drink or smoke or use profanity. She firmly believed in the teachings of the Bible and made a strong effort to instill these beliefs in her children. However, she did not fit in with the strict fundamentalists that were somewhat common in the older generations that lived on the Flat. She wore make-up, she loved to play cards and she was quite tolerant of a wide range of religious views.

It was always my belief that my father attended church mainly to please my mother and to enjoy socializing with those attending. He was suspicious of most preachers and would never have many good things to say about their sermons. He thought that most preachers went into the ministerial field because they were too lazy to make an honest living. After church was over each Sunday, my parents would have contrasting views on the preacher and his sermon.

My parents would also get into heated arguments over the Bible and its teachings. Although my dad believed in God and in sections of the Bible, there were many parts that he refused to believe. He would happily show Mom scientific literature on prehistoric animals and carbon dating methods showing how these animals had to be much older than what the Bible stated the earth was. My mother would never give an inch in these arguments and would quickly show him a certain verse in the Bible to try to prove her point.

The old church on the Flat.

There seemed to be a distinct difference of religious philosophy between age groups on the Flat. The older generation were more likely to embrace the more strict beliefs regarding dancing, makeup, profanity, card playing, smoking, drinking and gambling.

The younger generation practiced some if not all, of these so called vices, although many attended the church on a regular basis. It was my opinion that, like my father, most of the younger group were mainly attracted to the church for its social offerings.

John Scott, one of my dad's uncles, was the religious leader of the community. A large, silver-haired man with a commanding presence, he tried to make sure that a minister would be available each Sunday for church services. When he couldn't round one up for the church, which didn't have a regular minister, he would often give some type of sermon himself.

John was a tireless promoter for the church. He would stand out on the large walk leading to the church and shake hands with everyone as they came out and thanked them for attending. He always had a compliment for any of the youngsters who had read a verse or sang with the youth group.

John's choice of ministers sometimes seemed misguided. Perhaps it was the smallness of the church or the fact that quality preachers were hard to find on short notice. Whatever the reason, his choices sometimes gave the congregation a wide variety of extremes when it came to hearing the gospel. I suspect that some of these men may have misrepresented their true occupation to John.

Some of these preachers were quite successful in lining their pockets with the meager assets of the congregation. One particular preacher spent about a month in the community, during which time he and his wife rotated their stays with different families on the Flat. In addition to receiving hams, canned foods and some cash from each one of his hosts, he would try to get people to sign a contract that they would give him a certain percentage of their crop in return for his prayers.

Another preacher apparently thought that he had found his own little isolated kingdom, a kingdom that he could rule with an iron fist. His invitations as a guest minister for a couple of Sundays gradually turned into about a three-month stay. His sermons, which had at first been only moderately conservative, gradually grew more fundamentalist in nature. One by one his pointed remarks hit too close to individual members of the congregation and attendance dropped off rapidly.

Apparently he pushed his dictatorial leanings too far, one Sunday, and his visits to deliver fire and brimstone sermons were discontinued. Perhaps his sharp lecture to the congregation following the church services prompted his dismissal.

He had just finished his sermon and had terminated services with a marathon prayer that had left those in attendance eager to relieve their long suppressed silence with some good old fashioned socializing. Since visiting after church was one of the main attractions to many of the members, it would often last up to a half an hour.

It was during one of these periods that the member's conversation was interrupted by the sharp pounding of the preacher's fist on the pulpit. After capturing the surprised attention of the members, a stinging sharp lecture was delivered on the sins of desecrating the inside of the house of the Lord with unimportant chatter. He went on to say that if visiting had to be carried on during the Sabbath that the congregation should carry their sins to the large, plank walkway leading into the church.

There was another preacher that must have thought that there might possibly be a singing talent scout hidden in the midst of the church congregation. He had a loud booming voice that would make the church walls vibrate as though they were being subjected to a high intensity earthquake.

His sermons were frequently interrupted by requests to turn to a certain page number in the hymn book. Then, rapidly flailing his arms like a choir director, he would overpower the piano and audience with a powerful rendition of the song. He would often race back and forth across the elevated altar and simultaneously point at the audience with a vigorous throwing motion of his arm as he would terminate a line in the hymn.

These eardrum-pounding sessions would leave this preacher temporarily drained of energy. After the song was completed, much to the relief of the congregation, he would slowly make his way back to the pulpit and resume his sermon with an exhausted, drained voice. His lung and voice recovering powers were amazing, however, as it would just be a matter of a few minutes before he would be recharged enough for another song.

This minister's singing was brought to an abrupt halt one day, much to the amusement of the younger members of the church. The youngsters were always forced to sit in the front church pew facing the altar. We would almost be hypnotized as we would watch this loud man dash back and forth across the altar only twelve feet from where we were sitting.

Some of us were sure that his rapidly-flapping arms would someday lift him into flight. Others were worried that the throwing motion of his arm would propel some hidden object into our midst. Regardless of the reasons, our eyes would be glued to his every move.

On this one day, an angry wasp provided an entertaining interruption to one of his loud songs. He was providing his usual bellowing rendition to "Brighten the Corner," when we noticed a wasp make a six foot drop from the church ceiling to the preacher's shoulder.

Perhaps the wasp had had enough of the loud singing. It was rapidly beating its wings as it inched its way towards our singer's exposed neck. We breathlessly watched the angry wasp search for a vulnerable spot to launch its attack, and then the preacher's upwardly-flapping arm apparently pinned the wasp to his bare neck.

Although the booming voice of our star was silenced, his motions were intensified. As the rest of the audience sitting further back in the church looked on in astonishment, our singing minister started slapping and clawing at his neck like an African witch doctor conducting a voodoo dance. Later, the minister laughingly explained to the audience what had happened.

One minister who visited our church a few times had two qualities that probably could have put him in the history books. He had a soft, monotone voice that quickly put all the restless babies in the crowd sound asleep. By the time thirty minutes had passed, every other individual in the congregation had also experienced some degree of head-bobbing.

Within forty-five minutes, snores from the members were overwhelming the voice of the preacher. George Kennedy once jokingly remarked that this minister once dropped his Bible during one of his sermons, and the loud sound of it hitting the floor gave many of the church members a severe whiplash as they came suddenly upright.

The minister's other trait was his tendency to preach too long. His sermons were characterized by his reading long passages in the Bible and then explaining their true meaning to the members. His favorite line after going past the normal quitting time was that his sermon would not be complete unless he finished explaining his last Bible reading.

John Scott and the preacher's wife would take turns emitting coughs and clearing their throat with increasing intensity as the sermons dragged on. It would usually take the action of John slowly rising to his feet and pulling out his pocket watch before our long-winded preacher would end his sermon.

One evangelist preacher invaded the small Cricket Flat community like rock festivals invaded many small towns in the 1970s. Equipped with battery-operated loud speakers that were ahead of their time, this minister and his talented group of singers and musicians provided the best show in years for the Flat residents.

Their night revival meetings at the church would attract a most of the community members. Perhaps it was their loud booming gospel music, which penetrated the normally quiet air of the rural community for miles around, that attracted many of the residents to their meetings.

This preacher was a tall, handsome man with dark brown hair. He had a trained, persuasive voice and he could present a compelling message to the church members. After building up the emotions of the members with loud gospel songs accompanied by the piano, an accordion and several guitars, he would start his sermon. Beautiful, soft singing by his two daughters would offer a gentle background to his persuasive voice, as he would abandon his pulpit to approach various members in the audience.

His soft, compelling voice would convince members, one by one, to follow him to a kneeling position by the altar. As the voices of his daughters would gradually increase in volume, one or more members of his traveling group would suddenly start stomping around on the altar and begin talking in tongues. This would often be followed by people suddenly jumping up and praising the Lord with emotional outbursts.

These sessions would often last well into the night, with some people wailing and speaking in tongues, all to the background of music, singing and the strong compelling voice of the minister.

This minister and his troops both gained and lost as they ended their lengthy stay. Their large van was well-stocked with hams, sides of bacon and other foods when they left. However, the preacher's two daughters ended up being local residents when they stayed and married two of the Flat's young bachelors.

The little old church was also blessed with several good ministers. A Pentecostal preacher, with the last name of Rundell, served as the church minister when he and his family moved to the community for several years. Rundell was a sincere, hard-working man and was one of the few ministers who gained my dad's respect. Rundell would often hold down jobs as far away as Weston, some fifty miles away, in making a living for his family.

Our little, white church could undoubtedly add many more stories than what I have told. The church, which was named the Mt. Pleasant Church, was built in 1903 when my great grandfather, Joseph Scott, initiated a petition in the community for its construction.

Environmentalists today could not have been more pleased with the way the church blended in with its surroundings. The 36 by 22 foot building with its steep-pitched shingle roof, seemed to be mothered like a little chick by several large ponderosa pines that helped protect it from the wind and the sun.

Its two-by eight-foot windows, three per side, gave those inside its walls beautiful north and south views of a countryside checker-boarded with stands of coniferous timber and cultivated fields. An elevated plank walkway led east from the church door to the edge of the county road some sixty feet away. A woven wire fence topped off with two rows of poles separated the churchyard from the edge of the county road.

Two outhouses and a small woodshed that seemed to fight for space amongst the pine trees were located to the west of the church. Four-inch shiplap, which always seemed to be well-maintained, covered the outside of the building.

The inside of the church was always in worse shape than the outside. Upright tongue and groove one-by-fours formed the first four feet of the walls. The rest of the inside was adorned with several layers of wallpaper that was badly cracked and blackened with smoke.

Unfinished wooden floors met an elevated carpeted altar on the west end of the building. A large woodstove, with its metal stovepipe feeding into a small brick chimney, was located against the south wall. Six kerosene lamps with reflectors lined two inside walls.

Weather did not seem to deter those that attended Mt. Pleasant Church. I remember one winter Sunday when it was snowing so hard that my folks debated whether church would even be held. However, they decided to attend on the chance that others would be there. After hitching our two horses to our sled, we bucked more than a half-mile of deep snow to reach the church.

I remember my parents being surprised when they saw six other horse teams tied to the pole fence in front of the church. Two or three men were shoveling the snow off the wide plank walk leading into the church and the distinct sound of someone chopping kindling for the fire penetrated the cold winter air.

We had to dodge a barrage of snowballs by some fun-loving youngsters as we traversed the freshly-shoveled path to the church. My dad got there just in time to open the church door for a man with a heaping arm load of kindling and pieces of pine pitch.

As we entered the church, several families still clad in winter wraps eagerly awaited the building of a fire in the large woodstove. It did not take long for a man to carefully arrange a pile of pitch and kindling and douse it with kerosene. The strike of a match followed by a mini-explosion soon led to a roaring fire as the women and children eagerly surrounded the stove.

Following a pattern often used during cold weather, the men quickly moved the pews into a semi-circle closer to the stove so as to be closer to the warmth of the fire. It was also decided, instead of the children's Sunday School being held in the far corner of the building, that we would also meet near the stove.

John soon beckoned to his daughter-in-law, Ella Scott, to take her place at the old church piano. Ella, a courageous mother of more than ten children, adjusted a pair of old glasses held to her head by a string cord and thumbed through an old hymn book until she had found the right page number. John selected, "The Old Rugged Cross," for the first hymn.

Thinking back, it must have been quite a feat for Ella to pound out any type of tune on a piano in temperatures below freezing. This piano, which was always home to spiders, mice and wasps, had not been tuned for a long time, and sounded it. Mouse nests would often have been cleaned out of its inside when the keys could no longer be depressed. Ella's playing would usually improve as the piano warmed up later in the day.

The blending of children's and adult's voices, coupled with the sound of the untuned piano, would not have won any prizes at an amateur hour contest. However, volume made up for quality as John led us through three or four songs before he initiated Sunday School services. The close proximity of the children's and adults' services led to two different lessons, as the high narrow windows provided us with the view of a raging snow storm.

Before long, the heat of the stove activated several wasps that habitually used the layers of wallpaper for their winter resting sites. These wasps always kept those in attendance on the alert as they dropped from the ceiling like small, parachuting infantrymen.

John served as minister that day since the bad roads made it impossible for a visiting preacher. Despite the bad weather we had close to normal services. The children even had their usual game of trying to push one another off the high church walk into the deep snow after church services. Our return home was just as difficult as our earlier trip, with the team bucking even deeper snow. Several other members that traveled much farther than we did exemplified the dedication to attend church services.

One particularly happy event that occurred at the church was the annual Children's Day gathering. This was held on the second Sunday of June, and consisted of a morning program in the church where local, talented persons performed. This was followed by a short service. At noon families would pile up several large tables in the church yards with their favorite dishes. After everyone filled themselves with delicious food, a minister would deliver another after-dinner service.

Probably the most impressive part of these events, in addition to the fine food, was the large turn outs. On some occasions the little old church could not hold the crowd. Those who had any type of roots connected with the church or the community would gather at these events. People who had had long-standing feuds would shake hands and socialize at Children's Day. A large contingent of children often met for the first time to play games in the churchyard and the surrounding forest of pine.

Once, I jumped into the limelight at one of the Children's Day services. Being subjected to many long-winded sermons by certain ministers had caused me to take any evasive tactics I could think of to avoid being trapped into listening for very long.

Since most of the after-dinner services were held in the church, I had carefully formulated a plan that would allow me to play outside with many of the children. Knowing that my mother would be looking for me to sit with her during the sermon, I climbed a large thick-limbed pine tree near the side of the church for a hiding place.

I had just barely reached a place in the tree where I would be hidden when I heard repeated calls from my mother. Pretending that I did not hear her, I struggled to find a comfortable spot to spend time in the pitch-covered tree. In addition to the sticky pitch and the thick limbs where I could not find a comfortable resting place, a steady string of fierce red ants had also made this tree their home. As I fought the ants and the pitch, I consoled myself that my discomfort in the tree would soon be over when my mother entered the church for the services.

My deceitful plan, however, was soon subjected to a two-pronged attack. My first surprise was that, instead of holding services in the church, it was decided to hold the services outside, due to the large crowd and the nice weather. In addition, the minister picked a spot directly beneath the tree I was in to preach his sermon.

This crushing blow was almost more than I could bear. The thought of fighting off the ants and the pitch for an hour almost made me willing to subject myself to the embarrassment of climbing down the tree directly behind the preacher and in front of the large crowd.

My decision to stay in the tree, partially dictated by my shyness, was soon to receive another jolt. As I listened to the minister talk beneath me I could soon tell that this voice did not belong to the man who had delivered the short morning service. It did not take me long to hone in on his identity. In a shocking moment of recognition, I realized that this was the long-winded minister that I had mentioned earlier who put the congregation to sleep before his sermons were over.

I soon realized that I was in a dangerous position. I would somehow have to entwine myself in the limbs in such a manner that I would not fall if I should be lulled into sleep by this minister's sermon.

Somehow, while struggling around in the tree I dislodged a clump of cones that had hung on from the previous fall. Although I did not know it at the time, one of the cones made a direct hit on the preacher's head. Looking up in the tree and seeing my squirming body, the minister said, "Come on down, Zacchaeus, and join the crowd."

Climbing down the sixty foot pine tree in front of the large crowd and the minister was my contribution to the afternoon talent show. As I quickly glanced around the large crowd it did not take me long to pinpoint my parents. They stood out like a sore thumb because they were the only people in the crowd that were not laughing. Their stern, cold stares sent an unspoken message for me to be seated between them for the rest of the sermon.

My humorous memories of this incident are always somewhat tempered by the memory of the spanking that I received from my father when we reached the private confines of our house.

The Mt. Pleasant Church also served many years as a site for holding youth Bible School classes. Hilda Scott, Obe and Gladys Scott's youngest daughter, acted as the main teacher at these classes for several years.

Hilda and three other students from Multnomah Bible School would come up during the summer months to conduct the program. At the insistence of my mother, I attended these classes on a regular basis until I was in the eighth grade. I would unsuccessfully argue with her that I should be able to quit this program when I grew larger than the teachers.

One of the regulars at church services was Gene Carver. Gene, who was described in an earlier chapter, pulled the rug out beneath several ministers with his droll manner and sense of humor. He would generally sit in a non-committal manner, speaking only when spoken to. His stolid appearance would often give the deceiving appearance that his speech and hearing were impeded. He seemed to have a vulnerable, sorrowful look that was perceived by ministers as a person ripe for salvation.

Gene's bearing seemed to attract new ministers, especially evangelists, like flies to honey. Here, they sensed, was a splendid target for displaying their conversion talents in front of the rest of the congregation. They would wrongly suppose that his speedy acceptance of Christ would act like a catalyst in stirring an emotional response by the rest of the audience. Gene's loud responses, however, usually left the preachers speechless and provided those in attendance with a good laugh.

One evangelist approached Gene after issuing a call for people to be saved. Putting one arm around Gene and raising the other one he shouted in a loud commanding voice, "Gene, do you know Jesus?"

Gene, looking back at the minister in a casual manner, shouted back with surprising loudness, "No, I have never personally met the man, but I have heard a lot about him."

Another preacher once asked Gene if he would walk up to the altar and pray with him. Gene answered back, "I walked to church and I am going to have to walk back and I am not going to do any more walking than I have to."

The following poem, called, "Mt. Pleasant Church," is written in dedication to my great grandfather, Joseph Scott, for his efforts in getting the church built.

Here I still stand but my beauty is fading fast.
I was well built but I simply can't last.
The rats and the mice make good use of me now.
My yard is eaten down by more than one cow.
Most of my trees have been taken away,
Where we often stood to sing and to pray.
My sturdy plank walk is scattered and broken,
The elevated walk where many words were spoken.
My wallpaper walls are hanging in shreds,
And the windows have felt many dreads.
My kerosene lamps are no longer there,
And my wood floors are scratched and bare.
There is a hole in my door that is big and wide,
To allow animal passage to the inside.
These are just a few of my ills up to date,
There are many more that I failed to state.
It was not always like this, looking back in history.
I first started out in 1903.
Joseph W. Scott and other men of Cricket Flat,
Cleared out a small spot in some pine habitat.
They labored long and sawed my boards from a mill,
That was owned by more Scotts at the base of a hill.
It did not take them long to make me complete,
With a pulpit, an altar and pews for a seat.
A large woodstove to keep persons warm,
In cold weather and the mighty snow storm.
Folks and times were different than we have today.
They needed a close place to worship and pray.
The church placed high on their priority list,
And attendance by their children they did insist.

They mined the forest for it trees for the mill,
And used the cleared land for its soil to till.
They labored long throughout the long week,
But on Sunday the Lord they did seek.
My crowds were large, I was in my prime,
In all weather, even Wintertime.
Children's Day crowds always gave me full joy,
With many adults and many a girl and boy.
Persons that had known me and moved far away,
Always honored me on this Children's Day.
Many different men of the cloth spoke from my hall.
They persuaded many to listen to God's call.
Many young children were directed towards God.
In my Bible School where many have trod.

My halls were used well for about forty-five years,
But as time passed by I began to shed tears.
My attendance was dropping, no one made repair.
I longed to return to more song and sweet prayer.
I knew I couldn't offer, like churches in town,
Expensive pipe organs and men of renown.
Choirs with fancy robes and windows with different hues,
With many full members willing to pay dues.
Better roads and better cars also did me harm,
They made it easy to drive from the farm.
Former members were courted with interests besides me,
I couldn't compete with all these things you see.
It was in 1955 that they closed my doors—
No more prayers, no steps on my floors.

I have no regrets; I am proud of my past.
I have memories that will forever last.
I served at a time when I was needed by most,
And I was most happy to be a good host.
My vessel was small and my facilities only fair,
But there is one truth that I must declare.
I served as an extension from one high above,
As a house for the his worship as well as his love.

Chapter 17

Hygiene and Health

Keeping clean and not offending your friends with body odor is much easier to do today than during the 1930s. The lack of bathing facilities, difficulties in heating water and in transporting it from the water source to the house were all factors that discouraged bathing. Very few homes had water piped into the house. Most had wells or springs where water was packed into the house in buckets.

Our original water system required us to pull the water some twenty feet out of our well with a rope and an attached bucket. The water then had to be carried approximately sixty feet to our house. Water that was heated had to be warmed on our old wood cookstove by a built-in heating reservoir in the stove plus large water-filled containers placed on the hot portion of the stove. A hot fire had to be kept burning in the stove in order to heat the water. Even with a hot fire it would take up to an hour to heat a significant amount of water.

Eventually we modernized our water system by putting storage tanks in our house attic and pumping the water into these tanks with a gasoline run pump. A hot water tank operated by heating coils in the firebox of our wood cooking stove, piped water to our sink. A small shower installed in my bedroom was included in this water improvement project.

Before these improvements, we employed a number of water-saving techniques, especially during the winter months. Taking what we called a bath involved the use of a chair and a large washtub filled with a rationed amount of water. Since the tub was small, adults had to stand up in the tub and use a wash cloth. Small children could sit down and enjoy a more normal bath. Usually, two to three persons would use the same bath water, with hot water occasionally being added. This type of bath was generally limited to one per week.

We also took sponge baths. This bathing operation included a small wash pan containing about two pints of lukewarm water and a wash cloth. You first washed your face and then your pubic and arm pit areas using the wash cloth and plenty of homemade soap. The sponge baths were generally taken every two days unless we were having company or going somewhere. During these times we would take the sponge bath just before this event occurred.

We always had a wash basin full of water sitting on a small table in the kitchen for washing our hands before meals and at other times. This basin usually contained unheated water that was changed two or three times a day.

During the warmer summer months the male members of our household often used our pond for bathing. Other residents also used ponds, creeks and watering troughs. It is amazing that we could use

The first pond built on the ranch in about 1936.

the pond that was also used by our livestock and not be infected with parasites and diseases that in today's time are considered dangerous.

Some residents, including my family, set up an outdoor shower using the sun for heating the water. A six-foot high stand was erected so it would hold a fifty gallon barrel. A faucet was installed in the bottom of one end of the barrel and an opening made at the top of the barrel for filling purposes. A small baled bucket with a number of small holes drilled in its bottom was hung on the faucet. When the faucet was turned on the water ran into the bucket and was distributed in a sprinkling action over the bather. The barrel would be filled in the early morning so that the hot rays of the sun would have time for heating the water. This was a pretty good system during the hot summer months, but it was sometimes quite a bit of work to hand-fill the barrel with water.

Some of the Flat's residents did not use water as regularly for bathing as we did. Some of the women and girls depended on strong deodorants and perfumes for masking body odors. A few of the men went long periods between changing clothes and bathing. One man wore long underwear year around and would only change when the garment wore out.

The old wooden-board constructed two-seater toilets were the common facility used by most of the Flat's residents, including our family. Our toilet looked like its builder had been in urgent need of its use when it was constructed. Warped boards covered with knotholes and large cracks dominated the building. One large knothole in the door about eye level from one's favorite sitting position gave its user a bird's-eye view of on-coming traffic. Montgomery Ward catalogs usually were placed within easy reach near the seat. A bucket of quicklime, generally used for reducing odors and flies, was located someplace on the floor nearby.

One never got too comfortable while occupied in the outdoor facility. It was an accepted practice to bombard the outhouse with any projectile that was handy while it was in use. Tree limbs were the most popular thing to throw, because they were most available and they made a very loud noise when they hit the building. If one happened to be reading a book while sitting on the throne, which was often done, the sudden impact of a large limb hitting the side of the outhouse was enough to cause a heart attack.

My dad got more than he bargained for one day when he decided to launch a large icicle at our outdoor facility. He had watched my mother enter the outhouse, and after waiting for an appropriate time he heaved a large icicle at it. The sound waves of the crashing icicle had hardly started penetrating the cold winter air when my mother exploded out of the little old house like an angry bear. With her bloomers down around her knees and blood running down her head, she charged towards the house and my dad like a wounded rhino.

Dad did not know whether to call for a doctor or run and hide as my crying mother bore down on him. He had once been charged by a bear and had been mauled by a mad sow, but he had never had to face a mad woman with blood in her eye. Finally, concern overcame fright as he helped her into the house for first aid.

His icicle had made several rotations in the air and then straightened up exactly at the right moment to make a clean entry into the large knothole in the door. Still on an unlucky roll, it made a direct hit on my mother's forehead just above her eye. She said that she thought Dad had shot her when the icicle first hit. She had to be taken to the doctor and have several stitches to close the wound.

She did get one concession out of Dad and the rest of the family from her accident. A new regulation was implemented on the Scott ranch that any throwing at the outhouse would result in the death penalty.

Another boy and I almost burned our outdoor throne down one summer day. We had made some crude cigars out of catalog pages and dockweed seeds and were painfully trying to smoke the foul-smelling mixture in the security of the outhouse. As we were choking and coughing and telling each other how good it tasted, we spotted my father zeroing in on the old toilet like a honey bee headed for its hive. After quickly extinguishing our homemade gems, we threw the remains down the toilet hole and left our den of iniquity before my dad arrived.

Feeling relieved that we had seemingly destroyed any evidence of our crime, we met Dad as he was getting ready to take his morning rest break. He had already started to open a book that he had brought with him. My father's stays in the rest station could often last up to one half hour as his rest stops were often combined with literary research. It was about fifteen minutes later when the motion of Dad's sudden charge out of the outhouse caught our eye.

Smoke was billowing out of every crack and knothole as my father went into his firefighting mode. He quickly grabbed a shovel from the nearby tool shed and quickly excavated a large hole in front of the outhouse in his attempts to smother the fire.

My friend and I were recruited to pack the water that was finally needed to completely kill our fire. It did not take Dad long to browbeat a confession from us. Years later Dad said that the smell of his pipe smoke had delayed his discovery of the fire. A sudden, intense heat on his bare bottom told him he was on a hot seat. I also ended up with a hot seat over this episode after my friend had left.

As one can imagine, trips to the outhouse during cold winter nights were often impractical for the female members of the family, especially my younger sisters. A large porcelain chamber pot partly filled with water was generally placed out by our heating stove for bathroom use during the night. Yellow snow near the back doors of most residences attested to the fact that most male members also did not make the trip to the outhouse during the night.

Packing the large chamber pot to the outhouse during the daylight hours was not the most prestigious job in the world. Unless my parents happened to be making a trip to the outhouse at the right time in the morning, the job of hauling this treasure usually fell upon the shoulders of Rosalie or me.

This task proved to be a powerful disciplinary tool used to keep us in line. Normally, Rosalie and I took turns with this chore. However, if one of us happened to get into trouble with the folks, we would get saddled with this task several times in a row as part of our punishment.

I used to really enjoy watching Rosalie packing this bowl full of goodies to the outhouse. She would first wrap a scarf around her face in a manner that would cover her nose. She then put on the thickest pair of gloves she could find. Acting like she was marching to her doom, she would turn her head to one side. She would then hold the pot at arm's length directly in front of her as if she were presenting a peace offering to a group of hostile Indians.

Rosalie would often try and hold her breath as long as she could during this trip. After she staggered back into the house and set the pot down, she would run into another room and start taking deep breaths as though she had just run five miles.

The pleasure of watching Rosalie pack the pot got the best of me one day. As she was walking away with her pot of precious cargo, the devil forced me to hurl a large snowball at her backside. My throw was almost as accurate as my dad's icicle throw as it landed with a resounding splatter on the back of my sister's neck.

The surprise of getting hit by the snowball triggered an instant response in Rosalie. The chamber pot and its contents were hurled straight up in the air like the eruption of Old Faithful in Yellowstone Park. In a crying rage, my sister tore off her outer garments and came racing back to the house. Between sobs of rage she wasted little time in telling my mother what had happened. My short, thirty seconds of fun earned fifteen straight turns of pot packing.

Maintaining a supply of clean diapers was always a chore for mothers with young children. Disposable diapers did not exist so mothers with small children had to keep a large supply of cloth diapers. My mother used to keep two large buckets of water for the cleaning and storage of soiled diapers. The diapers were cleaned out in the first bucket and then allowed to soak in the second bucket until they were run through the washing machine.

The washing machine was much different from the ones today. It consisted of a large tub that contained an agitator. Like today's machines, this was were the clothes and soap were deposited. A swinging arm contained a set of facing rollers called the wringer. Clothes were fed into these turning rollers from the large wash basin and the pressed-out water fed back into the basin.

The clothes that were fed through the wringers ended up falling into a large container of rinse water. The washing machine was powered by a small gasoline engine that filled the washing room with dangerous engine smoke. The clothes then had to be fed back from the rinse water through the wringers again and deposited in a large clothes basket.

The clothes were hung on a wire line for drying. During the summer and the dry periods of winter, clothes were hung outside. During stormy weather in winter a folding drying rack constructed of small dowels was set up in the house for drying clothes.

Washing clothes was an arduous job that required packing lots of water and heating it on the old wood cookstove. Also standing over the smoking washing machine, filling it with water, and running the clothes through the wringer was a tiring and dangerous job.

On several occasions women on the Flat got their hair or breasts caught in these wringers. They could be in real trouble if they could not immediately hit the shut off lever on the wringer. The old saying, "Catching your tit in the wringer," has a factual foundation. My mother once got her hair caught in these tight-pressing rubber rollers. Fortunately, the engine died when her head was pulled up against the base of the rollers. However, she did have quite a time pulling her hair back out of the wringer.

Since there was so much work involved in washing clothes, several methods were employed to reduce this chore. Infants—at least in our family—were potty-trained at an early age. Undergarments were not changed nearly as often as most families do today. Work clothes were not washed as often, either.

Some families left their sweat-saturated work clothes out in a rainstorm and then allowed them to dry again before wearing. Others would let their dirty work clothes soak overnight in a watering trough. My mother had a stiff bristled brush she used to brush the dirt out of our coats. Some families had a bucket of soapy water that they soaked their dirty socks in. They would then wring them out by hand and let them dry.

Most families, including ours, made their own soap from hog fat. Fatty portions of the hog were cut into two to three inch chunks and cooked on the stove until most of the fat had liquefied. This grease was then poured into another container and mixed with wood ashes and lye. Some families would also add a cheap perfume to this mixture. This liquid mixture was then poured into large square metal pans to a depth of about one inch. Before the mixture had completely hardened it would be cut like fudge candy into soap bar-sized chunks.

This soap was an all purpose cleaner. We used it for bathing, for washing clothes and for washing dishes. We found out the hard way that one had to be careful when washing dishes; they had to be rinsed and dried thoroughly. Any trace of soap left on eating ware would cause diarrhea. When used in the washing machine, my mother would shave off thin flakes for mixing in with the clothes.

One of the by-products of this soap was the section of pork fat that did not liquefy. These crisp crunchy chunks, which were edible, were called cracklings. A commercial variety of this product called pork rinds can be purchased in stores today. These cracklings kept for long periods of time and provided tasty snacks for the family.

Medication and illness during the 1930s and early 1940s were quite different from today. Doctor and hospital visits did not occur as often because of costs and availability. No one had even heard of medical insurance and probably could not have afforded if it had been available. Doctor and hospital costs were only a fraction of what today's costs are. Families relied more on home remedies than purchased medication. Most of the modern antibiotics were not available.

The sub-standard roads and lack of adequate vehicles that had caused Flat residents to be self-sufficient in food supplies also caused them to ride their illnesses out or treat them with some surprisingly effective home remedies. My mother had quite a variety of methods that she used to treat our various ills or make us more comfortable while we were riding out an illness such as the flu, chickenpox, measles, strep throat, mumps and common colds. The following list shows some of the remedies she used:

Insect bites and stings and itching from chickenpox and measles: Treated with a thick paste of baking soda and water.

Croup, flu, whooping cough: Treated by making a miniature tent out of a sheet and placing boiling pots of water mixed with Vicks VapoRub inside the tent on a chair. The ill patient would stay inside the tent for extended periods of time. Also used calcidun pills.

Congestion from colds: Rub Vicks VapoRub on chest and neck areas and then lay warm towels on areas covered with medication.

Burns: Crushed raw potato was held on the burn with a piece of clean white sheet. Another treatment was Vaseline smeared on the burned area. Yet another treatment was smearing the affected area with lard.

Cuts: Any of the following—Iodine, Mercurochrome, turpentine, methiolate, alcohol, hot water. Old sheets were cut into strips for bandages.

Puncture wounds, sprains and boils: Mix Epsom salts in hot water and soak injured area.

Sore throats: Gargle with any of following—salt and hot water, honey, vinegar and lemon juice mixed with hot water, Listerine.

Indigestion: Drink a glass of a mixture of water and baking soda.

Earache: Blow cigarette smoke in ear, put couple drops of sweet oil in ear.

Fever: Any of the following—cold bath, wet wash-rag on forehead, aspirin, enema with cool water.

Constipation: Any of following—drink one glass of prune juice, take milk of magnesia, enema with warm soapy water.

Headache: Any of following—aspirin, rub forehead, massage back of neck, lay down and close eyes.

Toothaches: Any of following—Put clove drops on tooth, hot or cold packs on side of jaw.

Probably the most hated form of treatment that my mother seemed to prefer for several different types of illness was the enema. Rosalie and I would often hide our sickness symptoms to prevent this dreaded treatment. Many of my faked illness symptoms that I sometimes used to skip school would disappear in a hurry when my mother would threaten to give me an enema.

My mother had a large rubber hot water bag that appeared to hold about two gallons. This bag had a six-foot rubber hose attachment that screwed into the bag opening. On the other end of the hose was a six inch syringe that was about one-half inch in diameter. This was the apparatus that she used to administer this dreaded treatment.

While I was pleading and screaming that there was nothing wrong with me, my mother would firmly order me to pull my pants down and drape myself face down over a chair. With my rear end elevated above my legs and head, I would fearfully twist my head around and watch her apply a generous supply of Vaseline to the syringe at the end of the hose that now appeared to be about two feet in length and about two inches in diameter. She would then grab this huge syringe and approach me like a mugger would come at a person with a knife.

By this time, in addition to my screaming and pleading, I would be shaking my rear end like a Can-Can dancer in the hopes that she couldn't hit a moving object After a few unsuccessful jabs at my gyrating bottom, she would hit her target with the thrusting motion of a Mexican bull fighter making his killing thrust. Then as she was making dire threats for me not to move she would raise the huge water bag up over her head and start squeezing it like a Swiss accordion player playing a fast polka.

At this stage, my agony had just begun. She would operate this large bag like a giant tire pump, and my stomach would respond in the same fashion as a flat tire being inflated. As I was still being barraged by her warnings not to move, I felt like the Amazon River was racing through me at ninety miles an hour. It would not take me long to start screaming,

"Stop! I can't hold anymore," and her stock answer would be, "Yes you can; we've just started."

The next part of this water intake process was what I called the waiting stage. As my mother wrung the last drop out of the bag, she would tell me to stay where I was for a while. By this time I would be feeling like a stick of dynamite whose fuse had just been lit. I rolled around on the chair, my hard stomach feeling like an over inflated basketball as I emitted desperate repeated screams, "I can't stand it any longer!"

The only thing that kept me there was my mother's repeated warnings, "If you leave too soon we will just have to do it over again."

The old title-author joke, "Race to the Outhouse," by Willy Makeit, would describe the next stage of the enema operation. After what seemed to be hours of agony, my mother would look at the clock and reluctantly say, "Well I probably should wait a while longer, but we will see if this works."

Then, like the little old Dutch boy pulling his finger out of the hole in the ocean dike, she would pull the syringe. My feet would spin on our kitchen linoleum like a high school kid doing a hot rod burn-out as I headed for the old outhouse.

I am sure that my later development into one of the fastest runners at Elgin High School was a result of these life and death dashes. I really don't think my mother ever found out if these enemas worked. We always told her they did so she wouldn't give us a repeat performance.

Another painful memory that all our family had was going to the dentist. Dental technology has certainly advanced in the art of reducing pain. Bill Cosby's funny recording on going to the dentist must have been based on actual facts when it came to describing dentists of earlier times.

We went to a dentist in Elgin by the name of Dr. Smith. He was a friendly, soft-spoken man with graying hair. My sister and I called him Painful Potter because of all the pain that he inflicted upon us. Apparently he had really good teeth and never went to another dentist, or he had a high threshold of pain, as he didn't seem to comprehend how much pain he was inflicting on his patients.

Dr. Smith seemed always to have the same line as he would examine a tooth. After some painful probing with a sharp-hooked instrument he would say, "There is the little rascal. Not too bad. This might hurt for just a little while, but its not enough to require deadening."

Then he would then grab you in head lock with one arm and crank up an old antiquated drill that sounded like a chainsaw. His old, dull drill would bounce up and down on my tooth like a jackhammer as the smell of hot, smoking flesh and enamel permeated my nostrils. Sharp pain from the vibrating drill would make me grip the arms of the dentist chair tightly as I fully expected the powerful pressure-packed drill to bust through my tooth into the flesh of my jaw.

"Now that was not too bad, was it?" Dr. Smith would say as he flushed particles of blood and enamel out of my mouth.

"We have just a bit of drilling to do and we will be done," he would go on to say. His little bit of drilling would usually end up being about thirty minutes worth of the old, hot dull, drill seeking out every nerve center that it could find in my tooth.

Deadening the tooth with a needle was almost as bad as toughing it out. Surface deadeners that are now wiped on before penetrating with a needle were not in existence then. Needles were larger and duller and really created a lot of pain when inserted into the mouth area.

Medical fees were much lower, in those days. Dr. Smith used to charge five dollars for a filling. An office call to a doctor usually ran from five to ten dollars. I remember my mother paying $150 for a stay in the La Grande Hospital, although I don't remember the length of the stay. Doctors often made house calls and home-delivered a lot of the babies born on the Flat. The era of cheap medical treatment and home remedies has probably disappeared forever as medical costs and dependence on prescription drugs continue to rise.

Chapter 18

The Big Blast

One of the most memorable incidents that happened on the Flat was the blasting of the big stump. My dad and I had been clearing land of tree stumps in a section of land located about one-half mile north of our house. We had been using the old Fordson tractor to pull out the stumps.

Most of these pine stumps, which ranged from 12 to 18 inches in diameter, required considerable work before the tractor could pull them out. We would generally have to dig down around the base and cut several of the lateral roots on one side of the stump before the tractor could pull it out. It was hard, time-consuming work digging down through the hard dirt and cutting roots off with an ax.

George Kennedy, who lived just a short distance from our clearing site, came over during our clearing operations one day and temporarily changed our method of stump removal. After watching us laboriously remove a few stumps, George said, "Let me show you an easy way to get rid of those stumps."

After borrowing our tractor and small trailer, it did not take George long to return with a large box of dynamite, blasting caps and fuses. He explained that his brother had given him a generous supply of the explosives and that Dad might as well use some. It did not take George long to dig under one of the larger stumps, place a portion of dynamite under the stump and rig it for detonation.

After lighting the three-foot long fuse, we all retreated to a spot behind our tractor and breathlessly waited for what Dad and I expected to be a loud, booming explosion. Instead all we heard was a muffled thump and the stump barely lifted out of the ground. Still, Dad and I were real impressed with how the stump and its roots had been completely separated from the ground with very little effort.

George quickly taught Dad the finer techniques of blasting out stumps and he left the rest of the dynamite with us as he departed for his house. Dad was a happy man as we removed stump after stump in a fraction of the time and effort that had been required before.

The biggest job that now remained was loading the heavy stumps on the trailer and hauling them off to a large pile at the edge of the field. Some of them were so large that we couldn't load them in the trailer and they had to be dragged off behind the tractor, hooked to a chain.

It was the next morning during breakfast that George, who had been invited in for coffee after he arrived at our house for a short visit, put my dad in trouble with my mother. After about ten minutes of conversation, which he monopolized, George said, "How is your dynamite operation going?"

This casual statement lit a fire under my mother.

"Dynamite! What dynamite project?" my mother asked in a worried voice. Dad quickly tried to change the subject, but the cat was out of the bag. Like a trained dog sniffing out drugs, mom soon got a modified version of our stump blasting.

George had barely left the house when my normally calm mother started lecturing my father in an emotional manner. After listing at least a dozen cases of persons that she had known that had received severe injuries from handling dynamite and caps, she lectured him on his lack of judgment in including me in this dangerous work.

Despite my dad's arguments on how much work the dynamite saved in stump removal, he finally yielded to Mom's passionate pleas and promised that he would not use the dynamite again.

My father seemed very dejected the next day as we went back to the old difficult method of stump removal. Every aspect of the stump removal project was going wrong. My dad dulled his ax several times when he hit rocks. The large tow chain that he used to hook on to the stumps kept breaking and many of the stumps were very difficult to pull out.

Apparently the run of bad luck and the ease by which we had removed stumps the day before was more than my dad could take.

"Don't say anything to your mother about this," Dad muttered in a low, guilty-sounding voice as he made preparations to start blasting again. It did not take long before the repeated low volume thuds of the dynamite filled the afternoon air. Dad's disposition seemed to improve immensely as the dynamite made short work of all but one of the remaining stumps.

This last stump was a pitch-hardened giant that had been cut many years before. Extending to at least four feet in diameter and standing nearly five feet high, this stump seemed to present an overwhelming challenge to any force that would dare to take it on. George, who was quite an expert on dynamite, had mentioned earlier that it would take quite a charge to remove this giant and advised Dad not to fool with it.

"Are you going to try and take the big stump out, Dad?" I asked as I watched my father studying the old stump.

"No, I think it's too big to fool with," replied my dad as he reluctantly turned and started to walk away from the giant.

He had not taken many steps before he turned around and said, "It would sure be nice if that thing was out of there." I knew then that my dad had made up his mind as he started digging a horizontal hole between two of the stump's extending roots.

"I guess it wouldn't hurt to give it a try," he said as he prepared a hefty load of dynamite and lit the trailing fuse.

The old giant didn't even quiver as the major force of the blast shot a bunch of dirt from beneath the stump. "I didn't think it would work; it's just too big," Dad stated as he again started to walk away. The old stump must have had an invisible string on Dad as he only went a few feet before he turned and prepared a slightly larger charge in the enlarged cavity beneath the stubborn monarch. The only thing that was different from the first charge, however, was that more dirt was blown out from below the stump's roots.

There was no hesitation on my dad's part the third time. He couldn't wait to set another deeper and larger charge. The situation had now developed into a full-blown struggle between my father and the stump.

I do not remember how many charges my dad unsuccessfully set off beneath his adversary.

However, I now knew the only thing that would stop my dad was to run out of dynamite. Apparently sensing he did not have enough dynamite for many more charges, he decided that he would go for broke. Throwing all caution to the wind, not to mention good sense, he took all the remaining dynamite sticks and carefully packed them in with dirt beneath the stump. Again we retreated to the sanctuary of the old Fordson tractor as we waited for the burning fuse to reach the dynamite.

What happened next had to be one of the most traumatic moments of my entire life. The previous blasts that had all been muffled explosions were no comparison to what assaulted our senses of sight, smell and hearing.

A loud, booming sound that sent shock waves against our ears and face and made the very ground under our feet tremble like an earthquake, invading the still country air like an atomic bomb. An instant curtain of dust and smoke temporarily blocked our view of the explosion site. Suddenly appearing above the wall of smoke and dust, our giant stump appeared like a huge octopus rising from the depths. The instant smell of burnt sulfur and dust filled our open mouths and noses.

The whole event—lasting only a fraction of a second—seemed to turn us into motionless statues. I remember my father, with his mouth wide open, standing with his eyes locked on the airborne stump.

The tremendous old stump, which was now exposed with its full complement of roots, was slowly rotating in the air like a helicopter blade in slow motion. Its tangled root mass, which was about twenty feet in diameter, seemed to hang motionless in space as it reached the crest of its 150-foot climb. Chunks of clay two feet in diameter, rocks and pieces of roots grabbed our attention as they fell from the sky like giant hailstones.

Despite the bombardment of missiles falling all around us, we were still hypnotized as we followed the path of the falling stump, zeroing in our position like a heat-seeking missile. The resounding crash of the stump landing some fifteen feet from where we stood by the tractor brought us back to reality. Perhaps my dad was thinking about the heaven above, as the first word that he uttered was "Jesus Christ."

Fortunately, neither one of us was injured during this incident. My dad's biggest concern was getting rid of this large stump and its large root system, since it stood out like a sore thumb in this open, cleared field. He was afraid that my mother would spot this huge new landmark and know that he had used the dynamite again.

The mass of wood was much too heavy for our small, under-powered Fordson to move. However, my dad's prayers were answered when we found the aged stump and most of its limbs had turned into pitch wood, which burned quite well. We spent most of the afternoon cutting off the roots and consolidating them into a spot around the stump so that the whole thing would burn fast and completely.

The stump's removal left a huge crater in our field that served quite well for the deposit of rocks that we cleared from our fields. My father did not share the story of the blasting incident with many of our neighbors; he never wanted our close call to be discovered by my mother. He did, however, have to field several questions from my mother and a few of our neighbors about what had caused the loud boom on Cricket Flat that day.

Chapter 19

Uninvited Guests

Living in an old house located in the middle of the woods left us vulnerable to a number of house pests. When we first moved in the bedbugs ruled the roost. After we had gone to bed and the darkness had settled in, the bedbugs would pour out of every crack and hiding place in the house to feed upon us.

It took about two weeks of vigorous treatment by my mother to control these insects. After talking with some of the neighbors, she found that rubbing kerosene soaked rags on some of the cracks in the wall and around the window sills would rid the house of these pests.

One of the hardest pests to control was the common wasp. These pesky insects always seemed to be present in low to moderate numbers. We never did find an insecticide that was effective on these stinging critters. We always kept several fly swatters scattered around the house for control. The fall of the year was when they were the worst. Sometimes when we were going to be out of the house for a few days we would leave a sulfur candle burning. This would temporarily kill them off, but there was always a new batch ready to move in.

Ants were always a problem during summer months. We had small red ants that would invade the kitchen cupboards. Putting kerosene along the trail where they were coming in would slowly discourage them. The first warm days of spring would bring thousands of large, black carpenter ants throughout our house. We could not sleep well at night because they would crawl all through our beds. Fortunately these invasions would only last a few days and most of them would then disappear.

Yellow jackets and hornets were always a major problem, especially when outside water supplies were scarce. We had to keep screen doors on all our entrances and keep them closed to keep these ill-tempered invaders out of the house. We did not dare leave open water containers or fruit peelings near our house because of the numbers of these insects that would be attracted to our buildings.

The house fly was much more common than it is today. Despite the screen doors, these insects would manage to invade every room of our house, especially the kitchen area. Rooms would have from two to five sticky fly catchers hanging from the ceiling. These catchers consisted of a twisted strip of flexible paper about three feet in length. This inch and a half wide strip would be covered with a powerfully sticky substance that was attractive to flies.

By the end of the day these strip catchers would be so covered with flies that not another fly could find a spot to land on them. The combined sounds coming from several of these fly traps resembled the humming of a church choir. When the strips were full it was always a delicate operation to take one down without getting it stuck in our hair or other parts of our bodies. Just about everyone that lived among these traps at one time or other had the bad experience of getting one in their hair. They were so sticky that it was necessary to cut the hair away from the trap with a knife or a pair of scissors to escape.

The invention of DDT proved to be our salvation in the fight against flies and a lot of other insects. This affordable compound, which we bought in powder form, would be mixed with water and generously sprayed inside and outside the house. Since we were told at that time that it was a perfectly safe product, families had no reservations on how or where it was used.

We used it in our kitchen, around the outside of our house, around our barn, and on our fields. Some families that had problems with head lice washed their hair with it. One farmer told how he mistakenly dumped a five gallon bucket mixture of this compound into his hog trough, thinking that it was milk. He said that the hogs, which quickly drank the mixture without blinking an eye, came to no harm.

Perhaps its greatest advantage to our cause was its persistence. After one or two sprayings around the house, we would not be bothered by flies for the rest of the summer. It was too bad that this chemical proved to be so harmful to certain wildlife species, since it was such an effective compound for controlling insects.

We also had some problems with the common mouse. These rodents did not have any problem finding a way to enter our old house. Our main method of control was keeping a generous supply of house cats around and in our house. We would sometimes be forced to set some mouse traps in areas that were not accessible to the cats.

Wood rats proved to be our worst problem, especially during the first few years on the Flat. This rat, which was about half the size of a cottontail rabbit, was a light gray, bushy-tailed rat with white underparts. It had long facial whiskers like a house cat, large round ears, and a strong, distinct, musky odor. It was primarily a nocturnal animal that loved to inhabit any type of structure built by man.

Woodrats do not have to depend on buildings for their survival, however, since they do quite well surviving in wooded habitats. Since we were surrounded by forested areas, we lived in a perfect location for sustaining large rat populations.

When my folks first moved to the Flat, it was their belief that our house was being used as a convention center for rats. My mother told how the rats kept her from having any sleep until my dad found and plugged up their access holes to the inside of the house. She mentioned how the rats would jump from the walls and land on their bed throughout the night. She related how the rats, which are also called trade rats because of their habit of packing off small household items and leaving something in exchange, would leave a large supply of fir cones on our kitchen table in exchange for various items that they would pack away.

Although my dad was successful in blocking the rats' access to the inside of our house, he was never able to completely block their entrance to the house attic. Their presence in our attic would also be a sure prescription for a sleepless night. We were never able to figure out how a small animal could be so heavy footed. They would sound like a herd of elephants playing a game of tag as their loud repeated thumps would continue through the night.

We found that the best method of control was to set a small leghold trap in a section of six-inch stove pipe. My dad would generally have about three of these pipes with their enclosed traps located in our attic. If a person had somehow managed to go to sleep while a rat was running around in the attic, he would soon wake up when our noisy rodent got caught in one of Dad's traps.

The loud banging on the stove pipe sounded like a teacher ringing a large school bell. Whenever a rat would get caught in one of Dad's traps, Dad would have to get up, go outside and climb up a ladder into our attic. He had a long, heavy-duty stick that he used to kill the rats and the loud thumping sounds of him hitting the rat would generally finish out the disturbing noises for the night.

Two badgers once created about two weeks of sleepless nights for our family. These badgers apparently thought that the tight quarters beneath our house offered a splendid retreat for their nightly mating sessions. They picked a spot beneath our bedroom floor to carry on their rendezvous. We never realized that a badger had such a vocabulary until this experience. Squeals, grunts, hisses and growls would drown out the noise of the wood rats from our attic all through the night.

Our two dogs, not to be left out of these nightly noise-making festivities unsuccessfully tried to reach the crawl space area where the badgers were. Only a large wooden beam separated the four combatants as they threw verbal insults at each other in the form of growls and barks. Likewise, only the floorboards separated this noise-making from the bottom of my parents' bed.

Needless to say, my folks were getting very frustrated with this situation. Not only was the noise a real problem, the badgers gave off a strong smell that resembled a skunk. Dad tried boarding up all the holes where the badgers were crawling in under the house. However, our night-visiting friends would simply dig a hole beneath the boards and crawl in anyway.

Several times he got up early in the morning with the plan of shooting the badgers when they left the house. This proved unsuccessful, too. His attempt at setting a leg-hold trap only resulted in catching one of our dogs. He was seriously considering taking a sound shot through the floor with his rifle when the badgers solved the problem, themselves, by leaving one morning and not returning.

Another incident involving a badger occurred several years later after we had moved to our new house. One of the drivers who drove the cream and milk truck had a pet badger that would often ride around with him on his routes. After seeing this badger, I was obsessed with the idea of obtaining one and making him into a pet. Not realizing that badgers had to be caught at a very young age before they could be tamed, I set my sights on any badger that I could catch.

My prayers were answered one day when our dogs cornered a badger in a culvert near our house. A friend who was spending the day with me helped rig up a wire snare on the end of a long pole and we embarked on our first badger-capturing project. Our prospective captive, which happened to be a large adult, was in a nasty mood as we made several unsuccessful attempts to get his tapering, short neck into our snare.

Finally, after about half an hour, we were able to tighten our wire noose over the badger's neck. The battle was not won, however. Our mad captive braced his front feet against the seams of the culvert and hissed and growled for a long time before my friend and I could even budge him. Finally, he choked down to a point where we were able to pull him out of the end of the culvert. Choking and gasping for breath, the badger rolled on his back and tried to dislodge the wire with his front feet.

It was only after the badger was rendered semi-conscious that we were able to put him in a large gunnysack and load him into the back of Dad's pickup. By this time, my friend was expressing some doubts about the prospects of turning this bundle of fury into a pet. Still remembering the truck driver, I was still convinced that our captive could be tamed. I figured that his unfriendly manner was brought on by the rather unpleasant experience of being captured and that, once we showed him we meant no harm, he would calm right down.

I finally decided that, since my folks had gone to town, we would take the badger into the house where he couldn't get away, and then release him from the sack. Having had good success in taming some of the farm animals by the use of feed, I had no doubt that this would turn our friend into a cuddly, submissive creature. It did not take us long to get our captive up to the house and haul the sack and its unwilling cargo into the kitchen. Placing myself in front of the sack with some of my mother's homemade bread, I instructed my friend to untie the string that was securing the sack.

I quickly found out this badger was not going to be anyone's pet. When my friend opened the sack I was ready to hand our badger some of Mom's bread. The badger wasted no time in heading in my direction. I realized just in time that the badger wanted me more than the bread. Determined to get his revenge, our released captive with blood in his eyes chased us around the kitchen and living room about three times before we finally took refuge on the kitchen counter.

We must have looked like two house cats treed by a dog as we looked down on our snarling friend. By this time I had decided that perhaps this particular badger was not cut out to be a pet. Just as I was beginning to wonder what my folks would think when they walked in the door, the badger decided that he would explore the rest of the house. We wasted no time in jumping down from our counter perch and running outside, fully expecting the badger to be on our heels.

After waiting outside for about twenty minutes, we finally decided that our unfriendly beast was not coming out. A cautious search soon revealed the badger had holed up in my folks' bedroom, beneath their bed. Whenever we approached the bedroom door, he would make a false charge and then retreat back under the bed. We finally decided to leave all the doors in the house open and pray that the badger would leave before my folks came home. We left the house for about an hour, and when we returned, we found that our prayers had been answered. My proposed pet had left.

We had barely straightened up the house after our confrontation with the badger when my folks returned. They sniffed the air and mentioned that there must be a skunk in the area. My dad saved the day, however, when he said that he had also smelled one the previous morning. I waited several years before telling my parents about the badger that nearly moved into their bedroom.

Chapter 20

Sexuality

Children living during the 1930s and early 1940s were not nearly as advanced in their knowledge and practice of sex-related activities as are today's children. Unlike today, sexual activities among preteens and early teens were very rare. Reaction with the opposite sex was generally confined to sitting together, holding hands and writing love notes. A much higher degree of shyness seemed to exist between boys and girls during that time period.

There were some more daring acts of sexuality that would occasionally occur in mixed groups. Some of the more mischievous boys would urinate in front of the girls on various occasions. These acts were usually reported to some authoritative adult and the guilty party would be punished. Some of the more outgoing girls seemed to enjoy giving the boys brief opportunities to view their undergarments while engaged in some sporting activity such as swinging or jumping rope.

There were a couple of girls in the neighborhood who displayed no shyness in telling dirty stories. They picked these stories up from listening to their fathers tell the same stories. These girls often did not understand the hidden sexual implications of these jokes and would not hesitate to tell them to a teacher or another adult. A story told by someone's dad one day often made the rounds of all the school kids the following day and then the kids would repeat it to their parents when they got home from school.

Once, one of these stories created an embarrassing moment for my mother. One Sunday afternoon, my parents had invited a fundamentalist preacher and his wife home after church for dinner and were making light conversation during the meal. The conversation had shifted to exchanging some humorous true stories.

The minister had just finished telling about some incident when I asked if I could tell a story that I had heard while at school. The unsuspecting adults all politely told me to go ahead. The story I told was the type that masked its sexually-related punch line to the last few words. Thus, my mother did not have an opportunity to stuff a dishrag in my mouth before I dropped the bomb shell on my attentive audience.

Apparently, my sexually-explicit story must have topped anything that had been told before, judging by the response it generated. My mother wasted little time in grabbing her favorite handle, which happened to be my ear, and taking me into the next room. Following a stern lecture on keeping my mouth shut for the rest of the meal, she returned me to the table. The minister then requested a special prayer in which he prayed that the devil and his wickedness would be driven from the schools.

This was one of the few times that my parents did not present a stern, unified front when dressing me down after the departure of company. My mother's long lecture on how I had embarrassed and brought shame on the family with my big mouth appeared to stimulate a different response in my dad. One of his suppressed coughs during Mom's lecture triggered an uncontrollable laughing spell, which he finally finished with the following statement to my mother: "Did you see the look on the preacher's face when Harlan ended his story?" He then, with tears running from his eyes, burst into another fit of laughing which finally prompted a weak smile from my mother.

I had my first crush on a girl when I was in the sixth grade. This girl, who was a minister's daughter, opened up a whole new world to me in understanding on how a boy could possibly want to associate with a girl for any other purpose than children's social playing.

Although we seldom spoke to each other because of our shyness, we would exchange affectionate glances during school hours. Love notes, in which we would express our earnest feelings, would be traded each school day. We reached the peak of our mutual attraction for each other when we briefly held hands while walking home from school one day. A move by her family into Elgin kept me from finding out how far our relationship would have progressed.

Being raised on a farm with farm animals gave most of the Flat's youngsters, including me, some knowledge of the mechanics of sex and about the birth process. Dad gave me my first rundown on the birds and the bees when I was about nine years old. My observations of farm animals plus Dad's lecture gave me a pretty good picture of the reproductive process.

My father told me that too much preoccupation with sex at a young age would stunt one's growth. He illustrated this by pointing to under-sized bulls that were allowed to breed at too young an age. He also pointed out several small-sized men in the community that he believed had been sexually active when they were too young. He further added that sexually-preoccupied young boys often ended up in mental institutions. Armed with this information, I was determined that any relationship with the opposite sex would be put on hold until I was 30 years old.

However, my dad's lectures did not keep my curiosity suppressed. Depictions of nudity or semi-nudity in the opposite sex in the form of paintings, photographs or magazines stimulated my interest like a biologist discovering a new species. Books or magazines containing sexually-explicit articles were also prized items.

Perhaps my keen interest in these materials was due to the fact that materials of this nature were not available in the stores or on television like they are today. Also, as mentioned in an earlier chapter, my mother was quite strict on the type of books or magazines that were allowed in the house.

I had my own library located in a dense thicket some distance from our house. This collection, which consisted mainly of True Magazines, True Confessions Magazines, and the lingerie sections of several catalogs, was carefully concealed beneath a large log. This was a favorite spot to take visiting neighborhood boys; I always felt safer when there was another pair of eyes watching for possible discovery by my folks. The prospects of being discovered reading this material always weighed heavily on my mind.

Another boy's mother caught her son and me looking at a sexually explicit book one time. The boy had discovered the book hidden away in his dad's chest of drawers and we had taken our treasure into the boy's bedroom for our own private review. The book's graphic illustrations had captured our undivided attention to the point that we did not hear the boy's mother tiptoe up behind us. Her gruff voice shouting, "What are you reading?" made us feel like two deer that had been surprised by a cougar. We were in a state of shock as she grabbed our book and asked us where we had gotten it.

The boy and I both felt like we had been caught robbing a bank. My friend explained to his mother where we had found the book. After a strong lecture and being detained in the boy's bedroom as our punishment, the boy's mother took the book and told us she would call us when our punishment time was up.

Hours rolled by as we restlessly waited for her call. Finally we opened the bedroom door and set out to find her in case she had forgotten us. As we entered the kitchen we saw her sitting at the kitchen table deeply engrossed in the illicit book. She looked almost as guilty as we did as she explained that she had forgotten we were still in the bedroom.

One of the most dramatic changes occurring in my life was when I met Bill. Bill (not his real name) gave me my first real exposure to another boy close to my age that lived outside the Cricket Flat community. I first met Bill when his parents spent an afternoon visiting my folks. Following this meeting, our parents would get together two to three times a year and his parents also attended the Children's Day program at our church.

Bill shattered many of my prejudices against town kids. Earlier, I have mentioned how our parents and other members of the community instilled in us the belief that we were much better and tougher than the youngsters raised in town.

Bill was just the opposite of what I had thought a town kid should be. He was about half a head taller, he was stronger, he could run faster, and he could throw a rock farther than I could. He had wavy, red hair combed straight back; something that I had always longed for.

Bill had a cocky self-assurance that instantly gained my admiration. He had a real neat-looking billfold containing several pictures of good-looking girls that he said were fighting to be his steady. He had neat clothes that were not too big for him. He had a scabbard containing a knife with an assortment of blades and tools. Bill soon captured my respect and admiration like no other member of my peer group had done.

Bill had another characteristic that captured my undivided attention. He convinced me that he knew more about sex than anyone I had ever met. I would breathlessly hang on each word he uttered as he described his latest sexual encounters. His graphic descriptions of escapades with girls ranging up to twenty years of age would have put a porno star to shame. I was shocked, but did not disbelieve him, when he told me how two, young, religious women that had sung in the Children's Day program had pursued him until he had finally satisfied their needs.

Bill also made me question some of the things that my father had told me about early engagement in sexual activities. My father had mentioned how one's growth would be stunted. As I looked at Bill, I wondered about my dad's theory. How could someone that had numerous sexual encounters every day be much bigger and stronger than I was?

My image of Bill was eventually shattered. After several visits, during which time descriptions of his sexual exploits continued to monopolize our conversations, his reputation was finally challenged. He and I had gotten together during the annual Children's Day event. He had been making some comments about a particular girl in attendance that had quite a reputation of promiscuity.

Although neither one of us knew this girl, we had heard of her reputation. In those days a promiscuous girl's reputation would spread through the county like a highly contagious virus. Bill made several eye contacts with this girl, who I will call Mary (not her real name) and bragged to me how she had returned his bold flirtatious stares.

It was later in the day when Bill and I decided that a thick grove of pine trees behind the church offered us some seclusion for some private conversation. Bill had convinced me that I should try one of the cigarettes that he had smuggled out of his dad's car and I was trying to act like the Marlboro Man as I puffed away on the cigarette. We had been there about five minutes when the well-known girl, Mary, and one of her friends, suddenly joined our company.

Mary, who was a well-endowed girl with long brown hair, was a couple of years older than we were. With conversation riddled with profanity, she introduced herself and her friend and asked if they could have a cigarette.

As the four of us puffed away, I could soon tell that the two girl's attention and conversation were mainly directed towards Bill. Before much time had passed, Mary had placed herself directly in front of Bill and was sending a barrage of flirting eye contacts at him. Suddenly, I heard her proposition him in a low whisper using the forbidden four-letter sexual word that had gotten me in trouble with my folks.

Mary's request left me in a queasy state. I did not know whether I should leave or stay. Although Bill's many stories of his sexual experiences had filled me in on what to expect, the thought of watching this type of act between two of my peers left me with an indescribable feeling. Would the other girl ask me? How long would it take? I finally decided that I would stay and watch my friend go into action.

The event that followed shocked me as much as Mary's offer to Bill. My normally self-assured friend now seemed to be in a state of shock, himself. His red-complexioned face looked like it had been dipped in a bucket of white paint. His earlier confident eye contact with the girls was now gone. His eyes, which were now shifting around like a wild bird in a cage, kept looking first at me and then in the direction of the church. Desperation seemed to be written all over his face and I anxiously waited for his next move. Suddenly turning from Mary's seductive stare, my friend nervously blurted, "I hear my dad calling me." He then raced off towards the church with the speed of a deer.

Finding myself alone with the two girls, I felt like a soldier on the battlefront, deserted by his platoon. Past visions of what I might do in an encounter with the opposite sex seemed to have deserted me in much the same fashion as my friend. I was still trying to get over the shock of what had happened during the last few minutes when I heard Mary say, "Are you going to be a chicken, too?"

Still showing some respect for my hero, I timidly said, "I hear my mother calling me," and raced off nearly as fast as Bill.

I never found out if my dad's theories on early sex were correct. I never did grow to be very tall. However, I never ended up in a mental institution, either.

Chapter 21

Subjective Ramblings

The previous chapter concludes the description of my childhood days. In this chapter I would like to depart from the past and give my subjective evaluation of some of the problems facing our youth today and some possible solutions. Also, I would like to offer some predictions on what may be facing us in the future relative to living standards and why we may have to go back in time to a simpler lifestyle.

I believe that the majority of today's parents do not have the necessary training to administer a well-balanced program of disciplining their children. In my opinion, we have allowed some well-meaning, so-called child experts with long-handled degrees to halt some traditional, proven methods of discipline.

State and Federal Governments have allowed child psychologists with liberal leanings in child discipline to set standards for the school and the home. These standards, which are pushed by laws and certain taxpayer-funded educational service agencies, are forcing unproven discipline methods on today's parents.

It is my opinion that we should take a hard look at some of these liberal training methods and consider reverting back to some of the stricter methods used by our forebears. I do not necessarily agree that corporal punishment is the answer for every child. However, there are certain children for whom I believe it is required as a last resort. I think we need it as a tool, coupled with consistency and love, in both the home and the schools.

A multitude of distractions compete for our time, both parents and children. This lack of time prevents the necessary bonding of the child to the parent. Many children now use other substitutes, such as other children, sports celebrities, movie stars, singers and other role models that may not be the best influence on the child. Parents need to set up schedules to spend more time with their children, whether it's working or some type of recreation.

Many of today's parents do not set up daily, routine chores for their children. Children at an early age need daily chores that they are made to perform. As they grow older, they need to be involved in progressively harder and more time-consuming jobs.

Unfortunately, minimum wage laws, liability laws and other government red tape discourage work opportunities for children. If I had my way I would set up the two following programs for children: allow certain occupations such as farming to employ children under seventeen years of age without having to comply with minimum wage or liability laws. In many cases, just the value to the child in learning how to work and accept responsibilities would be adequate compensation. Second, I would initiate a program where public agencies could set up summer work camps for children ranging from twelve to eighteen years old. Again these programs would not have to adhere to minimum wage laws. Low wages and room and board would be adequate compensation for the work ethic the child would learn.

Tightening budgets in our high schools are resulting in the gutting of non-college occupational programs. We should remember that the majority of our high school students do not go on to a four-year college. High schools should beef up—not eliminate—these programs.

Reduced school budgets should be expected, so an array of innovative methods must be employed to preserve needed programs. Volunteer teachers from various trades and retired teachers could be used as resources, and employing students for janitorial and grounds work are other ideas that might help. We could also use brighter students for some teaching, and use senior students for driving buses. We could increase the use of computers in teaching, as well. As an ex-school board chairman, I will probably get criticized by some school employees for mentioning these ideas.

Today's four-year colleges are pricing themselves out of the average family's reach. If trends continue, only the very rich will be able to attend without scholarships. We need to set up satellite stations, at least one in each county, where the major colleges can transmit classes by television. A minimum of instructors would be needed to administer tests and operate the equipment. Students would be able to get a large portion of their credits from these satellite courses before transferring to a college, say for their final year. This would greatly reduce college costs by allowing the students to board and room at their parents' home during most of their college career. Technology will soon be in place for this type of arrangement.

I am afraid the law of supply and demand is on a collision course with the average family's living standards. Although politicians ignore the problem, the average income after costs of living have been deducted, is already declining. Students of economics acknowledge that our easy ride with a fully-stocked pantry is rapidly coming to a halt. Families living during the 1950s through the 1970s probably reached the peak of what we can expect as an average family income.

The basic problems—I call them the four Fs—are Forestry, Farming, Fisheries and Fuel. All of these commodities have one thing in common. They must meet increasing demands from consumers at a time when their supplies are diminishing. Our vast ocean fishery and commercial salmon runs in the Northwest have been sharply curtailed by over-fishing and habitat destruction. Our vast forests have been over-cut to the point where sustained yields are being lowered. Giant aquifers that provided cheap water for irrigation are being rapidly pumped down. Oil, which is the lifeblood of the world, will eventually be in short supply.

As these commodities diminish, their costs in the form of food supplies, building materials and fuels will all increase to the consumer at a higher rate than gains from wage increases. Families will have to tighten their belts and, in my opinion, revert back to a more conservative lifestyle.

Most families could save a lot with better food management. Cook more at home rather than buying fast foods. Develop more cold storage facilities to take advantages of sales on meats and vegetables. Plant a few fruit trees in your back yard and grow a garden. Then can or freeze the produce that you grow. Watch the sales on non perishable produce and buy in volume.

There are several ways to economize when buying a house. If one is handy with tools, buy an older house and remodel it. This is a lot of work but it builds equity in a hurry. Some young couples buy an older mobile home in a mobile home park for $12,000 to $18,000, for little down, pay it off in five years, and then use the equity to make a down payment on a regular house.

Also, mobile homes are much better than they used to be. Many of them can be purchased for a low down and $200 to $300 per month. This is much better than putting out $500 to $600 per month for rent. Many families in the 1930s shared houses. It can be done with some sacrifices.

Most families can save a lot of money on cars and transportation. Buy a used two- to three-year old car or pickup with low mileage. Stay away from sports cars—they drive up your insurance rates. Do you really need two cars? Do you need a four-wheel-drive pickup to use for recreational activities one month out of the year? Can you carpool to work? Have your car serviced regularly. It pays off in the long run.

Many families can save a lot on what they spend on recreation. If you have several kids and are living on a tight budget, stay away from ski sports, both snow and water, and golf. Good economy sports are swimming, picnicking, fishing and hiking. Camping trailers can be expensive. Tents and propane stoves are much cheaper. If you buy a boat, buy a small one that you can easily tow with your car. You can often get good buys on fishing tackle and camping gear at garage sales. Plan your vacations close to home to eliminate travel costs.

Throw all your credit cards away but one and use it only in emergency situations. Credit cards are probably one of the worst thing there is to get families in financial trouble. Pay cash for appliances and furniture, when possible to save interest charges. Don't let your pride stand in the way when it comes to buying secondhand. You can buy some good clothes and other used items at Salvation Army stores and other secondhand trading posts.

Don't overspend your budget or go in debt on Christmas presents. Families often shower their kids with too many toys that are often worn out or broken within a week. Direct your spending towards necessary items like clothes or needed household items.

Insurance is a necessary evil that is the biggest rip off today. Medical insurance is a staggering expense to young families. There are many low-income families that simply can't afford it. However, if you have many assets, I would suggest you get minimal coverage with a high deductible from a good, well-known company. Don't maintain collision coverage on older cars. Make sure your house insurance is listed for replacement costs.

Last but not least, make a family budget listing your main items first, such as food, clothing, transportation, and monthly payments, and in entertainment with what is left. Make sure you allow so much for an emergency savings account, at least ten percent of your monthly salary.

These practices are ones that I have used all my life and I can attest to their usefulness when trying to stay within a budget. I hope that my pessimistic predictions do not come true at too rapid a rate. In conclusion, I would like to thank the readers of this book for sharing a period of my life and hope that my advice can be used.